EVENT MANAGEMENT

for Tourism, Cultural, Business, and Sporting Events

LYNN VAN DER WAGEN
BRENDA R. CARLOS

PEARSON

Prentice
Hall

Upper Saddle River, New Jersey 07458

Library of Congress Cataloging-in-Publication Data

Van der Wagen, Lynn.
   Event management for tourism, cultural, business, and sporting events /
by Lynn Van der Wagen and Brenda R. Carlos.
         p.   cm.
   Includes bibliographical references and index.
   ISBN 0–13–114938–5
1. Special events—Planning.   2. Special events—Management.
I. Carlos, Brenda R.   II. Title.

GT3403.V38 2005
394.2—dc22

2004010178

Executive Editor: Vernon R. Anthony	**Manufacturing Manager:** Ilene Sanford
Editorial Assistant: Beth Dyke	**Manufacturing Buyer:** Cathleen Petersen
Senior Marketing Manager: Ryan DeGrote	**Creative Director:** Cheryl Asherman
Senior Marketing Coordinator: Elizabeth Farrell	**Senior Design Coordinator:** Mary E. Siener
Marketing Assistant: Les Roberts	**Cover Designer:** Michael L. Ginsberg
Director of Manufacturing and Production: Bruce Johnson	**Cover Illustration/Photograph:** Getty Images
	Composition: Pine Tree Composition
Managing Editor: Mary Carnis	
Production Editor: Bruce Hobart, Pine Tee Composition	

Pearson Prentice Hall™ is a trademark of Pearson Education, Inc.
Pearson® is a registered trademark of Pearson plc
Prentice Hall® is a registered trademark of Pearson Education, Inc.

Pearson Education LTD.
Pearson Education Australia PTY, Limited
Pearson Education Singapore, Pte. Ltd.
Pearson Education North Asia Ltd.
Pearson Education Canada, Ltd.
Pearson Education de Mexico, S.A. de C.V.
Pearson Education—Japan
Pearson Education Malaysia, Pte. Ltd.
Pearson Education, Upper Saddle River, New Jersey

10 9 8 7 6 5 4 3
ISBN 0-13-114938-5

To Rudy, Chad, Clint, and Melissa
for your encouragement, love, and devotion

CONTENTS

PREFACE

Atlanta Success Story
By Absolutely Atlanta

The Project

Deliver a Powerful Presentation

Create an Environment of Celebration

Transform an Active Aircraft Paint Hangar into a Beautiful Ballroom

Reveal the Stunning New Paint Scheme of the Boeing 777 to 7,000 Members of the Press and Employees of a Major Airline

The Challenge

Only 3 Weeks Lead-Time until the Event

Secure FAA Permits for Our Crew to Enter a Highly Secured Area of Atlanta's Hartfield International Airport

Hide a 250-foot-long by 220-foot-wide Commercial Aircraft

Create Hanging Points for Lighting and Sound Equipment in a Hangar with 5 Hard Slick Metal Walls

Cover 54 Feet of Paint-Splattered Walls

The Experience

Magical Wonderment!

Soft Lighting

Beautiful Fabric Draped Along the Wall

Time-Lapse Video Showing the Evolution of the Aircraft's Interior and Paint Scheme

Confetti Cannons Dramatically Explode

Blinding Light Pours into the Hangar as the Door Quickly Draws Back.

The Striking New Boeing 777 Gleaming in the Sun!

The Results

An Amazing Success!

A Dramatic Introduction to the Transformed Brand Identity

A Bridge into the Future

A Lasting Impression on the Press and Employees

Corporate and Brand Enthusiasm

Used with permission Global Events

Whether you're involved in creating an event such as the one listed above, which introduced over 7,000 members of the press and employees of a major airline to a new product, organizing a walk/run for a charitable event, or working on a local blues festival, the event management industry is full of excitement. Certainly no one day in the life of an event manager is ever alike. The event business is a dynamic one that is not free from frustration—but in the end, most event managers believe that they have the best job on earth.

The event and convention industry is a $100 billion industry and currently employs 1.5 million people. This has precipitated the increase in the popularity of studies of event management. For those who are looking for an exciting career, where their organizational skills and attention to detail along with their creativity can be fully utilized, this is an industry that is attracting many of the country's brightest students.

As an author who has written about the hospitality and event industry for the past decade, it has been my privilege to be able to compile this text. I have many people to thank. First and foremost I would like to thank Lynn Van Der Wagen. It has been a rewarding experience to adapt her original text, which was published in Australia. Thanks goes to Lynn for providing a number of photos that were used in this text. To Vern Anthony my Prentice Hall/Pearson editor and his staff who have shown tremendous interest and support for this work. To Ed Sanders, my mentor, who has always believed in me and helped me to grow in the industry. To the many associations, organizations and professionals that freely shared their data and ideas with me. Their examples are what make this text come alive and truly represent the U.S. market.

Most of all I must thank my dear family, who are the reason that I want to work hard and improve myself. Rudy, you're the best. Chad, Clint, and Melissa I appreciate your support. Mom and dad too, you taught me that I can accomplish anything I set my mind on as long as I'm willing to put in the required work.

And finally, a special thanks to all the students and educators who will turn to this book. I have kept you in mind during every phase of writing this manuscript. It is my hope that this book will become a great resource to you. May all your events be successful!

Brenda R. Carlos

The event planning and management industry has an extremely positive future. In addition to the usual corporate meetings, trade shows, and conferences, the event planning industry has also gotten involved in the advertising and branding efforts of their clientele. The usual methods of "interruption marketing" that advertisers use such as television commercials and also direct e-mail marketing are all being tuned out by savvy consumers. Devices such as "TIVO" wipe out commercials entirely. A new form of entertainment marketing called 'advertainment' has emerged. This highly interactive form of marketing blends the branding element of traditional advertising with live, interactive events that are extremely virile, extremely targeted, extremely economical, and best of all extremely measurable. Event Planners who can identify their clients branding strategies and can bring their expertise of running the logistics of live events have a very positive future. Any marketing majors who are looking for a growing and lucrative niche should definitely consider a career in event branding and experiential marketing."

Larry Jaeger
President
Events Xtraordinaire (www.eventsx.com)

Chapter One

INTRODUCTION TO EVENT MANAGEMENT

During his speech at the closing ceremonies Sunday, he said that the "people of America, Utah and Salt Lake City, you have given the world superb Games." Earlier in the day, IOC President Jacques Rogge told reporters that the Salt Lake Organizing Committee "has done a superb job," citing success in transportation, technology, security and even the weather.

Ratings for television coverage around the world of the Games "have exploded," Rogge said, citing as an example the seven million viewers a day in Germany tuning on to the curling competitions.

Rogge wasn't so generous in his comments about the 1996 Summer Games in Atlanta, the last American city to host the Olympics. "The last Games in Atlanta were not good Games—bad organization. This has been corrected here."

Deseret News, *February 25, 2002*

On completion of this chapter, you will be able to

- explain the unique characteristics of an event;
- classify and describe events according to size;
- classify events according to type;
- discuss relationships between event managers and other stakeholders; and
- discuss some of the ethical issues relevant to event management.

*T*he aim of this book is to assist you in your training to become an event manager of the highest caliber. Many of us have observed events, most of us have participated in events, but few of us have managed events. As an event manager, you are there to do far more than just observe. You are there to ensure the smooth running of the event, to minimize the risks, and to maximize the enjoyment of the event audience. The demands on an event manager are far greater than one would expect.

The preceding example focuses on the importance of sound management and the complexities of organizing an event. In most cases, careful attention must be given to transportation, technology and security, and a host of other elements. Whereas the Games in Utah will go down in history as a success, the Games in Atlanta will be remembered by some as less than perfect, because of the "bad" (according to IOC President, Jacques Rogge) organization of the management team.

Financial risk is also an important concern of the event manager. Events are generally extremely expensive, with high expenditure required over a very short period of time, and there are far higher levels of uncertainty about revenue and profit than there are with the average business.

In the case of voluntary and charitable events, of which there are many in every community, the risk is that the time invested by individuals will be wasted and that their objectives will not be achieved.

Finally, one of the most important things about an event is that it is often a highlight of a person's life. This occasion is not to be taken lightly. A significant birthday, a wedding, or an anniversary is so important to the main participants that nothing must go wrong. If something does go wrong, it cannot be easily rectified. For instance, a wedding at which the power fails because of overloading of the electrical supply cannot be repeated. The offer to "come back again at our expense" just doesn't work! Events are often a "once in a lifetime" experience. The event manager therefore carries enormous responsibility for ensuring that the event, however large or small, is a success because there is often only one chance to get it right.

From what we have discussed so far, events are characterized by the following:

- They are often "once in a lifetime" experiences for the participants.
- They are generally expensive to stage.
- They usually take place over a short time span.
- They require long and careful planning.
- They generally take place only once. (However, many are held annually, usually at the same time every year.)
- They carry a high level of risk, including financial risk and safety risk.
- There is often a lot at stake for those involved, including the event management team.

This last characteristic is crucial, since every performer, whether athlete or entertainer, wants to deliver his or her best performance. The bride wants the day to be perfect in every way. The marketing manager and the design team want the new product to be seen in the best possible light. Consider for a moment how much easier it is to run a restaurant (where you spread your risk over a number of days and a number of customers) than it is to run a one-time, big-budget product launch—particularly if this launch has 500 key industry players and the media are in attendance, and if it is taking place at a unique location with unusual demands for logistics, lighting, sound, and special effects.

The 2002 Winter Olympics held in Salt Lake City, Utah, were certainly a once-in-a-lifetime experience.
Source: Used with permission of IOC/Olympic Museum Collections.

Having pointed out the level of demand for the event manger and thus the possible downside of the profession, it is important also to point out that the event industry is one in which people (the event audience) tend to have the time of their lives. Making this outcome possible and sharing this with them is extremely gratifying. The work is demanding, exciting, and challenging, and it requires a fine-tuned balance between task management and people management. As the newspaper article illustrates, an event manager must bring together a team with clearly defined responsibilities for all aspects of the event, including unexpected crises. The team needs to be both organized and flexible. Events can be unpredictable and do require quick thinking that is based on a sound knowledge of procedures and alternatives. Decision making is one of the most important skills of the event manager, and those with first-class analytical skills are highly sought after by most industries.

Professor Donald Getz (1997), a well-known writer in the field of event management, defines special events from two perspectives, that of the customer and that of the event manager, as follows:

- *A special event is a one-time or infrequently occurring event outside normal programs or activities of the sponsoring or organizing body.*
- *To the customer or guest, a special event is an opportunity for leisure, social or cultural experience outside the normal range of choices or beyond everyday experience.*

Another well-known author, Dr. J. Goldblatt (1997), defines special events as "A unique moment in time celebrated with ceremony and ritual to satisfy specific needs."

In this book, the emphasis is on a wide range of events, including "special events," as defined before, and more common events such as sporting events, corporate meetings, conventions, expositions, parties, festivals, carnivals, and prize-giving ceremonies, which may not meet the definition "outside the normal range of choices."

Classification of events can be done on the basis of size or type, as shown in the following sections.

Size of Events

In terms of size, events may be categorized as follows.

Mega-events

The largest events are called mega-events, which are generally targeted at international markets. The Olympic Games, World Cup Soccer, and the Superbowl are good examples. The Superbowl, for which, in 1967, there were 30,000 tickets unsold, now sells out before the tickets have been printed and also accounts for the sale of 30,000 hotel rooms. It is televised to an audience of 800 million and adds $300 million to the local economy. All such events have a specific yield in terms of increased tourism, media coverage, and economic impact. Some cities are continuing to meet a legacy of debt after hosting an Olympic Games. Salt Lake City, Utah, was fortunate, however, as with all events of this size, it is difficult to calculate the costs accurately with so many stakeholders (mainly government) involved.

Relief was not the emotion that pervaded State House chambers Tuesday when the Salt Lake Organizing Committee paid off its $99 million obligation to Utahns.

Pride emanated from the packed room. But even more prevalent was a sense of thanks. In fulfilling the promises of three generations of Olympic leaders that the 2002 Winter Games would not leave taxpayers in debt but would leave a legacy, Romney reserved special praise for the volunteers.

Mike Gorrell, The Salt Lake Tribune

Although the size of the Olympic Games in terms of expenditure, sponsorship, economic impact, and worldwide audience would undoubtedly put it in the category of mega-event, it is worth comparing its size with, for example, that of the Maha Kumbh Mela (which translated means the "Great Urn Fair"), the largest religious gathering in history. During the 2001 event, approximately 70 million Hindu pilgrims converged on the Ganges and Yumana Rivers in Allahabad, India, for a sacred bathing ritual that devotees believe will purify and break the cycle of reincarnation. The gathering takes place every 12 years. The 2001 festival, described as the "Greatest Show on Earth," was arguably the largest gathering of humanity ever for a single event.

Regional Events

Regional events are designed to increase the appeal of a specific tourism destination or region. FAN Fair, the world's biggest country music festival, held annually in Nashville, Tennessee, the Kentucky Derby, and Arts in the Park, a Memphis art festival, are all examples of tourist destinations achieving market positioning for both domestic and international tourism markets through their annual events. Although Mardi Gras is celebrated in cities around the world, it's hard to imagine the annual celebration not being held in New Orleans, since it has been historically based there. This event attracts local and international visitors to New Orleans and has a significant positive financial impact on the city. The annual National Cherry Blossom Festival in Washington, D.C., is another good example of a regional event.

Major Events

These events attract significant local interest and large numbers of participants, as well as generating significant tourism revenue. As an example, Chinese New Year celebrations are held in many capital cities. In Honolulu, the event includes many festivals and traditions for the New Year, including the Lion Dance, Lantern Festival, parades, and Dragon Boat races. Friends and relatives of the Chinese community often visit at this time.

Most major cities have a convention center capable of holding large meetings, trade shows, and conventions. Chicago's McCormick Place is known as North America's premier convention facility and attracts more than 4 million trade and public show visitors annually. The McCormick Place Complex comprises three state-of-the-art buildings and has a combined total of more than 2.2 million square feet of exhibit space, 1.6 million square feet all on one level, making it the nation's largest convention center.

Following is a listing of some of the shows scheduled in 2003, which gives an idea of the magnitude of the large meeting and convention industry business. An asterisk before an entry indicates that the event was open to the public.

Chicago Boat, RV & Outdoor Show
The International Housewares Show
International Air-Conditioning, Heating & Refrigeration Show
*Carquest World of Wheels '03
ProMat
Aventis Awards, Launch Meeting
*The New Super Sale
*Chicago Automobile Show
*World Discount Club Show & Sale
Customer Relationship Management
*International Cluster of Dogs
*Supercycle Show & Parts Expo
Chicago Dental Society's Midwinter Meeting
National Manufacturing Week
Building Service Contractors Association International
*Chicago Chevy Vette Fest
Global Shop
Association of PeriOperative Registered Nurses
American College of Cardiology (Heart House)
*Voll Expo
*An Expo for Today's Black Woman
Risk and Insurance Management Society
CSI at Construct America
*Import Revolution
CMM International
American Urological Association, Inc., Annual Meeting
The 2003 Supermarket Industry Convention & Education Exposition
International Fancy Food & Confection Show 2003
Digital Solutions Forum
All Candy Expo
Annual Restaurant, Hotel-Motel Show
The ASI Show
American Society of Clinical Oncology
AAVS/SVS 2003 Joint Vascular Meeting
NCTA National Show
Retail Systems/VICS Collaborative Commerce

National Plastics Exposition
*John Hancock All Star Week Fan Fest
Institute of Food Technologists
Kehe Food Distributors, Inc.
*Hot Import Nights
The National Hardware Show Building Products Exposition
*Extreme Autofest
ICCMCRM/Field Solutions
Islamic Society of North America
Life@50+: A Celebration of You
National Safety Council
Interscience Conference of Antimicrobial Agents of Chemo-therapy
The Motivation Show
Frontline Solutions
PPAI Business Forum & Marketplace
*Import Xpression Showcase Tour
Council of Logistics Management
Graph Expo
Club Industry
National Association of Convenience Stores
International Sanitary Supply Association
American College of Surgeons
National Minority Supplier Development Council
American Meat Expo
World Wide Food Expo
National Association for the Education of Young Children
American Speech Language Hearing Association
Fabtech
Workers Compensation & Disability Conference & Exhibit
Annual Meeting of Radiological Society of North America

Minor Events

Most events fall into this last category, and it is here that most event managers gain their experience. Almost every town, city, country, and state in the United States host annual events. For example, Rhode Island, our smallest state geographically speaking, lists on www .visitrhodeisland.com 234 annual festivals including the Newport Winter Festival and the Miller Lite Hall of Fame Tennis Championship, as well as the Wickford Cup Race (a race for plastic sailboats). In the category of agricultural fairs and expos, there are literally thousands of

Anchorage appeals to every taste and every style. From festivals and arts activities, to sporting events, theatrical and musical performances, visitors will always find something exciting to experience in Anchorage, Alaska. The list below highlights a few of the many activities taking place throughout the next year.

OCTOBER 2003

Johnson/Nissan Hockey Classic

October 17–18, 2003

See four top-ranked college teams compete in this fast-paced hockey tournament. For more information, please call (907) 786-1230 or explore online at www.goseawolves.com

NOVEMBER 2003

Carrs/Safeway Great Alaska Shootout

November 28–30, 2003 (Thanksgiving weekend)

Famous basketball tournament featuring some of the finest college teams in the United States. The women's tournament features University of Alaska, Brigham Young University, Clemson, and Mount St. Mary's. The men's tournament features University of Alaska, Duke, Houston, Liberty, Pacific, Purdue Seaton Hall, and Southwest Texas State. For more information, please call (907) 786-1230 or look online at www.shootout.net

JANUARY 2004

WinterFest at Alyeska Resort

January 30–February 1, 2004

Alyeska Resort hosts the annual outdoor celebration of winter with fun activities for all ages including the Polar Bear Plunge, snowboard competitions, the Mountain Bike Slalom, wine tasting, evening parties and kid's games and activities. For more information, please call (907) 754-1111 or visit www.alyeskaresort.com or email info@alyeskaresort.com

FEBRUARY 2004

Symphony of Seafood

February 7, 2004

Get a taste of Alaska! Experience a showcase of new products made from wild Alaskan salmon and other delectable seafood, and vote for the People's Choice Award during the public tasting. Creative seafood dishes are featured throughout January at many local Anchorage restaurants. For more information, please call (907) 276-7315 or visit www.symphonyofseafood.com or email afdf@compuserve.com

Fur Rendezvous Winter Carnival

February 20–March 7, 2004

It's wild. It's wacky. Let's Rondy! The sixteen-day winter festival features many favorite activities such as the Fur Rondy Grand Parade, Snowshoe Softball, Ice Bowling, Fur Rondy Melodrama, Snow Sculpture competitions, and the Miners and Trappers Ball just to name a few! For more information, please call (907) 274-1177 or visit www.furrondy.net or email info@furrondy.net

MARCH 2004

Iditarod Trail Sled Dog Race

March 6, 2004

More than 1,000 dogs line up on Fourth Avenue in Anchorage to start the world's most famous dog race. Mushers trek 1,049 miles by dog sled following old gold rush trails in what is known as "The Last Great Race On Earth" from Anchorage to Nome. For more information, please call (907) 376-5155 or visit www.iditarod.com or email iditarod@iditarod.com

Tour of Anchorage

March 7, 2004

Glide along the city's many downtown ski trails during this annual race—a premier marathon that is part of the American Ski Marathon series. For more information, please call (907) 561-0949.

APRIL 2004

Alyeska Resort Spring Carnival

April 17–18, 2004

The Alyeska Spring Carnival celebrates its 27th year, which wildly welcomes spring with great skiing, zany events like the "Slush Cup," prizes and activities, a beach party, food, drinks and fun. For more information, please call (907) 754-1111 or visit www.alyeskaresort.com or email info@alyeskaresort.com

Native Youth Olympics

April 24–26, 2004

More than 100 young people from across the state of Alaska come together in Anchorage to demonstrate and compete in their favorite Native games. The Native Youth Olympics is an amazing demonstration of Alaska Native tradition. For information, call (907) 265-5986.

(continued)

Figure 1–1   A Selection of Anchorage Events for October 2003–September 2004.

JUNE 2004

IBEW Ship Creek King Salmon Derby

June (TBA)

Fish for king salmon and win great prizes in downtown Anchorage. For more information, please call (907) 276-6472 or visit www.anchoragederbies .com

Wild Salmon on Parade

Kicks off with King Salmon Derby

Hook into this outrageous school of fish! Twenty-one wacky, whimsical, and definitely wild, artistic designs are swimming through downtown Anchorage in a sea of culture. Can't wait to glimpse these flashy fish? Virtual tours are available online www.anchorage.net

Alaska Run for Women

June 5, 2004

Since it's inception, the Alaska Run for Women has raised more than $1 million to fight breast cancer. Nearly 5,000 women participate each year in the five-mile and one-mile runs.

Juneteenth

June 11–19, 2004

A celebration of freedom and diversity with three days of fun for kids and families.

Mayor's Midnight Sun Marathon

June 22, 2004

The Mayor's Midnight Sun Marathon is always held the Saturday closest to June 30th. Celebrate Solstice by taking part in the Mayor's Midnight Sun Marathon which features five events: 26.2 marathon, 26.2 marathon walk, half marathon, five mile fun run, and the youth cup. For more information, please call (907) 343-4474 or visit www.goseawolves.com or email mceleaji@ci.anc.ak.us

JULY 2004

Girdwood Forest Faire

July 4–6, 2004

This annual event features a parade and fun run. Arts and crafts booths weave throughout the forest. There are food, games, music and fun for all ages, as well as the Midnight Sun Paragliding Fly-In and 5K Fun Run. For more information, please call (907) 566-9039.

Bear Paw Festival

July 7–11, 2004

Eagle River hosts the 19th Annual Bear Paw Festival. The celebration features a parade, 5K Fun Run, carnival, classic car show, Miss Bear Paw Pageant, Slippery Salmon Olympics, quilt show, auction and the Teddy Bear Picnic. For more information, please call (907) 694-4702 or visit www.cer.org

AUGUST 2004

Anchorage Silver Salmon Derby

TBD (depending upon Fish and Game)

More than $10,000 in prizes and daily drawings will be given away. Tickets available at CARRSTIX outlet and during the Derby at the Ship Creek Derby booth between the Comfort Inn and the railroad station. Proceeds benefit Foster Grandparent and Senior Companion programs. Catch a big one at Ship Creek in downtown Anchorage. For more information, please call (907) 276-6472 or visit www.anchoragederbies .com

Alaska State Fair

Palmer Fairgrounds

Aug. 26–Sept. 6, 2004

Enjoy Alaskan food, music and crafts, along with agricultural contest, concerts, the Alaska State Rodeo, the demolition derby, and much more! For more information, please call (907) 745–4827 or visit www.alaskastatefair.org

SEPTEMBER 2003

5th Annual Alyeska Blueberry and Mountain Arts Festival

September 4, 2004

Enjoy a weekend full of great food, wine, creative arts and rousing folk music. For more information call (907) 754-1111, online at www.alyeskaresort. com or email info@alyeskaresort.com

FOR MORE INFORMATION:

These events are subject to change. Please visit www.anchorage.net for a complete event listing or call (907) 276-4118.

Source: Reproduced with the permission of the Anchorage Convention and Visitors Bureau.

county, state, and regional events held each year, the largest being the Texas State Fair, which draws over 3 million attendees each year. The Texas State Fair utilizes the services of over 15,000 volunteers and has a waiting list of thousands of additional eager volunteers. In addition to annual events, there are many one-time events, including historical, cultural, musical, and dance performances. At one such event, parents were proudly watching their tap-dancing offspring performing in their expensive, colorful costumes. Their proud expressions turned to dismay when several dancers landed on their rear ends, having slipped on a wet stage. Quick-thinking organizers covered the stage in a mixture of soft drink and cleaning powder, a solution that enabled the show to go out without danger of slips and falls to the performers—all in a day's work for the event team! Meetings, parties, celebrations, conventions, award ceremonies, exhibitions, sporting events, and many other community and social events fit into this category. Figure 1–1 gives a sampling of regional events held during a one-year period in Anchorage, Alaska.

Types of Events

In terms of type, events may be categorized as follows.

Sporting

The United States recently hosted one of the world's largest sporting events, the 2002 Winter Olympics, with people around the globe tuning in to watch. The opening ceremonies alone were rated 57 percent higher than NBC had for Sydney's Summer Olympics opening ceremony and 49 percent higher than CBS for the winter games in Nagano, Japan. The success of the 2002 Winter Olympics, held in Salt Lake City, Utah, can be attributed only to a management team, who despite a rocky start, laced with controversy, knew how to pull off such an extravaganza.

Sporting events are held in all towns, cities, counties, and states throughout the nation. They attract international sports men and women at the highest levels. Tennis, golf, baseball, football, basketball, downhill ski racing, and car racing are just a few examples. These major events are matched at the local level by sporting competitions for players at all levels. For example, the Pro Am, held annually at most golf courses, allows members to play with professional golfers. This event is usually the highlight of the golfing calendar and requires considerable effort by the team supporting it, including the PGA, the club committee, the club manager, the club professional, ground staff, club administration and catering.

Two very different types of sporting events: the America's Cup Race (shown below), which is a worldwide yacht race held every four years, and a Peewee Soccer Tournament in Austin, Texas.
Source: Tom Raymond/Getty Images Inc./Stone Allstock.

Source: Stephen Dunn/Getty Images, Inc./Allsport Photography.

Entertainment, Arts, and Culture

Entertainment events are well known for their ability to attract large audiences. In some cases, the concerts are extremely viable from a financial point of view; in others, financial problems can quickly escalate when ticket sales do not reach targets. Timing and ticket pricing are critical to the financial success of such events. According to the 2002 edition of the *Statistical Abstract of the United States,* published by the U.S. Census Bureau, 31,700,000 individuals attended Symphony Orchestra Concerts in 2000, the latest year that data were available. Also, 11,700,000 people attended Broadway Show Road Tour performances, and 6,700,000 attended the opera. In fact, 9.4 billion was spent on attending cultural events. Many U.S. art galleries and museums hold special exhibitions that meet the earlier definition of an event. The American Association of Museums reported that 865,000,000 people visit U.S. museums each year. These statistics don't even touch on the thousands of local art fairs and music festivals held in every corner of the country each year.

Commercial Marketing and Promotional Events

Promotional events tend to have high budgets and high profiles. Most frequently they involve product launches, often for computer hardware or software, perfume, alcohol, or motor cars. One such marketing activity dazzled attendees with its new launch motorbikes riding overhead on tightropes, with special-effect lighting.

The aim of promotional events is generally to differentiate the product from its competitors and to ensure that it is memorable. The audience for a promotional activity might be sales staff, such as travel agents, who would promote the tour to their clients or potential purchasers. The media are usually invited to these events so that both the impact and the risk are high. Success is vital.

Meetings and Exhibitions

The meetings and conventions industry is highly competitive. Many conventions attract thousands of people, whereas some meetings include only a handful of high-profile participants.

Festivals

Wine and food festivals are increasingly popular, providing a particular region the opportunity to showcase its products. Small towns such as Kenniwick in Washington state and Mountain View in California attract interest with their food and wine festivals. Many wine regions hold festivals, often in combination with musical events, such as the Portland Jazz Festival. Religious festivals fall into this category, too, and the United States' multicultural community provides rich

A balloon artist captivating a child at an Irish Festival.

opportunities for a wide range of festivals. Chinese New Year and Championship Native American Pow Wow at Traders Village, Texas, are good examples.

Family

Weddings, anniversaries, bar mitzvahs, and nowadays, divorces and funerals all provide opportunities for families to gather. Funerals are increasingly becoming big events with nontraditional coffins, speeches, and even entertainment. It is important for the event

Even a small garden wedding must run smoothly to be a success.

manager to keep track of these changing social trends. For example, Asian tourists are a big market for the wedding industry, with many couples having a traditional ceremony at home and a Western wedding overseas. Hawaii competes with many other international destinations for this market.

Fundraising

Fairs, which are common in most communities, are frequently run by enthusiastic local committees. The effort and the organization required for these events are often underestimated. As their general aim is raising funds, it is important that children's rides and other such contracted activities contribute to, rather than reduce, revenue. Sometimes the revenue gained from these operations is limited. There is also the risk that attendees will spend all their money on these activities and ignore those that are more profitable to the charitable cause. A number of legal requirements must be met by the charitable fundraiser, and these are covered in Chapter 4.

Miscellaneous Events

Some events defy categorization. Potatoes, walnuts, wildflowers, roses, dogs, horses, teddy bears, and ducks all provide the focus for an event somewhere in the United States. The following list shows some of the events held in Texas each year and demonstrate how varied these can be in terms of size and type:

Nolan River Dog Show
Annual Southwestern Exposition and Livestock Show & Rodeo
Martin Luther King Parade
Frontier Days
The Annual Texas Cowboy Poetry Gathering
Mardi Gras of Southeast Texas
Parade of Quilts
Annual North Texas Irish Festival
Annual Redbud Day & Romp
Annual Joy Ride Rod Run
Tons of Suds for Scleroderma
Springfest—Wine, Art and Food Festival—Texas Style
Annual Texas Storytelling Festival
Bayou City Art Festival
Annual Azalea Festival
Annual Bluegrass Jamboree

RioFest
Houston: Texas Hot and Spicy Festival
Scarborough Faire, the Renaissance Festival
Rio Grande Valley Onion Festival
Kerrville Easter Festival and Chili Classic
LBJ Ranch Roundup
Spring Gardening Festival
Windfest
Poteet Strawberry Festival
Great Texas Birding Classic
Texas State Championship Fiddlers Frolics
Arbor Daze
Freer Rattlesnake Round Up
Annual Bluebird Festival
Texas Crawfish Festival
Denton Cinco de Mayo
Annual National Polka Festival
Rockport Festival of Wines
Stockdale Annual Watermelon Jubilee
Annual Fishing Fiesta
Parker County Peach Festival
Annual Great Texas Mosquito Festival
Sahawe Indian Dancer's Summer Ceremonials
International Apple Festival
Ballinger's Annual Tractor Pull
Annual State Fair
Muzikfest
Annual Official Shrimporee of Texas
Fredricksburg Oktoberfest
Marshall Fire Ant Festival
McKinney Dickens of a Christmas

It has to be said that the most common events are community related and that they are run on a fairly small scale with voluntary support and sponsorship. These events provide the potential event manager with invaluable experience, as well as the opportunity to contribute to their community. Every event has a purpose, and the theme is generally linked to the purpose. Analysis of even the smallest event can provide valuable insight into the general principles that apply to managing all events.

The Event Team

An event manager is generally supported by a team that grows enormously as the event draws near. A planning team of 12 that works together for a year can explode into a team of five-hundred for the short period of the event. This phenomenon has been termed the "pulsing organization" by A. Toffler, who coined the term to describe organizations that expand and contract in size. This is particularly appropriate for organizations such as the U.S. Open Tennis Championships, since they surge in numbers for a short period every year. The second example comes from the 2002 Olympic Winter Games where the head of catering had a small team working with him to negotiate contracts with caterers in the lead-up to the Games, with his team expanding to over 200 (including volunteers) in the month before the Games. And there was only one opportunity for the whole group to be together for a training session!

Having just mentioned contractors, it is important to note that the event manager typically works with a number of contractors. These could include any or all of the following:

- venue managers
- stage managers
- lighting, audio, and video companies
- decorators and florists
- entertainers
- employment agencies
- rental companies
- public relations and marketing consultants
- security companies
- catering companies
- cleaning companies
- ticketing operations
- printers

For some events, the manager is also required to become a liaison with government agencies at a range of levels, from local government through to federal government. Local councils deal with event planning and approval; state governments sometimes provide approvals for traffic and policing; and the federal government gives advice on protocol for international dignitaries. These relationships will be explored further when looking in more detail at the planning and staging of an event (Chapters 9 and 11).

*C*ode of *E*thics

As with all modern professions, the presence of a code of ethics can enhance the reputations of those involved and can assist customers to feel confident in their choice of event manager, supplier, or contractor.

The International Special Events Society (ISES) has the following code of ethics:

- *Promote and encourage the highest level of ethics within the profession of the special events industry while maintaining the highest standards of professional conduct.*
- *Strive for excellence in all aspects of our profession by performing consistently at or above acceptable industry standards.*
- *Use only legal and ethical means in all industry negotiations and activities.*
- *Protect the public against fraud and unfair practices and promote all practices which bring credit to the profession.*
- *Maintain adequate and appropriate insurance coverage for all business activities.*
- *Maintain industry standard of safety and sanitation.*
- *Provide truthful and accurate information with respect to the performance of duties. Use a written contract stating all changes, services, products, performance expectations and other essential information.*
- *Commit to increase professional growth and knowledge, to attend educational programs and to personally contribute expertise to meetings and journals.*
- *Strive to cooperate with colleagues, suppliers, employees/employers and all persons supervised, in order to provide the highest quality service at every level.*
- *Subscribe to the ISES Principles of Professional Conduct and Ethics, and abide by ISES By-laws and Policies.*

*C*ase *S*tudy

A group of university students decided to hold a rock concert in the mountains in June and advertised the concert on the Internet. Three bands attended the three-day concert, and there was twenty-four-hour music. One young girl described the entire situation as living hell, although why she stayed is unfathomable. "The dance area was in a valley and to get a drink of water you had to climb a steep hill. Even then, the water was dirty and brown. The restrooms were so far away that nobody bothered to use them. The music pounded all night

Summary

In this chapter we have introduced you to some of the unique characteristics of events, one being that they are often one-off or annual occurrences, thus creating a high level of risk. This characteristic means that the event team has only one opportunity to get everything right. Most events take months or even years to plan, depending on the type and size of the event. And their focus varies, from the strictly commercial product launch to school sporting and art competitions that aim to raise funds with the help of the local community.

and the floor in the cabin we were in vibrated so you couldn't sleep. My friend got sick and there was no medical help. The organizers didn't have a clue. They just wanted to make a fast buck."

- What are some of the things that could go wrong, or have gone wrong, at similar events?
- List three ways in which the organizers were negligent.
- List three ways in which the event could have been improved.
- This event was described to the authorities as a cultural festival. Do you think it belongs in that category?
- The legal compliance issues of such an event will be covered in a later chapter. However, what are some of the ethical issues involved in this event and in others?

Activity

Investigate two events (ideally two that are quite different from each other), and describe them in detail. You might like to do your research on the Internet, starting with one of the state tourism Web pages such as www.travelsd.com (South Dakota's tourism Web site), www.chicago.il.org (the city of Chicago's Web site), or www.visitrhodeisland.com (Rhode Island's Tourism Web site); or you could visit your local council.

Links

www.kumbhallahabad.com/ (Maha Kumbh Mela Festival)
www.ises.com (International Special Event Society)
www.bigtex.com (Texas State Fair)
www.travelsd.com
www.chicago.il.org
www.visitrhodeisland.com

Chapter Two ➤➤
CONCEPT AND DESIGN

The Daddy of 'em All™ is the World's Largest Rodeo & Western Celebration. Cheyenne Frontier Days was established in 1897 in Cheyenne, Wyoming and will attract over 1,800 contestants, competing in nine performances for $1 million in total prize money in 2004. Since its inception Frontier Days has focused on volunteerism, civic participation, attracting visitors to Cheyenne, WY, providing a festive spirit for all involved and running a stellar rodeo.

The rodeo's history dates back to the late 1800's when the country was trying to recover from tough economic times. Cheyenne's Mayor William Schnitger was looking for some way to stimulate the economy of his dusty little town in the high-plains desert. About that time a passenger agent with the Union Pacific Railroad Company came through town and encouraged both the mayor and the editor of the local newspaper to put on a festival or fair. The railroad employee thought this would make Cheyenne a destination and increase traffic on the railroad.

Not only has Cheyenne Frontier Days helped to put the town on the map, it continues to stimulate the local economy and has become the world's largest outdoor rodeo.

www.cfdrodeo.com

On completion of this chapter, you will be able to

- establish the purpose of an event;
- develop a theme and decor that is consistent with the purpose;
- analyze the needs of the event audience;
- review financial and other resources;
- identify an appropriate venue to suit the purpose of an event;
- establish the timing and duration of an event; and
- review the logistical requirements of an event.

Volunteerism and community support are the backbone of Cheyenne Frontier Days that injects millions of dollars into the region's economy. The rodeo is held the last week of July each year and includes 40 bull rides, 28 bareback rides, 28 saddle bronc rides, 15 rookie saddle bronc rides, a wild horse race involving 16 three-man teams, among other events. The support of more than 2,500 volunteers contributes to the execution of this event and its long-standing success. It is an excellent example of a concept that has worked and continues to work.

Steer wrestling at the rodeo.
Source: Reproduced with the permission of Cheyenne Frontier Days.

In this chapter we will look at event concept and design—the creative element that inspires many to embark on careers in event management. Although it is absolutely essential to be creatively inspired, it is likewise essential to understand that innovative ideas must also be reasonably practical owing to the limitations of cost, venue, and safety. The other limitation on creativity is the taste of the client. In some cases, the client needs to be carefully guided in his or her choice of venue and theme, and both the event organizer and the client must have a clear idea of the event's purpose.

Let's look first at the elements of an event that have an impact on the development of the overall concept.

Developing the Concept

There are numerous elements that need to be considered in developing an event concept. They include the purpose of the event, the event theme, the venue, the audience, available resources, the timing of the event, and the skills of the team. The most important of these elements is the purpose, although the purpose is strongly linked to the theme and the venue.

Purpose of the Event

The purpose of the event should drive all the planning. For example, if you were running a conference for financial planners, there could be two quite different purposes:

1. To facilitate an exchange of information, bringing participants up-to-date with the latest changes in financial planning software products.
2. To achieve a memorable out-of-body experience for financial planners in order to develop a positive association with a new software product.

To achieve the first purpose would be quite straightforward, as this would require a fairly standard meeting or convention. Fulfilling the second purpose, however, would be more difficult. For this unforgettable experience, you would need a unique venue and carefully planned activities that the participants would enjoy. At the same time, the product would need to be reinforced constantly so that attendees would leave with an inescapable association with it. To have the fun without the positive association would defeat the purpose.

The focus of the first of these purposes is **information**, whereas that of the second is **entertainment.**

Although for many events the main purpose is making a profit, for many it is not. The Bix Beiderbecke Memorial Jazz Festival held in Davenport, Iowa, has been an annual event for over thirty years. Its purpose is to keep alive the memory and musical accomplishments of the city's native son, Bix, who was a cornetist, a pianist, and a composer. This festival is an excellent example of an event with a **community** purpose.

Theme of the Event

The theme of the event should be linked to the purpose. Moreover, it should be completely compatible with guest needs and consistent in all respects. Most events adopt a color scheme that is repeated on all items produced for the event, such as tickets, programs, uniforms, decor, posters, and merchandise. This technique helps attendees to identify with the theme.

The 2002 U.S. Open was an example of a fully integrated event venue and theme. The Open adopted the theme of "Heroes," since it took place within days of the first anniversary of the 9/11 tragedy. All marketing materials incorporated the theme. The U.S. Open is the largest annually attended sporting event in the world and includes five major championships—men's and women's singles, men's and women's doubles, and mixed doubles.

Bix Beiderbecke Memorial Jazz Festival

HISTORY

The Bix Beiderbecke Memorial Society was founded in 1972, in Leon Bismark (Bix) Beiderbecke's hometown of Davenport, Iowa. The purpose of the Society is to help keep alive the memory of this musical genius alive. Bix received lasting worldwide fame as a cornetist, pianist, and composer. The Society also believes that jazz is a national treasure and that it should be preserved.

Many have called Bix "an enigma." After all, how probable was it that a mostly self-taught young man from the mid-sized Iowa town on the Mississippi River would ever play and compose such incomparable music?

Bix was born on March 10, 1903, blazed like a jazz comet through the "Roaring 20's," and died, worn out and deathly ill on August 6, 1931, at the age of only 28.

How likely was it that he would be little more than an asterisk to the Jazz Age, if that, or that in more recent years he would be the subject of three films, at least five books, countless magazine and newspaper articles, and conversation wherever jazz fans and musicians gather?

In his biography *Sometimes I Wonder,* friend and fellow musician Hoagy Carmichael wrote, "He was our golden boy, doomed to an untimely end." Hoagy also said, "In Harlem, in Hollywood, in the Chicago South Side, in Le Jazz Hot joints in Paris where the city folk come to listen to his records, they still talk of Bix Beiderbecke." An unknown jazz musician perhaps summed up the essence of Bix: "Once you hear him blow four notes on that horn, your life will never be the same."

ANNUAL FESTIVAL

The first Bix Beiderbecke Memorial Jazz Festival was held in 1972. Each year the festival, fondly referred to by many as the "Bix Bash," draws thousands of fans from throughout the United States and even foreign countries where Bix was known and revered as a jazz legend. It is generally held over a four-day period in late July.

Davenport, Iowa, on the banks of the Mississippi River, is part of the Quad-Cities, a metropolitan complex of about 350,000 with ample hotels, motels, and venue sites as well as air transportation (Moline, Illinois, International Airport). The area goes all out to make visitors feel welcome.

There are always at least nine bands alternating between various venues, and concert prices are extremely reasonable. Board members and over three hundred volunteers donate their time and energies to make the "Bix Bash" bigger and better every year. Board members see the Society's goals, in addition to paying tribute to the genius of Bix, as including educating young people to the traditions of jazz through lectures and seminars and by actually learning and playing the music. The Bix Beiderbecke Youth Band is made up of young musicians selected from area high schools and is always on hand to demonstrate its proficiency at the festival.

FUNDING

Putting on an annual festival the size of this musical tribute to Bix is tremendously expensive, and ticket fees alone cannot begin to sustain it. The festival's success is dependent upon grants, sponsors, and donations large and small from Bix fans and supporters. www.bixsociety.org

There are an endless number of potential themes, limited only by your imagination and the size of the customer's pocket. Some examples include the following:

- historical
- geographical and cultural
- sporting
- film, music, and entertainment
- artistic
- food
- objects (i.e., flowers, animals, boats)

When coming up with ideas for a theme, it is most important to consider the range of suitable venues available, keeping in mind the constraints of budget and other considerations.

A hall transformed into a jungle theme complete with a carved ice bar. *Source:* Reproduced with the permission of IceCulture.

Venue for the Event

The event manager needs to carefully consider the planning implications of choosing an unusual venue in preference to a standard
venue requiring decoration only to match the theme. Lighting, sound,
and catering also provide challenges in unusual settings. This treatment will become more evident in the logistics section later in this
chapter and in Chapter 3. The following are examples of unusual
venues:

- demolition site
- parking lot
- tunnel
- museum
- research facility
- amusement park
- orchard
- vineyard
- aquarium

There are over six hundred convention centers located throughout the United States. (See the Internet address in the Links section at
the end of this chapter.) In addition, in most cities there is a host of
meeting rooms available for events. Many of these venues provide
enormous flexibility and can be readily transformed to meet the requirements of the theme. The range is extremely wide—from hotel
banquet rooms to theaters to sporting venues. When considering the
choice of venue, the event organizer needs to look at a number of factors, including the following:

- potential to fulfill the purpose of the event
- ambience
- location
- access by public transportation
- parking
- seating capacity
- features (such as stages)
- cost of decoration, sound, and lighting
- cost of labor
- logistics of setting up
- food and beverage facilities
- safety

There are many, many factors that need to be taken into account in selecting an event venue, but the overall strategy should be to aim for the best possible fit with the client's and the audience's needs at the lowest possible cost. If all stages, props, carpets, seating, portable kitchens and refrigerators, and so on have to be procured, the cost will be very hard to justify—even if the venue seems perfect in other ways.

Event Audience

When organizing an event, the needs of **all** participants must be considered before finalizing the concept. At a recent event, a well-known wheelchair athlete was invited to give a presentation attended by several thousand people. The event center was unable to provide a ramp to the stage for her wheelchair and wanted to compromise by asking members of the audience to lift her chair onto the stage. This treatment was clearly unacceptable. In the example of the entertainment-based event held for the financial planners (conservative stereotype!), an organizer would be wise to challenge normal behavior and to encourage participation in unusual activities. However, great care would need to be taken to ensure that such an audience was not pushed beyond its conservative limits. At a similar event, an event coordinator found that persuading the audience members to wear unusual hats was all that it took to break them out of their normal patterns of interaction. Of course, every audience is different, and the event manager needs to go with the flow and to direct the event to meet audience response. This method can involve sudden changes in plan.

Financial Considerations

The topic of financial management will be covered in detail in Chapter 7. However, it is an important consideration at this early stage of event concept and design. Initial financial estimates can get out of control very easily, and the choice of event concept can certainly contribute to this problem. Otherwise good ideas should be knocked on the head at an early stage if they do not appear financially viable, because it is possible to come up with concepts that are startling in their simplicity and that are also cost effective. This is where the creative and the rational aspects of the event manager's abilities can come into conflict. Very often the creative aspect wins—sometimes at the expense of the company's profit on the event.

Timing of the Event

The timing of an event is often linked to the season or weather. For example, a food-and-wine festival would be better programmed for early autumn than for mid-summer when the heat would be intolerable for both the audience and the vendors. And mid-winter is certainly not the time to hold a flower show. Although this might seem obvious, it is surprising how often events are programmed to occur at very unsuitable times. The timing of sporting events is, of course, limited by the sporting season and their traditional competitions. Broadcasting the event to international audiences is another consideration. Evaluation of an event concept must take into account the following four time-related factors:

1. season
2. day of the week
3. time of day
4. duration

Generally, the weather does affect an event. Depending on the type of event, too much snow or not enough snow in the case of an outdoor winter festival could determine the success of an event. Rain or high temperatures can affect summer festivals. Events that are scheduled too close to holidays or to other community events may have poor attendance. Certain times of the year seem to have an over-supply of events. Wise event planners take into consideration the time of year, normal weather patterns, and already scheduled events that may draw attendees away.

Event Team, Contractors, and Other Stakeholders

The skills of the event team and, just as importantly, the contractors, such as lighting technicians and catering staff, are an important consideration in terms of concept development. Because staff who are working at most events have very limited opportunity for training, job breakdowns and task sheets become essential aspects of planning. In addition, stakeholders such as the police, emergency services, and the Environmental Protection Agency, as well as the local transit authority, have all sorts of requirements that could challenge the feasibility of an event, and these must be investigated.

Analyzing the Concept

The following elements will be covered only briefly here, since they are revisited in a number of later chapters. The aim of introducing them in this chapter is to raise awareness of the problems and pitfalls that can occur if they are not considered at this early stage of concept development. In addition, if not dealt with, they can have a negative impact on the event manager's creativity.

Competition

Prior to involvement in any event, it is essential to conduct an analysis of your competition. This involves looking at the timing and duration of other events, even if they are unrelated. Because people have limited disposable income, festivals and events tend to be nonessential items in most family and tourist budgets.

Regulations

A wide range of laws and regulations have an impact on the staging of events, and these can severely limit creativity. As a simple example, releasing balloons into the atmosphere is considered environmentally unfriendly. Parking, traffic, and neighborhood impact, especially in terms of timing and noise, are all aspects that require the event manager's liaison with local or state government.

Marketing

How to sell an event is a very important part of the initial planning, the timing of your marketing efforts being crucial. Do you advertise months beforehand, or the day or the week before? Will the audience turn up on the day? How can you encourage them to do so? What medium should be used for advertising the event (local TV, radio, magazines, newspapers, direct mail, etc.)? The key is to know your audience and to become visible to them. Should you sell tickets in advance? (Many events actually have no advance ticket sales.) All these questions require the decision-making skills of the event manager or the event management team.

Community Impact

The impact of an event on the local or wider community and others is a major consideration of the planning stage. Because local lobby groups can create extreme difficulties for the unprepared event organizer, it is absolutely essential that community benefits are explained and that other impacts are considered as part of the event proposal.

Risk

At this point you must be aware that for most events, the weather is the greatest risk to attendance and enjoyment. (You will be reminded of this fact at several points throughout this book.) Measures to counteract the impact of weather are essential aspects of event feasibility planning. You must also be aware that insurance premiums will be linked to the perceived risk to the safety of participants.

Revenue and Expenditure

Finally, losing money is the fastest way to get out of the event business. For this reason, the event concept (and the investment in event design) needs very careful analysis.

esigning the Event

Consistency and links to the purpose of the event are all essential parts of the creative process in designing an event. The following are the main creative elements that must be considered.

Theme

As Goldblatt (1997) points out, the theme should ideally appeal to all senses: tactile, smell, taste, visual, and auditory. If the aim of the event is to create a unique and memorable experience for the audience, then appealing to all the senses will contribute positively to the outcome. Keep in mind; once again, the needs of the audience when planning, for example, what music will be played. As we all know, taste in music and desirable sound level vary enormously from one audience to another.

Layout

This creative element is so often given far too little consideration. Consider events that you have attended in which you have felt socially uncomfortable. Your discomfort was generally the result of being in too much open space or of being in a cramped space, having too much light or not enough light, or having just a limited opportunity for people to mix. The worse scenario is being seated at a long, wide table where you are too far away to talk to those opposite and are stuck with people you have little in common with on your left and right. And to add insult to injury, the venue is ablaze with bright lights. Worse still is the cocktail party in a huge ballroom where a small circle develops in the center—not small enough, though, for everyone to talk. The audience needs to comfortably fill the venue to create a positive ambience.

Decor

Fabrics, decorative items, stage props, drapes, and table settings can all be rented; moreover, it is generally worthwhile investigating these options before deciding on the event theme, since renting items can reduce costs enormously. Floral arrangements need to be ordered from florists experienced in larger events. In many ballrooms, floral arrangements are elevated above the table, on tall stands, so that they can be seen across the floor. Careful placement of floral arrangements should be made when being used to decorate the tables, so that guests can talk to each other more easily. Floral arrangements provide a dramatic effect.

Suppliers

Good relationships with suppliers of all commodities will ensure that only quality products will be received, including the freshest flowers and the best produce that the markets can supply. During most large events, suppliers are pressed for the best quality from all their customers at a time when volumes are much larger than usual. This is a situation in which a good long-standing relationship with a supplier is invaluable. It was reported that in Atlanta during the 1996 Olympic Games, people could not buy tissues or towels anywhere. The planners of the Olympic Games in Australia planned early (especially the menus), allowing farmers and other suppliers to sign contracts well in advance. According to a report in *Hospitality News,* The Compass Group (official catering services supplier) for the 2002 Winter Olympics held in Salt Lake City had the job of feeding over 125,000 people daily, including the athletes, members of the worldwide media, judges, and officials. In anticipation of the large crowds, Compass Foods ordered 400,000 hot dogs, 275,000 pounds of Certified Angus Beef, 275,000 bottles of water, 30,000 pounds of cheese, 18,000 pounds of pasta to be consumed, and so on.

The decor has to be carefully considered for a special dinner event.

Technical Requirements

Few people would have attended an event or a meeting where there wasn't a single technical glitch. Speakers put their notes on their laptop, and the screen starts changing at a phenomenal rate. Screensavers come on when the speaker goes on too long, the presentation is halted, and file names appear on the screen. Although none of these problems are caused by technical support, there are ways in which they can be reduced. Technical glitches by the contracted company are unacceptable. Microphones must have backups, the power supply must be assured, and stages and video screens must be visible to all in the audience. There is no substitute for wide-ranging experience, and this is a key attribute that should be sought when choosing technical contractors. New technology, especially anything used to demonstrate new products, needs to be tested thoroughly, through many rehearsals. A backup system is essential.

There are times when a particular event concept should remain just that and be carried no further, because it is technically impossible.

Entertainment

For some events, entertainment is central; for others, it is peripheral. The most important thing is that the entertainment should suit the purpose of the event, not detract from it. The needs of the event audience must be carefully considered when making this decision. A clown creating balloon art is something one would consider for a children's party. However, the same idea (with different designs) could also work extremely well at a product launch while attendees are waiting in line for breakout sessions.

Catering

Nothing makes participants at an event more frustrated than delays in service and poor quality food—except, perhaps, lack of restroom facilities! Whereas guests may have patience with other delays, they will become very agitated if hours are spent in long lines, especially if these are away from the action. Food quality and selection are notoriously bad, as well as outrageously expensive, at many events, and planning must take this factor into account. These days an espresso coffee cart can be found every few yards at most events, reflecting changes in the expectations of the audience and event managers' response to this change. Creative event planning frequently requires unique or unusual food and beverage products, and these can take time to find. They may even need to be imported. Time means money, as does importing, and both can contribute to an escalation in costs.

Logistics of the Concept

The following logistical elements must be taken into account when considering an event concept:

- Access to the site (For example, can vehicles come close enough for off-loading or to park?)
- Physical limitations (For example, will the size or shape of the stairs make it impossible to move heavy equipment?)
- Dimensions of site (Is it too high, too low, too narrow?)
- Refrigerated storage (Is it sufficient?)
- Physical space for food preparation (Is it too small?)
- Restroom facilities (Are they fixed or portable?)
- Cleaning (Is it contracted?)
- Catering (Will there be any physical problems with transporting, storing, and serving food?)
- Safety (Are emergency services, exits, fire procedures, first aid, and so on, all in place?)
- Potential damage to the site (Is there a danger of flowerbeds being trampled?)
- Provision of basic services (Are water and electricity turned on?)

This chapter illustrates the careful balance required between the creative and rational aspects of decision making when considering an event concept. Brainstorming by the planning team will generate ideas, but these then need to be considered as to their feasibility in terms of the issues raised in this and subsequent chapters.

Case Study

One event planner was asked to plan a woman's fortieth birthday party. The woman's husband wanted a party that would be unique and memorable not only for his wife but also for all who attended. He was thrilled with the idea of a luncheon harbor cruise. The planner was to arrange for the boat rental and catering and to decorate the boat on the morning of the party.

As it turned out, there were three complications. The first was the weather. It rained, and they could not use the top deck of the boat, which was wonderful, but only on a sunny day. This limitation meant that the downstairs area became quite crowded. The harbor was also quite choppy, and a few people felt seasick because of the small swell.

The thing that the planner really hadn't thought through carefully enough was the needs of the children who accompanied their parents. The older ones were just bored and not difficult to manage. The toddlers were a disaster. Mothers were on the run all afternoon keeping up with their toddlers, who wanted nothing more than to climb over the rails. But by the end of the afternoon, it was the mothers who were ready to throw themselves over!

Finally, the cruise lasted too long—long enough for some of the party to drink too much and long enough for others to get desperate for dry land and peace and quiet.

The outcome of this event was a real lesson to the event planner in planning for the audience (everyone who came), in selecting the venue, and in timing. An evening party would have ensured that at least the toddlers would have been left at home.

- What were the three complications?
- How could these problems have been avoided?
- What would you suggest for a family party for a fortieth birthday?
- List the types of events affected by weather.
- What are some general suggestions for avoiding weather problems?
- How can you keep young children amused when they are part of an event?
- What would have happened if one of the guests invited to the cruise had been in a wheelchair and there was no access ramp to the boat? (What about accessibility on the boat? Would the guest be able to move the wheelchair freely around the boat? What about the bathrooms; would they be wheelchair accessible?) The ADA's Web site (Americans with Disabilities Act) may be helpful; see www.usdoj.gov/crt/ada.

Activity

Start a collection of images that will inspire future event designs. These may come from a range of sources, including magazines, gift wrap, table napkins, cards, and posters. All will give you ideas for themes and color schemes. You may also like to begin to investigate colors and textures by looking at fabric samples.

*L*inks

www.cfdrodeo.com (Cheyenne Frontier Day Rodeo)
www.bixsociety.org (Bix Beiderbecke Memorial Jazz Festival)
www.usdoj.gov/crt./ada (Americans with Disabilities Act–ADA
    Homepage)
www.specialevents.com (Buyer's guide provides links to florists, en-
    tertainers, fireworks, furniture, etc.)
www.conventioncenters.us

*S*ummary

In this chapter we have looked in detail at the event concept because it is essential that this be workable right from the start. We have stressed the importance of determining the purpose of the event in conjunction with all stakeholders. Early in the process it is also necessary to identify the potential audience as well as the financial and other resources required to support the event. The event concept can then be further developed to include the theme and the decor, and a suitable venue can be selected. We also pointed out that any logistical requirements of the event must be identified early in the planning process. The purpose, theme, audience, and venue need to be compatible elements for the event concept to be successful.

Chapter Three ❧

FEASIBILITY

▼▼▼▼▼▼▼▼▼▼▼ *The 2001 London New Year's Eve celebration was cancelled due to transportation and security concerns. The organizers of the event, police and the mayor's office couldn't reach final agreements. London has had the reputation of hosting one of the world's largest and grandest New Year's Eve celebration in the world. But there were too many unanswered questions left during the final planning stages, so London's Lord Mayor cancelled the event.*

On completion of this chapter, you will be able to

- discuss the feasibility of event concepts;
- analyze the factors that contribute to feasibility;
- look at infrastructure and other event requirements that have an impact on feasibility;
- look at a range of risk factors that could have an impact on feasibility; and
- identify ways in which risk can be minimized.

*T*his article clearly illustrates the issues associated with feasibility and risk. There are many events worldwide that are cancelled as a result of risk, and financial risk not the least. Careful analysis of feasibility and detailed analysis of potential risks are essential when looking at the feasibility of an event. Anticipating risk and planning preventive measures can reduce the liability of the event management company. In the end, however, the event should not go ahead unless there is an unequivocal "Yes" to the question "Is this event feasible?"

*K*eys to Success

The following keys to success were developed by Ernst and Young, advisers to the Olympic Games, the Emmy Awards, and the PGA Tours (adapted from Catherwood and Kirk, 1992):

- Is the event a good idea?
- Do we have the skills required to plan and run the event?

- Is the host community supportive?
- Do we have the infrastructure in the community?
- Can we get a venue at a price we can afford?
- Will the event attract an audience?
- Will it attract media support?
- Is it financially viable?
- Are the success criteria reasonable?

These questions will be used in this chapter to look at the topic of feasibility. In addition to the nine questions listed, we will ask one final question, "What are the risks?" Risk management is one of the most important concerns for the event manager. As mentioned in the first chapter, events can go spectacularly right, but they can also go spectacularly wrong. For an event manager to be involved in an event that goes wrong is not only career limiting but also catastrophic. The opportunity to run another event will not occur, and thus an alternative, vastly different career will need to be considered. This is particularly the case if people are injured or if the event proves to be a financial failure. As mentioned earlier, risk for most business operations is spread more evenly than it is for the event manager or the event management organization. A bad day's trading for a company that trades all year is not as problematic as a bad day's trading for a one-day event! In order to consider the questions posed by Ernst and Young, we will focus on two very different examples: the issues that were raised prior to the 2002 Winter Olympic Games and a proposal for a very small local event, a weekly farmers' market.

Is the Event a Good Idea?

Although this question appears quite simple, there are many event management teams that ask this question more and more frequently as the event draws near. The measure of public support for the 2002 Olympic Games far exceeded the organizers' expectations as evidenced by robust ticket sales. After only a few days into the games, officials from SLOC (Salt Lake Olympic Committee) announced that they had already passed their $180 million goal for ticket revenue, selling 94 percent of 1.6 million tickets. By the end of the games, reports were given that ticket sales far exceeded all expectations. No doubt the organizers had asked the preceding question many times in the months leading up to the event—and hopefully before they made the bid—only to have their doubts resolved at the last minute when record ticket sales were reported. It is a major question for any city bidding for the Olympic Games, and one that needs to be carefully considered at an early stage of the process.

In the case of the farmers' market, the organizers must first determine the purpose of the event. Is it to raise the profile of the area and its products? Perhaps the purpose is to raise funds for charity? Or is it a straightforward commercial venture? No matter what the answer, the organizing committee must then consider carefully if it is a good idea by asking the questions that follow.

Do We Have the Skills?

Criticism of the Salt Lake Organizing Committee for the 2002 Olympic Games and related stakeholders was well documented in the press in the years leading up to the games. However, any doubts were quickly resolved when the games proved to be an outstanding success, demonstrating that the wide range of skills required did exist. The skills required to run a farmers' market are largely administrative. If, however, the concept was developed as a charitable fund-raising event, it would be necessary to carefully consider the ongoing time and commitment required by the volunteers to sustain the event on a weekly basis.

Is the Host Community Supportive?

Some cities and states tend to feel ambivalent about hosting an Olympic Games. The citizens of Colorado voted against holding the Winter Olympic Games in 1976. The people as a whole must commit

The farmers' market got it together, but there were a few obstacles along the way.

to significant expenditures and inconvenience, and some business and residents undoubtedly experience negative consequences. For example, there were constant complaints about the roadwork being done leading up to the 2002 Olympic Games. With a new light-rail system being added and improvements being made to highways that feed into downtown Salt Lake City, the roads were in turmoil for a number of years leading up to the Olympics. There was the belief among some that the funds could have been better spent on schools and hospitals with urgent problems. However, those with an interest in the tourism industry and an understanding of the economic potential of the games were far more positive. An analysis of community support must take the opinions of all such stakeholders into account.

A weekly farmers' market would probably generate little opposition from residents unless vendors were noisy when setting up early in the morning. However, local food retail stores might be quite antagonistic, since the farmers' market would not be faced with the same overheads and could thus provide competition through lower pricing. On the other hand, the market could attract visitors from outlying areas and a few tourists, an outcome that could lead to increased trade for the retail outlets. Most studies show, however, that tourists visiting festivals and markets tend to do so on impulse, so it would not make sense to base planning on the tourism potential of such markets.

Do We Have the Infrastructure in the Community?

The infrastructure required for an Olympic Games is enormous, airport facilities being a good example. Although Cape Town in South Africa put in a bid for the 2000 Olympics, most agreed that the infrastructure would never have been able to cope with an event of such size. Bid cities generally have to make a commitment to infrastructure development in order to win the games and are then faced with the issue of the viability of these venues after the games have left town.

Transportation and parking are generally important considerations. However, in the case of the farmers' market, these would not be problems if the market was held in a country town where open spaces are in abundance.

Can We Get a Venue at a Price We Can Afford?

For most event organizers, the cost of the venue rental is a key consideration. Many are tempted to save money by renting tents or canopies and using temporary accommodations, but this method can prove a false saving, since the decor, lighting, electricity, and catering are generally more expensive and more risky. The benefits of function rooms include tried and tested facilities, safety plans and insurance, as well as numerous other features. The expertise of venue managers cannot be underestimated, and that expertise can contribute to the technical success of an event. With an entertainment event, the location and the cost of the venue can have a critical impact on pricing and promotion.

The cost of the venue is also dependent on the time for which it is required. In some cases, the time needed for setup and dismantling is quite long, necessitating higher than expected rental costs. Car and boat shows are good examples, with huge demands on the logistics of setting up. Goldblatt (1997) refers to these as time/space/temp laws, pointing out that the actual physical space governs the time required. He cites the examples of a Superbowl at which 88 pianos had to be moved onto the field during half-time. Loading area access and storage are other considerations. And security is of particular concern because high-priced items can turn up missing; it was reported that a new model car disappeared from the floor of an Australian car show and was taken for a 375-mile joyride!

The costs incurred by a farmers' market for its venue would be minimal compared with the enormous cost of the purpose-built venues suitable for events like the 2002 Winter Olympics. Nevertheless, these costs are just as important a consideration for the market as they are for organizers of any Olympic Games. Despite the fact that such venues remain a lasting legacy for the host city, their long-term financial viability is always an issue of concern.

Will the Event Attract an Audience?

The location of the event venue or site is crucial for attracting the numbers you require to make the event successful. In the case study at the end of this chapter, you are given a list of potential events, and then you are asked to rank them in terms of their feasibility. All are located in different towns and cities, and a study will have to be made of the local population, as well as of the domestic and international visitors who may be attracted to the event. Identifying the audience is a key issue for event managers in planning an event.

Market research into current trends is essential for event feasibility planning. An extensive range of reports is available from tourism commissions at both city, state, and federal levels. For example, findings from a report on the seniors market show that this age group is a tourism market segment with significant potential. These statistics, combined with data from the U.S. Census Bureau, report on the changing demographics (including age groups) of the U.S. population, and clearly point to the size of this market now and its potential in the future. Seniors are living longer than ever before. They are staying healthier longer and are pursuing active lifestyles.

Returning to the example of the farmers' market, this concept could be expanded to include the whole spectrum of organic foods and health products and so become a highly feasible event targeted specifically at seniors. The location would need to be in an area in which the demographic group is large and continues to grow, and the venue would need to have facilities that cater for seniors, such as easy parking, not many stairs, and so on.

Figures 3–1, 3–2, and 3–3 illustrate the demographics of four randomly selected cities in Los Angeles County. As is apparent from Figure 3–1, West Hollywood's population is aging in comparison with that of the broader areas of Los Angeles, Torrence, and San Fernando. It has a higher than average number of people in the age 65 and over demographic. At the other end of the age scale (Figures 3–2 and 3–3), the percentage of people in the 0–9 and 10–19 year demographics in West Hollywood is lower than those of the other areas compared.

In view of these statistics, a strategic ten-year plan for an annual event would target the age group showing the highest growth rate in West Hollywood, in this case people aged 65 and over. Targeting a declining age group would reduce the feasibility of the event in the long term.

Figure 3–4 shows the population distribution by suburbs in twenty randomly selected cities in Los Angeles County, and this information could be used effectively to indicate the feasibility of an event designed to attract a large local audience. Of the suburbs shown, Torrance, Downey, and West Covina are the most populous suburbs and would thus appear to be the best locations for an event of this nature.

Will the Event Attract Media Support?

Media support is essential. Whether the event will attract national and international attention, as in the Olympics, or a local radio station or a hometown newspaper depends on the type of event. Smart organizers take a look at the different media outlets that are available.

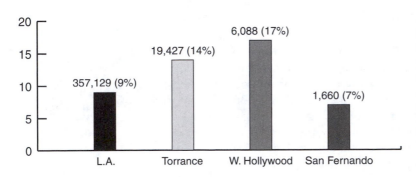

Figure 3–1 Percentage of Senior Citizens (over 65 Years) in the Population of the City of LA Compared with Three Suburbs
Source: Data from the U.S. Census Bureau (2000 Census). lapl.org (go to databases; statistics; Databook for LA county Table II)

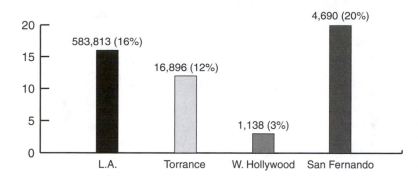

Figure 3-2 Percentage of Children (0–9 Years) in the Population of the City of LA Compared with Three Suburbs
Source: Data from the U.S. Census Bureau (2000 Census).

They try to determine which outlets their possible attendees use to get their news. For example, if the event is a children's fair, then the organizers should try to determine which television stations, radio shows, newspapers, and magazines the parents are most likely to use in that community. Press releases, guest appearances, and even advertisements should then be targeted at those media outlets.

In the case of the farmer's market, it would be best to approach local newspapers to seek their support. Stories and images, with a focus on the value to the community, the local farmers, and the management of risks, would need to be provided to stimulate both media and community interest in the event. A special feature, including advertisements by exhibitors, would be the type of proposal that would be well received at the local level.

Is the Event Financially Viable?

An event that is financially viable and that brings benefits to the community can outweigh most objections. One that is not viable will have a short life span. The farmer's market would be unlikely to make huge profits or generate substantial charitable funds, but it might contribute to community spirit and provide intangible benefits to the local population. For example, it might enhance the reputation of local

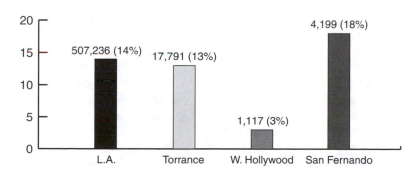

Figure 3-3 Percentage of Young People/Teens (10–19 Years) in the Population of the City of LA Compared with Three Suburbs
Source: Data from the U.S. Census Bureau (2000 Census).

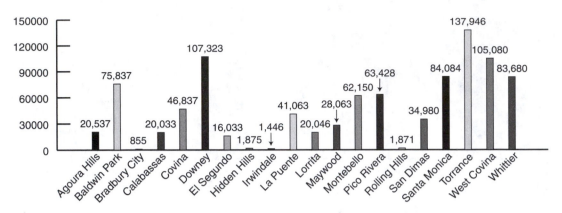

Figure 3-4 Population Distribution with Selected Cities in Los Angeles County
Source: Data from the U.S. Census Bureau (2000 Census).

agricultural products, thus attracting investment in the farm-grown concept. Fees charged to the vendors would need to cover all expenses associated with the event, since there would be no charge to visitors.

The Olympic Games held in Montreal in 1976 left a lasting debt for the Canadian people. What began as a glorious vision turned into a financial disaster, and one that took the people of Quebec almost twenty years to pay off. Through planning errors, misjudgments, and strikes, as well as suspected corruption, the estimated cost of $124 million rose to an incredible $1.5 billion. In contrast, in Australia, the New South Wales taxpayer was free of debt after the Sydney 2000 Olympic Games, which also reaped additional benefits for the people of Australia. As reported in the *Salt Lake Tribune* soon after the 2002 Winter Olympics, Mitt Romney, president of SLOC (Salt Lake Organizing Committee), appeared before the Utah House of Representatives and paid off its $99 million obligations to the state of Utah, "fulfilling the promises of three generations of Olympic leaders that the 2002 Winter Games would not leave taxpayers in debt but would leave a legacy."

For most events, the decision as to what price is to be charged to visitors or spectators, and when the decision is made, is critical. Tickets cannot go on sale the day after an event is over, nor can the merchandise that was produced for the event. The failure to sell T-shirts, caps, and CDs will mean lost revenue for the event. Even the concession outlets that sell food and beverages do not get a second chance at sales. For these reasons, both the decision on price and the timing of this decision are extremely important in ensuring that the event audience reaches a viable level.

In Chapter 7, on financial management, the concept of a break-even point will be discussed. For the event manager, careful attention to budgeting will provide a reasonably accurate idea of the costs involved in running the event, and this is essential in making a decision as to what to charge for tickets. Before ticket prices can be determined, it is helpful to understand the local market and the consumer's perceptions regarding value for money.

However, not all events are ticketed: an exhibition, for example, involves renting booths to exhibitors, and the price charged for exhibiting is based on the cost of staging the exhibition and the likely number of exhibitors. For nonprofit events, financial decisions involve keeping within the budget, which may be established by another body (for example, the nonprofit organization's board of directors). When a client is paying for the staging of an event, the event management company would develop a budget for the event based on very clear expectations from the client as to the benefits expected from the event. Often the event management company earns a fee and the client is ultimately responsible for the cost of the budgeted items and any variations.

Are the Success Criteria Reasonable?

The criteria on which the success of events is judged vary widely. The Olympic Games is generally judged on feedback from the international audience. Although feedback from the athletes on accommodation and sporting facilities is important, the continuing sponsorship of the games is the result of the response of the world television audience. This is clearly one of the most relevant criteria for the continued success of this mega-event.

The farmers' market could encourage local growers to develop entrepreneurial skills and to produce and market a differentiated product. This has already been done by many regional wine growers, such as the wine growers from Wenatchee, Washington, who participate in the WAWGG (Washington Wine Grape Growers) Annual Meeting, Convention, and Trade Show held in Yakima, Washington. Wines from Wenatchee that used to be considered a regional choice are now being marketed and served throughout the country and abroad. Change in consumers' perception of a region's products is difficult to measure, as is the increased confidence of the local producers. These are known as intangible outcomes and seldom form part of the success criteria, which tend to be more tangible results, such as improved sales. Increased exposure to Utah was one of the intangible outcomes of the 2002 Winter Olympic Games.

A wedding is an interesting event to analyze in terms of success. Should its success be judged on the criteria of the bride, the groom, the parents, or the guests? Were there elements of the wedding (such as lack of compatibility between the bride's and the groom's

Like many other cities, San Francisco's local farmers come together every Saturday for a farmers' market. Despite the event's low-key appearance, it takes a host of volunteers to keep the market going on a weekly basis.
Source: AP/Wide World Photos.

families) that could not be managed? And just about everyone attending has a point of view about the decor and color scheme.

The criteria for success need to be established before the event takes place, as it is against these that the feasibility of the event is analyzed.

What Are the Risks?

This final question is the most important of all, because failures, and even fiasco, are always possible.

Brainstorming, in order to reveal all of the possible risks associated with an event, and then ranking them, is the first step. Risks may include the following:

- heavy weather, wind, and/or rain
- flooding
- fire
- collapse of buildings or temporary structures
- accidents involving workers and/or the event audience
- crowd control
- security of participants and VIPs
- food poisoning
- breakdown in water supply or power supply

Contingency planning, in order to deal with potential risks, is the next step. And the third step is that policies and procedures must be put in place to deal with every possible eventuality. In Chapter 8, we will discuss risk management in more detail, with particular focus on priorities and operational plans designed to minimize risk.

The IACC (International Association of Conference Centers) has set international standards for operations, facilities, equipment, and management for small- to medium-sized conference centers (20 to 50 people), and many conference venues around the country are adopting these as a benchmark. This type of accreditation is reassuring for the event organizer and an excellent method of reducing many of the most common risks. Links to this association are listed at the end of the chapter.

To briefly summarize, the aim of the event organizer is to improve feasibility and to reduce risk (see Figure 3–5).

The SWOT Analysis

It is traditional, and important, to do a SWOT analysis for every event. This involves analyzing the strengths, weaknesses, opportunities, and threats of the event or event concept.

S   **Strengths** are the internal strengths of the organization, for example, the enthusiasm and commitment of volunteers, the specialist knowledge of the lighting engineer, or the wide range of products available for planning themes and decor.

W   **Weaknesses** are the internal weaknesses of the organization, for example, the skills and knowledge of the management committee or their lack of availability for meetings.

O   **Opportunities** are the external favorable things that may occur, such as new sponsorships or unexpected positive publicity.

T   **Threats** are also external: competition, poor publicity, and poor crowd behavior would all be classified as threats.

Figure 3–5   Aim of the Event Organizer.

Improve feasibility   Reduce risk

Summary

In this chapter we have compared two very different types of events and in the process have shown that asking simple questions can help you to determine the feasibility of an event concept. Questions need to be asked about the financial viability of the concept, the demographics of the audience, the infrastructure required to stage the event, and, of great importance, the potential risks. We have also discussed the contribution of community and media support to the success of an event. An evaluation of an event's success or otherwise, based on criteria established in the planning stages, should be carried out after the event. Some events are measured by profits, others by the level of community support they attract.

Essentially, the idea of improving the feasibility of an event is to improve the strengths of the organization (and the concept) and to maximize the opportunities. Likewise, acknowledging potential weaknesses and dealing with them will minimize the risks. Assessing potential threats and introducing contingency plans to circumvent them will also improve the feasibility of the event.

Case Study

Use the questions provided in this chapter and any other relevant ideas or information to discuss the feasibility of the following event concepts. Then rank them in order, from most to least feasible.

- Agricultural Show in December in Lawrence, Kansas
- Flower Show in Pasadena, California, in February
- Wedding on an island off San Francisco Bay in July (with tents)
- Red Earth Native American Arts Festival in Oklahoma City, Oklahoma, in May
- Creole Dance Festival in New Orleans in July
- Marathon in Denver, Colorado, in January
- Food and Wine Festival in Napa Valley, California, in December
- Wildflower Show in Tucson, Arizona, over the Easter weekend
- Spring Break Celebration at Virginia Beach, Virginia, in April

Activity

List the advantages and disadvantages (and thus the feasibility) of the following event durations:

- one session on one day
- sessions on multiple days
- annual session on multiple days

Use an example for each in your discussion, which should be based on some of the concepts in this chapter and in Chapter 2.

Links

www.lapl.org (go to databases; statistics; Databook for LA county
    Table II for the statistics used in Figures 3–1, 3–2, 3–3, and 3–4)
www.iacconline.com (International Association of Conference Centers)
www.icca.nl/index.htm (larger exhibition centers)

Chapter Four

LEGAL COMPLIANCE

While the press reported that the party was a disorganized, wild bunch of teenagers running an illegal rave party at which drug dealing was rampant, this was not the case. The party had been carefully planned with approvals sought from the police and local authorities and had met requirements for liquor licensing, security and amenities. Showers, water and first aid were all provided. The event was supported by a range of sponsors and had taken two years of planning.

Event Organizer

On completion of this chapter, you will be able to

- explain the laws and regulations that may have an impact on event planning;
- identify the bodies from whom approval is required or support is needed, to stage a particular event;
- explain the legal compliance requirements of an event;
- identify insurance premiums and fees that need to be paid; and
- describe the contracts required between event organizers and other parties, including subcontractors.

This case study clearly illustrates the dilemmas faced by event organizers of rock concerts. In this case, the organizers not only had sought all approvals but also had the support of the police and the city where it was to be held. It is easy to see, then, why event organizers must ensure that they comply with the relevant legislation. For example, if you were organizing a music event, it would be necessary, among other things, to obtain permission in compliance with the Federal Copyright Laws and to pay fees to satisfy copyright agreements with song writers and publishers.

This chapter will cover all the necessary requirements, such as music licensing, food safety plans, the building of temporary structures, entertainment in public places, and road closures.

There are three levels of government in the United States—federal, state, and local—and there are laws and regulations at each of these levels that may require compliance (see Figure 4–1). For example, federal law gives the legal drinking age as 21 years of age. When

Federal Government (Federal Law)

State Government (Laws of States)

Local Government (Regulations)
(Counties, Cities,
Towns)

Figure 4–1 Levels of Government and Sources of Law

serving alcoholic beverages at the event, you must comply with that federal law. If you're holding your event in a park, then the permission from the local (city/town or sometimes the county) would need to be sought. Generally, the first place to start is at the local level. Call the local mayor's office, and describe the event. The office will generally give advice on all legal compliance and will direct the event management team as to what other departments within the city must be notified, such as the police, the Environmental Protection Agency, if applicable, park's department, and so on. Some cities have event planning policies that include all relevant regulations, as well as higher-level legal compliance requirements.

In Appendix 2 , the outline for an event proposal provides prompts for a range of legal requirements, some of which may not be applicable, for example, to the organization of an indoor event. However, this general outline gives you the main cues for event planning and for meeting legal obligations.

Relevant Legislation

The principles of the major acts and regulations relevant to event management are covered below in the next sections, in general terms.

Local Government Acts and Regulations

There are a number of local government regulations that may apply to events. These vary considerably from one area to another. Some city councils have detailed guidelines, whereas others have less formal requirements. The size of the event largely determines the detail required in the submission, since smaller events tend to have a lower impact on the community.

If an event has already been held in one area, with approval, it may still be necessary to obtain approval for a second similar event in another location. Likewise, if the event covers more than one jurisdiction, additional proposals may need to be submitted.

If the event requires the building of permanent structures, all necessary building permits would be required. Application for the use of the premises and property for entertainment may also be necessary. Plans would need to be developed for the erection of temporary structures, and approval would need to be sought for them.

Approvals are required by most cities for the following:

- using loudspeakers or amplifiers in public spaces
- installing amusement devices
- singing or providing entertainment in public places (fees would also apply)
- using a building or structure for entertainment
- building a temporary structure

City councils are also very concerned about cleaning programs during and after the event, noise and disturbance of local residents, and traffic management.

Business Registration

Each state has different requirements for registering a business. Most states do require that every business be registered, whether you're a corporation, partnership, limited liability company, limited liability partnership, or an association. Small business development is encouraged, and there are agencies such as the SBA (Small Business Administration) that will provide advice and assist with the formalities in all states.

Entertainment Industry Legislation

Licenses for the entertainment industry cover agents, managers, and venue consultants. The disbursements of fees, as well as trust accounts for performers, are covered by this type of legislation. There is also a code of ethics. Entertainment industry legislation allows for complaints to be heard and resolved regarding payments to performers, agents, managers, and venue consultants.

Music Copyright

The right to use music in business or commercial operation as well as in a public setting requires permission according to U.S. copyright law. There are two ways to obtain permission. The first and easiest way is to go through a performing rights organization. These organizations represent songwriters and publishers and their right to be compensated for having their music performed in public. There are three performing rights organizations in the United States: ASCAP,

BMI, or SESAC. By obtaining a license from these companies for the songwriters and performers whom they represent, music users can legally play any song from their repertory. Without a license, music users would be in danger of copyright infringement. Since an artist or publisher can be represented only by one performing rights organization, it is generally important to obtain licenses from all three organizations if a variety of music is to be used at the function. The fees, although nominal, recognize the copyright and commercial value of music. The fees vary according to the use of the music (from background music, live performances, music played at free or benefit concerts, etc.). The other way to obtain permission is to go directly to the owner of the copyright for each specific piece of music. Although it is fully permissible, most event managers would find that method to be very expensive and time consuming.

Liquor Licensing

In general, this legislation covers the age of drinkers, the venues, and the situations (for example, with meals) in which alcoholic drinks can be served, as well as the legal hours of alcohol service. Liquor must be correctly labeled and sold in legal measures. A sign must be displayed to say that it is an offense to sell or supply liquor to, or obtain liquor on behalf of, a person under the age of 21 years. The licensee must be able to show that reasonable steps (including requests for identification) have been taken to ensure that minors have not been served alcohol.

Federal Trade Commission Act

The Federal Trade Commission Act aims to ensure that advertised goods and services are provided in accordance with the advertising. This act protects the consumer against misleading advertising and deceptive conduct. A consumer (or a client) can sue under this law; that is, one cannot engage in conduct that is liable to mislead the public as to the nature, the characteristics, and the suitability for the purpose or the quality of any services. The contract for services to be provided in the organization of an event thus needs to be extremely explicit.

Federal Equal Employment Opportunity Laws

These laws protect employees and customers from discrimination on the basis of factors such as race, color, religion, sex, age, or national origin. They also prohibit employment discrimination against qualified

A liquor license is required to serve alcoholic beverages. New York Food Fair.
Source: Rafael Macia/Photo Researchers, Inc.

individuals with disabilities in the private sector, as well as in state and local governments.

Clean Air Act

Under the watch of the Environmental Protection Agency (EPA), which develops and enforces regulations, this legislation allows prosecution for those contributing to the pollution of the air.

Noise Control

Noise is a troublesome problem for festivals and events, since by their very nature they attract crowds, with entertainment events being particularly problematic. It is therefore essential to check noise limitations in terms of allowable decibels and the times during which loud music is permitted. (Check with the local jurisdiction.)

Clean Water Act

Discharge of sewage, oil, and other waste into water systems is illegal, and our waterways are protected by the Federal Water Pollution Control Act.

Safe plating of food. These carts are designed to be stored in refrigerators.

Safe Food Handling

Under the direction of the FDA, National Food Safety Programs provide guidelines for safe food handling (www.foodsafety.gov). Contract caterers should be required to develop a food safety plan covering food safety at all stages of delivery, preparation, and service. This step is necessary to guard against bacteria that may develop if food is left standing after delivery, or during preparation and service, and not kept at an appropriate temperature. Buffets where food is left unrefrigerated are notorious for high bacteria levels. Generally, food needs either to be kept cool or to be heated to a hot temperature. The mid-temperature range is the most dangerous. A qualified caterer and his or her employees should know all about food hygiene and should follow correct procedures to avoid contamination. A food safety plan should be part of any catering contract, which should also include menus and prices.

Charitable Fundraising

Some states have a set of registration forms, requirements, and procedures for fund-raising. These regulations are needed to

1. promote proper management of fund-raising appeals for charitable purposes;
2. ensure proper record-keeping and auditing; and
3. prevent deception of members of the public who desire to support worthy causes.

A person who participates in a fundraising appeal that is conducted unlawfully is guilty of an offense. Authority is required to conduct a fund-raising appeal, and this is obtained by applying to the relevant body in your state. *Fund-Raising Regulation: A State-by-State Handbook of Registration Forms, Requirements and Procedures,* by Seth Perlman and Betsy Hills Bush, is a good resource for event managers. Another source for a state-by-state listing of requirements can be found by going to www.raffa.com. See Figure 4–2, which offers suggestions for documenting contributions given to nonprofit organizations.

Insurance

The most important insurance required by an event management company is general and product liability insurance. Claims against this insurance can be reduced by careful risk analysis and prevention strategies. Cities often require a certain level of insurance for minor events and another level of insurance for major events. As with most other local government requirements, these may change from one

Charities must send written acknowledgements of donations and contributed property worth $250 or more. Nonprofits should send a written document and retain a copy for its records. The acknowledgement must include:

1. Amount of cash contributed (or description, but not the value of property other than cash).
2. Whether or not the organization provided goods or services in exchange for the contribution. An exchange of goods or services reduces the tax deductible amount by the retail value of the good or service exchanged.
3. Additionally, if goods or services were provided in exchange for the contribution, the acknowledgement must include a description plus a good faith estimate of the value of the good or service exchanged.
4. Additionally, if goods or services were provided in exchange for the contribution, the acknowledgement must include a description plus a good faith estimate of the value of the goods and/or services provided.
5. Acknowledgement of an "intangible religious benefit" if true of the goods or services provided. An example of this would include admission to a religious event.

Excerpted from *Handbook for Starting a Successful Nonprofit.* Used with the permission of the Minnesota Council of Nonprofits 2001 (www.mncn.org).

Figure 4–2   Documenting Contributions

city or municipality to another. Assets and motor vehicles also need to be insured. See Figure 4–3, which shows a disclaimer that could be used by the organizers of a race event.

Essentially, the person who signs this disclaimer is taking responsibility for his or her actions. However, from a legal point of view, there is nothing to stop the contestant from making a case for negligence against the race organizer. Clearly, it would have to be shown that this negligence led directly to the injury, and the extent and impact of the negligence would then be investigated. In other words, an event organizer cannot avoid liability for negligence by having participants sign a disclaimer. The person has the right to sue in any circumstances, and the case would be judged on its merit.

The following disclaimer is aimed at reducing the liability of a race organizer:

1. *I, the undersigned, hereby waive any claim that I might have arising out of my participation in this event and fully accept all the risks involved.*
2. *This waiver shall operate separately in favor of all bodies involved in promoting or staging the event.*
3. *I hereby attest and verify that I am physically fit and have sufficiently trained for this event. I agree to be bound by the official rules and regulations of the event.*
4. *I hereby consent to receive medical treatment that may be deemed advisable in the event of injury or accident.*

Figure 4–3

In addition to public liability insurance that must be taken out by the event management organization, all contracts signed with subcontractors, such as a company that erects scaffolding, should also include a clause requiring the subcontractor to hold a current policy covering them against liability for incidents that may occur. As you can see, there are a number of different stakeholders who are potentially liable, and the event organizer therefore needs to limit his or her own liability by managing risk and ensuring that subcontractors are also insured. In the following article, the honorary vice president of Clowns International advised 70 members to take out insurance against potential claims for custard pie injuries!

> *Clowns gathered at a special Big Top conference last week—to discuss the legal risks of chucking pies. They got serious as they discussed whether circus audiences sitting in the front row were willfully placing themselves in the line of fire. Clowns fear they could be liable for compensation if a member of the public got it in the face.*
>
> International Express, April 10, 2001

Other insurance policies that should be considered are errors and omissions policies (for any claim for breach of professional duty through any act, error, or omission by you, your company, or your employees) and climate insurance against rain and other climatic occurrences that might have an impact on the event. Clearly, climate insurance is extremely expensive, and the process of demonstrating the impact of climatic conditions on attendance is quite onerous.

Since insurance is a key issue these days, it is wise to exchange copies of insurance policies with the venue managers. When you pick a site for your event that is not normally used for entertaining, be clear on who is responsible for the insurance. Be sure that you haven't exposed yourself and your volunteers to lawsuits by choosing an unprotected site. In the case of sporting events, it is important that participants sign a liability waiver form.

Security Legislation

This legislation provides for the licensing and regulation of persons in the security industry, such as crowd controllers, bouncers, guards, and operators of security equipment. In general, most states license security personnel through the Department of Public Safety. At this point, there is not a nationwide standardization, and each state has its own requirements for training.

Occupational Safety and Health Act

This legislation is designed to save lives and to prevent workplace accidents and injuries in order to protect the health of America's workers. The legislation has specific requirements for employers to provide safe workplaces and safe work practices. This topic will be covered in detail in Chapter 15.

Workers Compensation Insurance

Workers compensation insurance, which is obligatory, covers treatment and rehabilitation of injured workers. Volunteers and spectators are not covered, since they are not paid workers. Instead, they would be covered under the organization's general liability insurance.

Taxation

For anyone running a commercial business (fee for service), compliance with taxation rules is essential. Most states require businesses to be registered. Go to www.sba.gov/hotlist/license.html for a listing of where to go to obtain a business license. Most counties maintain an office for licensing issuing officers and will give advice on all types of taxation applicable, including all payroll deductions that need to be held for paid employees. Qualified charitable bodies and some educational institutions may have tax-exempt status. It's always best to consult with an accountant as you set up your business or organization.

Stakeholders and Official Bodies

Some of the following bodies may require detailed plans or briefings, depending on the extent of their involvement in an event.

Police

Oftentimes the venue or site officials will demand that a certain number of police officers be present during your event. In some areas, the city will dictate the number of officers that you will need to have on hand, often depending on the crowd expected. It is wise to contact the local police if you are collecting large sums of cash or expect more than a couple hundred people. Some venues will have their own security staff or may even contract with a security force. In that case, the security coverage would be part of your contract with the venue. It is a good idea to send a packet of event information to the local police chief, including schedules, maps, contact numbers, press releases, and so on.

Any impact on traffic because of an event must be discussed with the police in advance. The staging of an important event in Washington, D.C., proved problematic when most of the guests arrived in limousines. The driveway was too small to accommodate them, and the traffic backed up for miles, resulting in the event program being delayed. This disruption had implications for the VIPs invited, including senior members of local and foreign governments, who missed flights and other engagements.

Emergency Services

In most cities, an event organizer should alert the fire chief ten days to two weeks prior to the event. Depending on the size of the estimated crowd, the local department will determine how many paramedics and other employees need to be on hand to assist in the case of an emergency. If the general public is invited to your event, then the emergency services are generally covered by the city's budget. Those services may need to be contracted out for private events.

If you plan to host athletic activities at your event, it might be wise also to contact your local hospital and Red Cross. Ask these organizations for safety instructions and required items to have on hand, such as strip bandages, stretch and gauze bandages, ice packs, and the like. It is best if paramedics or health personnel be in attendance at athletic events.

Contracts

This final topic is the most important in this chapter and could become a book in its own right. The effectiveness of the contracts between the parties involved in an event is crucial. Specifications need to be incredibly detailed in order to avoid disputes. Clarity and agreement between all parties is essential. The contract provides the basis for variation in price every time the customer has new demands. For this reason, time invested in the writing of the contract will reap rewards and often resolve legal disputes. Professional legal advice is essential for a new event management business. (See Figure 4–4.)

Many events involve a range of contractors for services such as catering, cleaning, sound, lighting, and security. While it is tempting for an event organizer to take on all roles, the benefits of employing contractors are many. Specialist organizations generally have more expertise and better equipment, they generally carry their own insurance, and they have a lot of experience in their particular field. By dealing with a range of contractors and using professionally prepared, well-negotiated contracts, the event organizer can dramatically reduce risk and liability. On the day of the event, the main role of the

- parties to contract
- deadline and deposit
- specifications (for example, space booked, timing, food and beverage, accommodation)
- services to be provided
- special requirements
- schedule of payments
- insurance
- cancellation
- termination/nonperformance
- contingency
- consumption
- confidentiality
- arbitration
- warranties
- signatories
- date

Figure 4–4   Content of Contract/Agreement

event organizer is to monitor the implementation of the agreed contracts.

Case Study

You and your friends are planning to have a party to celebrate the end of the college year. Your plan is to hold the party at the parking lot of the school's football stadium, but if it rains, you will hold it in your garage. Invitation has been informal, and you aren't sure how many students have actually been invited. Everyone will bring his or her own alcohol, although a few of the people will be under twenty-one. A friend with a sound system is bringing it along, and you have decided to charge everyone who attends $5 to cover your costs. Another friend who runs a catering company will provide munchies and will charge $2 per plate.

- Is permission required to use the parking lot, and if so, from whom?
- What are the implications of charging an entry fee? Would you recommend this?
- Should the police be told about the party? (Is there any chance that uninvited people may turn up?)
- Do you need a liquor license if alcohol is not sold?
- Who is responsible for underage drinking?
- What would happen if a fault in the wiring caused someone to be electrocuted?
- What are the limitations on the use of a sound system, either at home or at the parking lot?

Summary

This chapter dealt with legal and related issues that must be considered during the planning of an event, including licensing and approvals. Legal compliance is one of the major risk issues for organizers of an event, and research into these requirements is essential. Tight contractual arrangements with the client and subcontractors are equally important, since these can ensure the financial viability of an event or can completely derail it. Insurances of various types are also required, including workers compensation and public liability; moreover, workplace health and safety should be a major consideration of any event organizer.

Activity

Investigate two venues that offer weddings, and compare their advertised services/products, contracts, and checklists from the point of view of the customer and the owner of the business. In addition, compare the contracts of the two venues in terms of the potential for misunderstandings to develop and legal disputes to follow.

Links

www.sba.gov (Small Business Administration)
www.epa.gov (Environmental Protection Agency)
www.ftc.gov (Federal Trade Commission)
www.nal.usda.gov/foodborne (Foodborne Illness Education Information Center)
www.foodsafety.gov (Government food safety information)
www.fstea.gov (Food Safety Training & Education Alliance)
www.raffa.com (Lists fundraising requirements for each state)
www.mncn.org (Minnesota Council of Nonprofits)

Chapter Five

MARKETING

Fan Fair 2002 was bigger and better than ever with an aggregate attendance of more than 126,500, making it the biggest crowd in Fan Fair's 31-year history. Enlarging the event and improving on the successes of Fan Fair's move to Downtown Nashville in 2001, "The World's Biggest Country Music Festival" provided more activities, more stars and more music for the fans to enjoy. More than 40 artists participated in the star-studded, nightly concerts at Adelphia Coliseum during the four days.

www.fanfair.com

On completion of this chapter, you will be able to

- describe the features of event marketing, including intangibility, variability, inseparability, and perishability;
- establish the features of an event product;
- understand market segmentation;
- analyze consumer decision-making processes;
- establish ticketing programs where required;
- promote and publicize an event;
- attract sponsorship for an event; and
- evaluate the marketing effort.

Fan Fair is one of America's best examples of an event that grows from strength to strength, gaining in popularity from year to year. It continues to enhance Nashville's image as a tourist destination. There are many music festivals in the United States, but few have had as much impact as this one. The reason for its success has a lot to do with marketing and what is known as the marketing mix—the combination of product (country music festival as opposed to rock festival), price, promotion, and place. The choice of messages and the channels of communication with the event audience are also important, and together these factors form part of the marketing strategy.

Marketing is important because it helps to attract an audience without which any event will turn out to be a nonevent! The event audience makes decisions about cost and effort to attend, and the audience weighs these against the benefits of attending. An understanding of the decision-making processes of the audience is therefore essential for anyone planning and promoting an event.

Nature of Event Marketing

Event products generally include a combination of goods and services, and so provide a challenge for those involved in event marketing. Some industries market products without a service component, for example, soft drinks where the focus would be on the product. In marketing computer equipment, however, there would be goods and services aspects of the product that might include hardware and backup service. On the other hand, when marketing something purely intangible, such as "Come for the atmosphere" or "Do you just want to have fun?" there is a large service component. In some respects it is far more difficult to market something that the customer cannot take home or physically consume.

The first feature of services marketing that makes it challenging, then, is its **intangibility.** Another feature of services marketing is that there is a higher degree of variability in the service provided, as well as in the response to the service provided. The service and the service provider are also distinguished by their **inseparability.** In other words, as an event organizer, you are very reliant on your staff, performers, and athletes to meet the needs of the audience. You have far less quality control than you would over tangible goods (such as soft drinks)—unless your training is first-rate.

In summary, the three features of services marketing are the following:

- Intangibility (such as fun, entertainment, information)
- Inseparability (such as the usher's service approach to the customer when product and provider are inseparable)
- Variability (such as different levels of service provided by different ushers or different responses from two or more customers to the same experience)

Some goods and services components of a conference are illustrated in Figure 5–1.

There is one final important consideration for the event marketer. A restaurant in a good location can rely on a level of passing trade. So, too, can a general store. This is not the case with an event, as the decision to attend or not attend is generally made shortly before the event and is irrevocable. If a customer decides not to attend, revenue to the event organizer is completely lost. This is not the case for the restaurant owner or shopkeeper, who may see the customer at a later date. An event, whether it is a one-time or an annual event, is highly **perishable.** Unsold tickets cannot be put out on a rack at a reduced price!

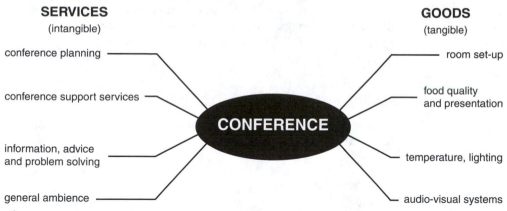

Figure 5–1   Goods and Services Components of a Conference (Product)

Services provided at events, then, are intangible, inseparable, variable, **and** perishable, presenting a number of marketing challenges, since value for money is generally an issue for the consumer.

Process of Event Marketing

The event marketing process is summarized in Figure 5–2. Ultimately the aims are to enhance the profile of the event (and associated sponsors), to meet the needs of the event audience, and, in most cases, to

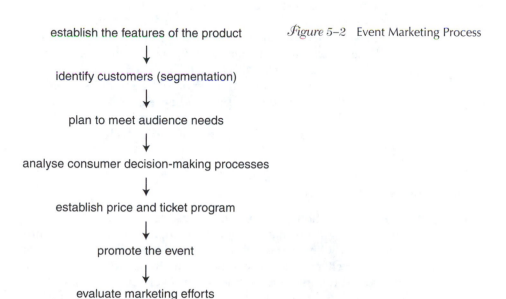

Figure 5–2   Event Marketing Process

generate revenue. Some festivals are fully funded by government bodies, and although they are not expected to raise revenue, they aim to attract a high level of attendance or interest as a minimum expectation.

Establish the Features of the Product

Each event offers a range of potential benefits to the event audience. These may include one or more of the following:

- a novel experience
- entertainment
- a learning experience
- an exciting result
- an opportunity to meet others
- a chance to purchase items
- dining and drinking
- an inexpensive way to get out of the house
- a chance to see something unique

Many marketing experts are unable to see past the main motivating factor for the event, which may be the opportunity to watch a professional tennis match. There may, however, be some members of the audience who have little interest in tennis but who are motivated by some of the other features of the product, such as the opportunity to see and be seen. Generally, people attending an event see the product as a package of benefits. Convenience and good weather, for example, could be benefits associated with an event product.

When marketing an event, therefore, alignment between the product benefits and the needs of the audience is necessary to guide the design of the event and the promotional effort. Pregame and half-time entertainment are good examples of adding value to the main benefit offered by a sporting event product.

Identify Customers

Market segmentation is the process of analyzing your customers in groups. Some groups may enjoy a particular type of country-and-western music. Others may enjoy line dancing. Yet others might visit just for the excitement and the atmosphere. It is absolutely essential to analyze the different motivations of the event audience and to develop a profile for each of these groups.

Having fun and meeting friends are all part of the enjoyment of attending an event like the Indy 500 in Indianapolis.
Source: William H. Edwards/ Getty Images, Inc./Image Bank.

Plan to Meet Audience Needs

Once you have identified your customer groupings, it is then necessary to ensure that all their needs are met. With the Fan Fair example, there may be a generation of older music enthusiasts who are looking for a certain type of entertainment, as well as a younger group (say aged 10 to 14) who need to be entertained, too, so that they can gain something from the experience. As another example, a "Symphony under the Stars" concert would attract many fans of classical music. However, many others would come for the atmosphere, and some just for the fireworks at the end. None of these customer segments' needs can be ignored. All audiences need food and facilities, but food and beverage may or may not be a high priority of a particular event audience. For some, the music is the highlight; for others, it is the hype of the event; and for still others, it is the food that is important.

Analyze Consumer Decision-Making

The next step is to analyze the customer's decision-making process. Research conducted in this area will produce information that is very useful in guiding promotional efforts.

Competitive Pressure (Positioning)

Competition from other forms of entertainment for a person's disposable income would need to be considered. The economic environment would also need to be scanned in order to understand factors

Decisions, decisions, decisions.
Source: Steve Mason/Getty Images Inc./Photodisc.

that might have an impact on discretionary spending on tickets, as well as possibly on travel and accommodations.

Motivation

Customer motivation has already been mentioned under market segmentation. Potential customers may have positive responses to some aspects of an event and negative responses to others, such as the distance to be traveled, crowding, and the risk of bad weather. Customers can be divided into decision makers, followers, influencers, and purchasers. Although in most cases the person who decides to attend (and perhaps take his or her family or friends) is the one who makes the purchase, there are situations in which the decision to spend money on an event is influenced by others. For example, if a teenager wished to go to a concert, the teen might exert pressure on his or her parents to make the purchase on his or her behalf. In this case, both the needs of the teenager and those of the parents would need to be met. Since teenagers would generally discourage their parents from attending, promotional efforts would need to ensure that parents perceived the concert to be a 'safe' environment. Those who tag along to an event are the followers. Each of these—the influencer, the decision maker, the follower, and the purchaser—would generally have different expectations of the event and would evaluate it differently.

Timing

This is the most important aspect of consumer decision-making since it has implications for the promotions budget. The issue is this: when does the consumer make the decision to attend? If the decision will be made two months before the event, you need to deploy all marketing initiatives at that time. If, on the other hand, the decision will be made the week, or the day, before the event, this timing will have important implications as to how and when the advertising and promotions dollar will be spent.

Purchase or Attendance

Finally, the desire to attend needs to be translated into a purchase action. If it is perceived that getting good tickets is going to be difficult, some consumers might not make the effort. In fact, for some festivals, there are no advance sales of tickets. This restriction means that the decision to attend is considered impulsive and that it would generally be made on the day of the event. Clearly, advance ticket selling means a better opportunity to plan for an event as well as a substantial boost to cash flow.

Establish the Price and the Ticket Program

Sale and distribution of tickets has been mentioned briefly before. Now it is necessary to consider that event attendance could be tied in to tourist travel to a destination. If this were the case, it would involve negotiations with a tour wholesaler, extending the time line for planning. Plans would need to be finalized long before the event, with price determined, brochures printed, and advertising done (sometimes overseas) well in advance. This package tour might also include airfare and accommodations.

The decision to attend any event is often impulsive and made on the day of the event.
Source: Bruna Stude/Omni Photo Communications, Inc.

Promote the Event

Having made the decision as to when it is best to promote the event, the next question is how to promote it.

Differentiation

Organizers must demonstrate the difference between an event, whether it is a concert, festival, street fair, or charity fun run, from other related leisure options. The consumer needs to know why this event is special.

Packaging for Effective Communication

The messages used to promote an event are extremely important. Usually there is only limited advertorial space for convincing all market segments to attend. Thus, the combination of text and images requires a lot of creative effort. If there is time and sufficient budget available, utilizing these communication messages with consumers is recommended.

There are many forms of promotion, including brochures; posters; banners; Internet advertising; news, radio, and television advertising; and press releases, to name a few types or marketing tools. Balloons and crowd-pleasers (people balloons with moving arms) are examples of eye-catching promotional strategies that you can use.

Evaluate Marketing Efforts

The effectiveness of all promotional efforts needs to be carefully monitored. With an annual event, for example, customer responses to the various types of promotions will guide promotional efforts in future years. Evaluation needs to be done systematically by asking questions such as "Where did you find out about the event?" or "When did you decide to attend this event?"

There are three stages at which research can be conducted: prior to the event, during the event, and after the event. The research can be qualitative, such as focus groups and case studies, or quantitative. In the latter case, the research generates statistics such as customers' expenditure at the event.

The Marketing Mix

In the final analysis, the marketing efforts need to be analyzed in terms of the marketing mix (see Figure 5–3). In other words, was the event positioned well, priced well, promoted effectively, and distrib-

PRODUCT/SERVICE

event venue

quality of food

quality of entertainment

cleanliness of venue

PLACE

ticket sellers

tour wholesalers

tourist information offices

venue

MARKETING MIX

PRICE

cost of ticket

cost of travel

time taken to travel

other inconvenience

PROMOTION

advertising

public relations

sales promotion

Figure 5–3 The Marketing Mix

uted through different channels efficiently? All these factors must work together if success is to be the outcome.

Positioning

The questions to ask are "Was the choice of event appropriate?" and "Was it positioned correctly in terms of competition?" For example, one would hesitate to run a food and wine festival in a small town when there was already an Oktoberfest at a larger town nearby.

Price

Pricing for an entertainment event is very tricky. It depends on the size of the potential audience and the selected venue. If the ticket price is too high and if the featured artist is not as popular as expected, then the half-empty venue will result in a dismal financial outcome. Pricing of food and beverage items is also an important consideration, because customers become annoyed if markups are excessive.

Promotion

Promotional activities need to be chosen carefully and timed effectively. Promotion is a costly exercise, radio and television advertising being two of the most expensive. Overall, the most cost-effective methods of promotion are feature articles in local newspapers and banners. Many events are promoted by tourism bodies and by tourism information offices at minimal cost. And increasingly, the Internet is being used as a source of information by the event audience.

Distribution

Tickets can be distributed as part of package tours, through ticket sellers (who take commission), or at the venue. In many cases, the event product is produced, distributed, and consumed at the venue. This arrangement contrasts, for example, with goods that are imported for sale and are ultimately consumed by the customer at home. The effectiveness of the channels through which an event is promoted and sold is a crucial aspect of its success.

Sponsorship

Sponsorship is one of the most common funding sources for staging an event. In some cases, the sponsor is happy to provide cash to support the event in exchange for increased profile and sales of the sponsor's products. In other cases, the sponsor provides "value in kind"; that is, the sponsor will provide free goods and services, again with the expectation that this arrangement will have a bottom-line benefit. For example, a newspaper sponsor may provide free advertising space. Some sponsors use an event to promote a new product, and, in this case, the whole event is aimed at developing customer awareness and loyalty. In all of these situations, the marketing messages must be consistent with the event and must be clear to the audience. An expensive party to celebrate the release of a new product is a waste of money if the audience cannot recall the name of the product a few weeks later, or worse, fails to purchase it.

Essentially, the sponsor identifies with the event, mainly through the use of his or her name and logo, and expects a return on the investment. It is thus essential to evaluate both the sponsor profile and the sponsor's sales, or any other sponsorship objectives, after the event to ensure that the sponsorship has been successful and that the sponsor's relationship with the event will continue.

There are a number of questions to ask before approaching a potential sponsor.

What Are the Benefits?

Can the sponsor's involvement lead to some benefit for the organization in terms of increased profile or increased sales? What other benefits are there? At what cost? Will it be time-consuming for their staff?

How Long Will the Association Last?

Is it possible to build a long-term alliance with the sponsor? Can an agreement be reached for perhaps a five-year sponsorship?

Jeff Gordon celebrates at Daytona International Speedway with Pepsi, Gatorade, and Dupont company logos visible. Many companies seek opportunities to have their name and logos seen at major events.
Source: David Taylor/Getty Images, Inc./Allsport Photography.

How Much Exposure will the Sponsor Achieve?

Will the sponsor's logo appear on all advertising? Will the sponsor have naming rights to the event, or will specific prizes be awarded for particular events by the senior staff? Will the winning athlete wear one the sponsor's caps when interviewed by television crews? Will the sponsor be named in the prize-giving ceremony?

Will the Sponsorship Be Exclusive?

Will this sponsor be the only one and thus clearly associated with the event? Or will there be a large number of sponsors?

Is There Compatibility?

Have the potential sponsor's competitors agreed to provide sponsorship, and will this arrangement lead to a conflict of interest? Is there compatibility between the sponsor's product and the event purpose (for example, if the purpose of the event was promoting a healthy lifestyle)?

Will There Be Ambush Marketing?

Are there organizations that will attempt to gain advertising mileage and sales from the event, despite their lack of sponsorship or other commitment? Will competitors' products be on sale at the event or in a nearby area?

Ultimately, the most important question of all concerns the sponsor's benefit from his or her involvement in the event. This consideration needs to be negotiated early in the arrangement, and a process for measuring sponsor objectives, such as recognition or purchase of the sponsor's products, needs to be put in place prior to, during, and after the event. When clearly audited records or professional surveys can demonstrate sponsorship outcomes, renegotiating sponsorship arrangements for subsequent events or for different events will be much easier, since success has been demonstrated in a tangible way. At the end of the day, the sponsor needs a report detailing all promotional efforts and the ensuing benefits, as well as photographs and success stories for postevent publicity.

Case Study

Using the concepts in this chapter, develop a very brief marketing proposal for five of the following events. When the proposal is complete, analyze the differences in the approaches you have suggested.

1. Newport Winter Festival. With over one hundred and fifty individual events, this Festival has grown to become "New England's largest winter extravaganza." Alive with sparkle and excitement, the Winter Festival offers a unique winter experience combining food, music, and entertainment, with fun for all ages. www.newportevents .com

2. Frederick Festival of the Arts. The Frederick Festival of the Arts presents a dynamic exhibition and shopping experience at a juried fine arts and fine craft market. The Festival also presents continuous live entertainment of music, dance and theater on three stages, a film festival and literary activities in Frederick, MD. www .frederickarts.org

3. The Las Vegas Comedy Festival. Whether you're an aspiring comedian, a fan of comedy, or someone who'd like to infuse humor into their communication skills, the **Las Vegas Comedy Festival** is for you! Whatever your ambitions, the **4-day festival** is jam packed with seminars, events and discussion groups that will help you tap into your comedic voice and get more laughs out of your ideas. www.lasvegascomedyfestival.com

4. The James River Writers Festival. The James River Writers Festival (JRWF) is an initiative begun by Richmond-area writers to link our city's professional writing ranks with accomplished and aspiring writers from Richmond, VA, as well as the rest of our state and nation. www.jrwf.org

5. The Palm Springs International Film Festival. Located in the beautiful Coachella Valley desert at the base of Mt. San Jacinto in southern California, the Nortel Networks Palm Springs International Film Festival is one of the largest film festivals in the country, screening over 180 films from more than 55 countries to an audience of over 70,000 from around the world. The festival also features cultural events, filmmaker tributes, industry seminars and an annual black-tie gala award presentation. www.psfilmfest.org

6. Diabetes Run. The Sheridan Community Diabetes Education Committee (SCDEC) and the Sundowner's Lion's Club are sponsoring the Fifth Annual Diabetes Run on Saturday, May 31st at Kendrick Park in Sheridan, WY. After the run, a special treat is planned in conjunction with SmithKline Beecham pharmaceuticals, Coca Cola, and many of Sheridan's local physicians. They will be teaming up to provide the runners and their families a grilled lunch and cold refreshments. http://mhsc.surfcommunications.net/news/releases/may272003.htm

7. National Restaurant Association, Hotel & Motel Show. This annual trade show brings together over 76,000 foodservice and hospitality professionals from across the nation and around the world to see and taste the newest products, equipment and services and to hear industry leaders share their insight. Educational seminars coincide with the trade show. www.restaurant.org

8. Virginia City Camel Races. What started as a hoax is now a tradition in Virginia City, NV. This is the 44th year that jockeys will mount high-spirited dromedaries for the Virginia City International Camel Races and the fun will begin again. www.renolaketahoe.com

Summary

In this chapter we have discussed the marketing mix for event marketing, including product, price, promotion, and place (distribution). Identification of consumer interest in the product and their decision-making processes form a key part of the planning of promotional efforts. Since most promotional budgets are limited, the expenditure must be timed carefully to ensure maximum impact. Sponsorship is one way of attracting funding or "value in kind," and this is an important element of the marketing strategy. Evaluating the marketing effort is essential, because it will facilitate planning of future events.

Links

www.fanfair.com
www.newportevents.com
www.frederickarts.org
www.lasvegascomedyfestival.com
www.jrwf.org
www.psfilmfest.org
www.restaurant.org
www.renolaketahoe.com

Chapter Six

PROMOTION

It's not too early to "saddle up" for the 97th anniversary National Western Stock Show Rodeo & Horse Show, Jan. 11–26, 2003.

The National Western will kick off with a pair of Mexican Rodeo Extravaganzas in the Coliseum on Jan. 11 and Jan. 12, followed on Jan. 13, 14 and 15 with three Professional Bull Rider performances in the same venue at 7:30 p.m.

PRCA ProRodeo action follows in the Coliseum with 22 performances from Jan. 16 through Jan. 22.

Ticketed presentations in the Events Center include Wild West Shows on Jan. 18 and 19, the $15,000 Invitational Freestyle Reining Competition and Grand Prix on Jan. 20. Evenings of Dancing Horses will be held on Jan 22 and 23 and four Coors Draft Horse Shows will take place on Jan. 24, 25 and 26.

All tickets also include free daily grounds admission for the livestock and horse judging and sales. Children's Ranchland, Barn Tours, commercial and education exhibits, the Coors Western Art Exhibit and much more are available with tickets.

The Western Stock Show Association continues to focus on its mission, which is to educate the general public of the agricultural industry, to provide agricultural marketing opportunities and to preserve the western lifestyle.

Reproduced with the permission of Western Stock Show Association (www.nationalwestern.com)

On completion of this chapter, you will be able to

- plan the promotional strategy for an event;
- develop a brand or an image for the event based on the theme;
- develop advertising materials and place them appropriately;
- manage publicity; and
- manage public relations.

The National Western Stock Show Rodeo & Horse Show, held in Denver, Colorado, is an example of an annual event similar to other annual events held in major cities. Agricultural shows continue to appeal to a wide audience ranging from rural farmers to city dwellers. For young children, the baby animal area is always popular, while sideshows and exhibits are perennial favorites. For rural exhibitors, these events provide the opportunity to have their livestock judged, thus increasing exposure and prices for breeding.

Promotion and public relations are a crucial part of the marketing of any event, as we have mentioned in previous chapters, and they will be discussed later in some detail. As part of the marketing strategy, event promotion involves communicating the image and content of the event program to the potential audience. Broadly, the aim of a promotional strategy is to ensure that the consumer makes a decision to purchase and follows up with the action of actually making the purchase. It is essential to turn intention into action, and this step is often the biggest obstacle of a promotional campaign.

There are a number of elements involved in promotion, including the following:

- image/branding
- advertising
- publicity
- public relations

Image/Branding

The first step for most events is the development of a name, a logo, and an image for the event. This includes the color scheme and graphics that will appear on all event material ranging from registration forms to tickets to merchandise. Image and logo are closely linked and need to be agreed on well in advance. Together they are referred to as "branding." Where sponsors are involved, it is essential to obtain their approval of the branding; otherwise, there could be conflict over the use of color or the positioning and size of logos. The design must meet the needs of all stakeholders, as well as appealing to the event audience, particularly if the design forms the basis for merchandise such as T-shirts and hats. A slogan is sometimes developed as part of the image for an event and is incorporated wherever possible. The result should be a consistency in theme and color scheme for all promotional materials. In most cases, the color scheme is also carried through to the decor, including signs, fencing, flags, table settings, banners, and posters.

Advertising

Advertising is the second element of the promotional strategy. It may take many forms, the following being some of the options:

- print
- radio

- television
- direct mail
- outdoor advertising/billboards
- brochures
- Internet

As part of the marketing plan, it is necessary to identify the market to be reached and then to establish where the people in the market live and which of the media would be most likely to reach them. When selecting the most appropriate media, cost is generally the biggest issue. Then you need to decide when to advertise—a month before, a week before, or the day before? Faced with budget limits and potentially expensive advertising, these are all crucial decisions.

When preparing an advertising budget, you should be aware that different time slots on radio and television cost vastly different amounts, as do different positions on the pages of print media. Local newspapers and local radio stations are always more cost-effective than national ones and are generally a more effective way to reach a local audience. Larger events may aim to attract international audiences, and if this is the case, you will need to clearly identify the potential overseas audience and perhaps develop a tourist package to include accommodations and other attractions. Partnership arrangements can often be reached with travel agencies, airlines, and hotels, as well as with state and national tourism boards that have agreed to support and promote the event.

The content of advertisements must be informative, and of most importance, it must inspire decision making and action to attend or purchase. Let's look at the following advertisement by an event company for its wedding rental products and services:

We provide six-arm gold candelabra in the Victorian style, silk flowers, tea lights, fairy lights, table overlays (in organza, Jacquard and cotton), chair covers with sashes and ceiling drapes. We set up for you.

In this advertisement there is a lot of information but absolutely no inspiration. A number of descriptive adjectives would certainly have enhanced the text, as well as the possibility of customers' buying their services!

In contrast, the advertisement for an unusual event following is much more creative. It would be very difficult to attract an event audience if only the facts of a blood donation were presented and if the promotional team has realized this by making this event into something not to be missed.

> **WE WANT YOUR BLOOD!**
>
> *Millard Clinic Blood Drive Week*
>
> *August 10–15 with the grand finale (don't miss this) on August 15 (10 a.m. to 9 p.m.) Greendale Clinic's last drive was a huge success. This year our target is 3,000 units of blood. Sponsors have donated ten major prizes as well as minor prizes for all other donors. Our top prize, a trip for two to Hawaii, will be presented at the grand finale. We will have a health advice booth, a complimentary espresso kiosk, food booths, a craft fair, children's entertainment, local celebrities, and a jazz band in the late afternoon. Attendance is free and all donors will receive a sponsor prize, and will be entered into the drawing for the major prizes. Parking is available on Grant St.*

Figure 6–1   Advertising brings excitement to an otherwise boring event.

The advertising message needs to meet the motivational needs of the audience at the same time that it assists the decision-making process by supplying the necessary facts.

Publicity

Free publicity for an event can be secured by running a careful publicity campaign with the media. This involves developing and disseminating press releases to journalists and then following up by telephone. Sometimes interviews with journalists will also be necessary. There are several points of contact. In the print media, these include the editor, the feature writers, and the editors responsible for individual sections of the newspaper or magazine. In the broadcast media, the people to contact include the station manager, the news announcers, and the radio personalities. For television, contact the program producer or director. In each case, the first question to be asked will be "What makes this event newsworthy?" and the answer to this must be clear.

The aim of a press release is to stimulate media interest in the event and thus achieve positive and cost-effective publicity. Many large event organizers post their press releases on their Web pages (see as an example the press release on page 82 of this chapter for the Susan G. Komen Breast Cancer Foundation Komen Race for the Cure®). For mega-events and regional events, a launch is usually held prior to the event to which the media and the stars of the show are invited. These occasions are used to distribute the press release. It is

Having your product name and logo visible at events is one very important form of advertising. *Source:* Bob Daemmrich/ The Image Works.

essential that a launch be well attended and that the media report the event in a positive way; otherwise, the effort will be counterproductive. In the case of smaller events, sending a press release to a local paper and to the local radio stations is generally the best option. Since the staff working on these smaller publications are extremely busy, it is advisable to provide them with a ready-to-go article, including photos, logos and quotations when possible. The following is an example of the sort of press release/article that would draw the attention of a local newspaper:

The Longest, Largest and Oldest Touring Bicycle Ride in the World

RAGBRAI®, The Register's Annual Great Bicycle Ride Across Iowa™, is an annual seven-day bicycle ride across the state. RAGBRAI is the longest, largest and oldest touring bicycle ride in the world. It started in 1973 as a six-day ride across the state of Iowa by two Des Moines Register columnists who invited a few readers along. It attracts 10,000 participants from every state in the country and many foreign countries. The RAGBRAI route averages 470 miles and is not necessarily flat. It traditionally begins along Iowa's western border on the Missouri River and ends somewhere along the eastern border on the Mississippi River. The starting and ending towns and the route across the state are changed each year and announced in early February in The Des Moines Register and on the website at www.ragbrai.org. Application materials will be available online November 15, 2003 for RAGBRAI XXXII which takes place July 25–31, 2004.

> *The people of Iowa truly make RAGBRAI the special event it is by opening up their towns and communities to the ride participants. The Iowa hospitality, the beautiful countryside, and the chance to get away from it all for a week make this bicycle tour the most memorable experience of a lifetime. To learn more about the event, visit the website, or call the RAGBRAI hotline at 800-I RIDE IA (800.474.3342).*
>
> RAGBRAI® and the Register's Annual Great Bicycle Ride Across Iowa™ are registered trademarks of the Des Moines Register & Tribune Company. Used with permission.

The following guidelines for preparing a press release will help to ensure that the reader sits up and takes notice:

- There must be something to appeal to the reader in the first two sentences: he or she must be motivated to read the whole press release.
- All the facts must be covered: what, when, why, and how. This is particularly the case for negative incidents. The reader wants to know what happened, when it happened, why it happened, and how things will be resolved. When something goes wrong, the facts are important because unsubstantiated opinion is dangerous. If the press release is promoting an event, all information such as the venue, date, time, and so on should be included:
  - The press release should be short and to the point (no longer than one to two pages).
  - Layout is extremely important.
  - Contact details should be provided.
  - Photographs should be captioned.
  - Quotes from senior staff and stakeholders (including sponsors) may be included.
  - If the press release is promoting an event, it should describe all potential benefits for the audience.
  - An action ending for booking or registering should include all necessary information.

Apart from free media publicity, it is also possible to obtain free exposure through a number of official tourism organizations, many of which are listed at the end of this book. They provide tourist information to visitors through tourist information offices or their Web sites at the state or national level. Brochures distributed to such offices or listings on their event calendars can provide valuable information to the potential (and sometimes very hard to reach) event audience.

Every effort should be made to ensure that the event is listed as widely as possible.

Public Relations

The role of public relations is to manage the organization's and the event's image in the mind of the audience and the public. This undertaking is mainly done through press releases as described in the previous section. These up-to-date information sources, together with photographs, provide the media with the background information they need to develop stories about the event. Media briefings can also be conducted before and during the event, particularly if high-profile people such as celebrities, entertainers and athletes can enhance the publicity.

One of the most critical public relations roles is to inform the media whether there is a negative incident of any description. For this reason, an incident-reporting system needs to be in place so that senior members of the event management team are fully informed, including the public relations manager, if this is a separate role. It may be necessary to write a press release or to appear in an interview if such an incident occurs. In some situations it is essential to obtain legal advice regarding the wording used in the press release. The public relations role can be a highly sensitive one, and in some situations, words need to be chosen carefully. A simple expression of regret, for example, would be more tactful than suggesting the cause of an accident.

Another, more positive public relations role is the entertainment of guests and VIPs attending the event, in some cases from other countries. In this public relations role, you need to be the following:

- attentive to the needs and expectations of your guests;
- mindful of their cultural expectations;
- flexible in your responses to their behaviors;
- informative and helpful as a host;
- proactive in designing hosting situations to meet the required protocol; and
- able to make easy conversation.

Particularly with overseas guests or guests of event sponsors, you need to know in advance who they are (official titles, correct names, and correct pronunciation) and where they come from. Of most importance, you need to know the reason why your company is acting as host to these guests, because often business objectives, such as sponsor product awareness or negotiations, are involved. Research is therefore essential to determine how to meet the needs of the guests and the expectations of, for example, the sponsors. According to Roger Axtell (1990), the effective multicultural host has the following attributes:

- being respectful
- tolerating ambiguity
- relating well to people
- being nonjudgmental
- personalizing one's observations (not making global assertions about people or places)
- showing empathy
- being patient and persistent

As you can see from the preceding, there are a number of roles for the public relations manager, or indeed for any member of the event team. The opportunity to sell an event occurs every time the telephone is answered or an inquiry is made by a potential customer. Because customer relations becomes the role of everyone involved in an event, training in this area is recommended. This training should focus in particular on the event information likely to be requested by the customer, a task that is more difficult than it sounds since plans are often not finalized until very close to the event. Training ties in closely with the planning process, and the distribution of information to all concerned right up until the last minute is very important.

There are a number of situations in which an event manager might become involved in public relations, including the following:

- making travel arrangements by telephone or e-mail
- meeting and greeting at the airport
- providing transportation
- running meetings
- entertaining at meals
- entertaining at events
- providing tours and commentary

If you have to lead a small group around the venue or the event, there are a number of additional recommendations:

- Plan the tour so that enough time is allocated to see everything.
- Advise your guests of your plan, however informal the group.
- Make sure that there is time for a break and refreshments.

- Provide maps so that people can get their bearings.
- Pause frequently so that the guests can ask questions.
- Be gracious—questions are never trivial or stupid.
- Make sure that everyone can see and hear.
- Treat everyone as equals.
- Speak slowly and at an appropriate volume.
- Be patient, and speak positively.
- Be flexible, and change plans if necessary.
- Be attentive to fatigue or boredom, and accelerate the tour if necessary.

In promoting an event, it is essential to analyze and understand the needs of the target market or markets. If, for example, one of the target markets is children aged 8 to 12, it is necessary to understand the motivations of this group and to match the product to these motivational needs. It is also necessary to keep in mind that the person purchasing the product may not be the consumer—in this case, it may be the parent—and promotional efforts need to assist with decision-making processes within the family. Likewise, a sponsor may be making a substantial investment in the event, and may have general, as well as specific, expectations of the event, which may or may not be consistent with those of the event audience.

To summarize, the task of promoting an event to the optimal audience at the most beneficial time is the first challenge. The second is to meet the needs of all stakeholders and to maximize public relations benefits to the satisfaction of customers at all levels.

Case Study

Using the press release in Figure 6–3 and any materials you can find on the history of the Lewis and Clark expedition, prepare one or more of the following promotional materials:

- a travel brochure attracting families to spend their vacations along the expedition sites
- a Web page (home page only) promoting the commemoration
- a press release listing some of the activities that are planned in conjunction with this bicentennial event

Links to tourism and other Web sites provided in the Links section that follows and in Appendix 1 will assist with your research.

For Immediate Release

The Susan G. Komen Breast Cancer Foundation Celebrates the Komen Race for the Cure®'s 20th Anniversary

World's Largest 5K Race Series Kicks Off 2003 Season With New Sponsor, Sets Course for Future Progress

Dallas–March 20, 2003—The Susan G. Komen Breast Cancer Foundation kicks off the 2003 Komen Race for the Cure® Series this month, marking the 20th Anniversary of the Foundation's signature awareness and fundraising program. Through Komen Race for the Cure® events, the Komen Foundation supports outreach programs to help women facing breast cancer today and invests in research that will one day find a cure for the disease.

The first event of its kind, the Komen Race for the Cure® was created in 1983 by Nancy Brinker, who established the Komen Foundation to honor the memory of her sister, Susan G. Komen, who died from breast cancer at the age of 36. In 20 years, the Komen Race for the Cure® has grown from one local race in Dallas, Texas, with 800 participants to an international series with 1.5 million people expected to participate in 2003. Today, with more than 100 race events in the U.S. as well as Rome, Italy, and Frankfurt, Germany, the Komen Race for the Cure® Series is the largest series of 5K runs/fitness walks in the world.

"Through the Komen Race Series during the last 20 years, we have made great strides funding community programs and innovative research grants that might otherwise be overlooked. And these events educate the public with a message that early detection provides a greater chance of survival and more treatment options," Brinker said. "Still, the Komen Race Series' anniversary reminds us that, despite these great successes, there is still work to do as many research and community grants go unfunded."

Funds raised by the Komen Race Series support non-duplicative breast cancer education, screening and treatment projects for the medically underserved in more than 100 communities around the world. In addition, the Komen Race Series is a major contributor to the renowned Komen Foundation Award and Research Grant Program, which has supported a number of the most significant medical and scientific milestones of the last 20 years. The Komen Foundation was an original funder of V. Craig Jordan, Ph.D., the scientist whose work resulted in the development of tamoxifen for the treatment of breast cancer, as well as Mary-Claire King, Ph.D., the researcher whose work led to the discovery of the first breast cancer gene mutation.

Thanks to a network of 75,000 volunteers across the country, the Komen Race Series touches people of all ages, races and backgrounds with life-saving messages about early detection and other breast health educational information. Race participants wear "In Memory of" and "In Celebration of" back signs to honor breast cancer survivors and those who have lost their battle with the disease. At each Komen Race event, breast cancer survivors wearing pink caps and T-shirts are celebrated for their strength and courage.

"The Komen Race for the Cure® is sponsored nationally by ten corporate and organizational partners. Their contributions ensure that the majority of the funds raised support breast cancer programs, services and research.

Figure 6–2   Outstanding Example of a Press Release
Source: For more information, contact, www.komen.org. Used with permission from the Susan G. Komen Breast Cancer Foundation.

For Immediate Release
Office of the Press Secretary

Presidential Proclamation

July 1, 2002 Nearly 200 years ago, President Thomas Jefferson sent an expedition westward to find and map a transcontinental water route to the Pacific Ocean. With approval from the Congress, Captains Meriwether Lewis and William Clark embarked on their legendary 3-year journey to explore the uncharted West. The expedition included 33 permanent party members, known as the Corps of Discovery.

Their effort to chart the area between the Missouri River and the Pacific Coast set these courageous Americans on a remarkable scientific voyage that changed our Nation. In successfully completing the overland journey between the Missouri and Columbia River systems, they opened the unknown West for future development. During their exploration, Lewis and Clark collected plant and animal specimens, studied Indian cultures, conducted diplomatic councils, established trading relationships with tribes, and recorded weather data. To accomplish their goals, the Corps of Discovery relied on the assistance and guidance of Sakajawea, a Shoshone Indian woman.

As we approach the 200th anniversary of Lewis and Clark's expedition, we commend their resourcefulness, determination, and bravery. This Bicentennial should also serve to remind us of our Nation's outstanding natural resources. Many of these treasures first detailed by Lewis and Clark are available today for people to visit, study, and enjoy. As the commemoration of this journey begins in 2003, I encourage all Americans to celebrate the accomplishments of Lewis and Clark and to recognize their contributions to our history.

NOW, THEREFORE, I, GEORGE W. BUSH, President of the United States of America, by virtue of the authority vested in me by the Constitution and laws of the United States, do hereby designate 2003 through 2006 as the Lewis and Clark Bicentennial. I ask all Americans to observe this event with appropriate activities that honor the achievements of the Lewis and Clark Expedition. I also direct Federal agencies to work in cooperation with each other, States, tribes, communities, and the National Council of the Lewis and Clark Bicentennial to promote educational, cultural, and interpretive opportunities for citizens and visitors to learn more about the natural, historical, and cultural resources that are significant components of the Lewis and Clark story.

IN WITNESS WHEREOF, I have hereunto set my hand this twenty-eighth day of June, in the year of our Lord two thousand two, and of the Independence of the United States of America the two hundred and twenty-sixth.

GEORGE W. BUSH

Figure 6–3   Lewis & Clark Bicentennial by the President of the United States of America
Source: Office of the Press Secretary of the United States of America.

Summary

In this chapter we have dealt with event promotion in more detail and have seen that branding or image is linked to the event purpose and theme, and that all of these aspects must be consistent and compatible in order to create the greatest impact on the consumer or event audience. There are many media options for advertising, and these are often determined by the promotional budget available. Advertising and publicity need to be carefully planned to ensure the highest possible level of attendance at an event. We have also discussed the public relations role, communication with the media and other stakeholders being important during the planning phases and equally important when there are problems or incidents that threaten the success or reputation of an event. A more positive public relations role is the entertainment of guests and VIPs for which certain attributes are essential, including tolerance, patience, persistence, respectfulness, and an ability to relate well to people of all cultures.

Activity

Select five advertisements for events, and analyze the differences, deciding which has the most audience appeal in terms of the following:

- attraction
- development of interest
- assistance in decision making
- ability to lead to action/attendance

Links

www.nationalwestern.com
www.ragbrai.org
www.komen.org
www.lewisandclarkexhibit.org
www.lewisandclark200.org

Chapter Seven
FINANCIAL MANAGEMENT

The Miami International Film Festival is just one example of an event that has experienced some financial woes. As reported in the Miami Today News, *the festival sponsored by Florida International University experienced a $220,000 deficit in 2002. The festival added screenings and venues but saw a decrease in ticket sales.*

Despite the bad press, the organizers feel secure that they can recover and carry on in future years. Part of their optimism is that they have risen from a deficit situation in the past. When the university first took over the festival in 1999 it was $100,000 in debt, but the university was able to pay off the debt three years earlier than planned.

On completion of this chapter, you will be able to

- develop an event budget, including income and expenditure;
- identify the break-even point in order to make pricing decisions;
- review and manage cash flow;
- produce a simple profit and loss account; and
- develop control systems for managing finances within budget.

Long-term financial results are an important consideration in event management. In the preceding case, part of the shortfall for the 2002 festival is being amortized (spread) across future festivals; however, in general, the aim of financial management is for all expenses to be recouped at the time of the event.

Not all events are profit oriented. For example, a promotion for a new product, such as a new brand of perfume, would be part of a major marketing initiative, with the expectation being long-term return through sales. The perfume company would meet the expenses associated with staging the event. Similarly, a party or celebration is usually paid for by the client. Good financial management by the event company will ensure that the quote given to the client at the beginning will at least cover the expenses incurred in staging the party—and hopefully make a profit for the company! In other cases, ticket revenue and other sales (such as from merchandising) are expected to exceed the expenses, thus delivering a profit to the organizers or investors.

The first step in the financial management of an event is to ask the questions that follow.

Is the Aim to Make a Profit?

There are many events that have a range of objectives that do not include making a profit. For example, street parades or music festivals may be offered to the public free of charge, the expenses being met by government agencies and/or sponsors. Often, goods and services are provided by businesses and individuals to assist in the running of an event, thus making it difficult to accurately estimate the actual costs. However, it is still essential that all other expenses are properly approved and documented.

When the objective of an event is raising money for charity, a target needs to be set, and, once again, both the expenses and the funds raised need to be accounted for correctly.

How Much Will the Event Cost?

In the example of the fund-raising event described before, as indeed for any nonprofit event, it is important to estimate how much the event will cost as well as to keep track of the actual expenses incurred. With every event, money changing hands must be properly documented, and, in most cases, the financial records should be audited. Expenses, or costs, include fees, equipment and venue rental costs, advertising, insurance, and so on.

What Are the Revenue Sources?

Generally, revenue is raised by selling tickets or charging admission fees. Merchandise sales also contribute to revenue. Merchandising items, such as T-shirts and caps, may be sold by the event organizer or under arrangement with the retailer whereby the event organizer earns a percentage of any sales. The same arrangement may occur with food and beverage sales.

How Many Tickets Must Be Sold to Break Even?

This is a critical question. In essence, it relates to whether you decide on a large venue, large audience, and low price, or on a small venue, small audience, and high price. This question will be discussed in more detail later in this chapter.

What Is the Cash-Flow Situation?

Events are fairly unique in that, for most, revenue comes in only on the day of the event. This arrangement means that all costs, such as salaries, office expenses, and fees, have to be met up front from existing funds. When ticket sales occur long before an event is staged, as they do with major concerts, this arrangement puts the company in the enviable position of being able to pay for its expenses from revenue while also earning interest on this money until the remaining bills become due. Very few events fit this category. Cash-flow planning is an essential part of the event planning process for the previously mentioned reasons.

What Control Systems Are Needed to Avoid Fraud?

All businesses are accountable, and systems need to be put in place to ensure that moneys are accounted for. Systems and procedures are needed so that every transaction will be recorded and all expenditures approved, including payment of invoices, handling of cash, paying of taxes, and so on. Cash management systems for the day of the event are often lacking, and it is not uncommon for registers to be left open, for staff to take handfuls of change without substituting notes and for bags of cash to be left lying around. This situation is clearly unsatisfactory.

How Will Legal and Taxation Obligations Be Met?

Employing the services of a properly qualified accountant will ensure that your organization maintains accurate records and meets its legal obligations.

The Budget

Preparing a budget is part of the initial planning stage. A budget includes projected revenue and expenditure from which an estimate of the net profit (or sometimes net loss) from the proposed event can be ascertained. It is a plan based on accurate quotes from all contractors and suppliers and on careful research to ensure that no expenses have been overlooked. It provides guidelines for approving expenditure and ensuring that the financial aspects of the event remain on track. The budget is part of the event proposal or the basis of the quote by the event management company to the client.

Several sample budgets are provided in Figures 7–1 to 7–4. As you will see, they vary considerably in the number of expense and revenue items, though the general principles remain the same. Note

Fixed Costs
Band
Dancers
MC
Stage crew
Costumes
Theme
   Decoration
   Sashes
Signage
   Entrance
Graphics
   Animation logo
Artwork and printing
   200 programs
Lighting
Sound
Vision
   Rear projection
   4.2 × 3 m screen
   Data projection

Freight and travel
Labor
   Setup
   Dismantle
Management fee
   Creation, production, supervision
   Management of evening

Total fixed costs

Variable Costs (based on 200 guests/pax)

Table decoration, say 21   @ $
Food   @ $ per head
Beverage   @$ per head
Band/entertainer meals 15   @ $ per head
Total Variable Costs

Contingency

GRAND TOTAL

Figure 7–1 Budget Items for Themed Dinner
Source: Reproduced with permission of Events Unlimited, International.

Income
Entry—corporate 40@ $
Booth rental
Merchandising
Raffle
Entry donations
Other donations
Total Income

Expenditure
Fixed Costs
Rentals
Structures
   50 team tents
   5 booths (food)
   3 booths (merchandize)
   1 official's booth
   6 security/first aid stations
   1 information booth

1 site office
1 children's sign
164 ft. of synthetic turf
Allowance for under panels for turf
Ticket box
3 flag poles
2000 Paper cups
3 fold-out tables
2 water thermoses
2 transport carts
Portable Restrooms
20 dual sex portable restroom
1 handicapped portable restroom
5 portable hand-washing basins
1 attendant
Equipment
Portable stage
Stage roof
Lectern

Figure 7–2 Budget Items for Relay Race Event
Source: Reproduced with permission of Events Unlimited, International.

(continued)

Stage skirting
10 rolls marking tape
Transport carts
Control
Scoreboard
Timekeeping devices
Rental of public address equipment including microphones, cords and stands
500 coded wristbands
Rental of 2 bar code readers
10 walkie talkie radio sets
4 phone lines
50 × 10 team numbers
70 vests for security officials
Start/finish air horn
1 winner's shield
10 winners' medals
500 competitors' ribbons
Staff
MC/announcer
Security
20 parking lot attendants
Labor for set up and tear down
50 race officials/including relief
2 emergency first aid staff
Photographer
Logistics
Garbage bins
Clean up and garbage removal
Power
Water
2 Gators for quick transport
Promotion
Printing
Design/artwork
500 entry forms
10,000 flyers
2000 programs
50 corporate prospectus

50 competitors' entry kit preparation
Stationery
1500 "show bags"
Signage
2 banners
20 directional signs
5 sponsor signs
50 team names for tents
Advertising
Marketing
Media Launch
Administration
Postage
Phone, fax, e-mail
Insurance
Permits
Children's amusements
Raffle prizes
Management Fees
For collection of team monies and database management; media coordination; coordinating and running the event, including budget development
Total Fixed Costs
Variable Costs (based on 40 teams)
Food & Beverage
Catering 1200 @ $
Buffet tables set-up
Beverage (4 hour package) 1200 @ $
Wait staff 40 @ $
Health drink for athletes
Ice water for athletes
Health food snack for athletes
Total Variable Costs
Contingency
Sub-Total
Total Expenditure
Profit

Figure 7–2   continued

Fixed Costs	**Liability insurance**
Venue rental	Included in general event insurance
Costs included in rental budget	**Printing**
Signage	Exhibitor manual—100 copies
Directional	Exhibitor guide—1000 copies
Large banner with rotating globe	Exhibitor lists and floor plan, large layouts
50 national flags	**Miscellaneous**
Lighting	Consumables
On banners, globe and flags	Estimate: postage, phone, e-mail, etc.
Name tags	Storage area
Exhibitors 300 @ $	Internet café—stand only with furniture
Visitors and other delegates 500 @ $	Internet café—IT equipment
Welcome display	Internet café—coffee bar estimate includes
Estimate: operators at reception and info desk	espresso machine
Exhibitor manual	Additional supervisory/security 36 hours @ $
Placed on website	Cost of stand
Preparation of Intranet site info	Travel, accommodations for exhibition and at-
Marketing	tendance at 8 meetings
To previous showcase exhibitors	**Total Fixed Costs**
Promotion to new database in conjunction	**Variable Costs (based on 20 booths)**
with promo	**Basic booth construction**
Setup/Teardown	10 × 10 per concept description @$
Rental of scissor lift	**Catering**
Exhibition function	2 days × 6 per booth @$
Wine and cheese evening sponsored by	**Total Variable Costs**
Onsite staff	Contingency
14 @ $	**Total Costs**

Figure 7–3   Budget Items for Exhibition
Source: Reproduced with permission of Events Unlimited, International.

the differences between fixed costs (these do not alter) and variable costs (these vary in accordance with the size of the event audience).

Management Fees

In many cases, an event organizer charges a management fee to oversee an event. As a ballpark figure for planning purposes, this is generally in the region of 10 to 15 percent of total costs. According to Larry Jaeger, president of Events Xtraordinaire, the industry has gotten a bit more competitive, so there are situations in which an event planner may look at business as an opportunity and get more aggressive on fees. Jaeger also reports that any fees in addition to what is specified in the project or any projects that are smaller in nature are billed on a per-hour consulting fee, which can be $125 or more per

Fixed Costs	
Fixed Costs	Programs (shell plus inset)
Venue rental	Reviews
Artists	**Onsite staff**
MC	Catering
Actor/scriptwriter	**Other rentals**
Singer/composer	Catering
Choreographer	**Gifts for special guests**
Technical director	**Photography**
Set designer	Digital camera
Makeup designer	**Video recording**
Props designer	Video camera rental
Production team	Tapes
Stage manager	**Setup/Teardown**
Asst. stage manager	**Freight**
Asst. technical director	**Airfares**
Costumes	**Ground transportation for guests and dignitaries**
T-shirts @ $ (+ 10% for extreme sizes)	**Accommodations and meals (2 days) for guests and dignitaries**
Sound	**Miscellaneous**
Copyright fees	Phone, fax estimate
Equipment rental	**Contingency**
Lights	**Management Fee**
Visual effects (for presentation and speaker)	**Total Fixed Costs**
Based on PowerPoint presentation and video	**Variable Costs**
Preparation of visual effects	**Catering**
Staging	Coffee on arrival @ $
Preparation of production detail	Mid-morning snack break @ $
Set backdrop, paints etc.	Lunch—sack lunches @ $
Props materials	Afternoon beverage service @ $
Expenditures	Pre-show canapé and buffet dinner @ $
Posters for theater	Total $ per head
Props	Second day breakfast @ $
Laptop and printer	**Total Variable Costs**
Printing	**Total Each Location**
Individual group labels	**Grand Total**
Invitations	

Figure 7–4 Budget Items for Music Event
Source: Reproduced with permission of Events Unlimited, International.

hour, depending on the region of the country. Although an event might have a low budget, it might still require considerable time and effort in its organization, and thus the lower end of the range, 10 percent, would simply not cover management costs. In that case, an event planner may opt for the hourly consulting fee.

Prior to contracts being signed, the event organizer should work out the tasks involved in the event, allocate staff to the various roles, and determine their pay rates in order to come up with a more accurate estimate of management costs and, therefore, the management fee to be charged. In some situations, the event organizer might wish to involve himself or herself in a collaborative entrepreneurial arrangement with the client whereby the management fee is based on income earned or sponsorship raised.

If a management fee is charged, the client is usually responsible for all pre-event payments to venues and subcontractors. The fee is for the management and the coordination of the event by the event organizers, and for their expertise, from concept through to execution.

Contingencies

Most event budgets include a contingency for unexpected expenses. This ranges from 5 percent of the costs (if the event organizer is confident that the costs are controllable) to 10 percent (if there are a number of unknown variables or the costs are uncertain).

Break-Even Point

To work out the break-even point, the event organizer has to estimate the number of tickets that need to be sold in order to meet expenses (see Figure 7–5). These expenses include both fixed costs and variable costs. Fixed costs, such as licensing fees, insurance, administrative costs, rent of office space, advertising costs, and fees paid to artists, generally do not vary if the size of the event audience increases; these costs are often called overheads. Variable costs increase as the size of the audience increases. If food and beverage were part of, say,

Figure 7–5   Break-Even Point

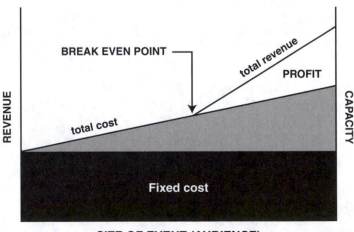

a conference package, clearly these costs would escalate if the numbers attending the conference increased. Once the total revenue is the same as the total expenditure (fixed and variable), then the break-even point has been reached. Beyond it, the event is profitable.

In the case of an exhibition, the organizer would be using the budget to establish how many exhibitors were needed to break even. The price charged for exhibiting could clearly be quite low if there were a lot of exhibitors; the price charged would have to be high if there were few exhibitors and if the aim were to meet the budget (particularly for fixed costs). However, this is not an altogether feasible way of setting prices or fees, since there is a maximum price that the market will bear and a minimum level at which the event becomes viable. This iterative process of analyzing ticket prices or fees charged and the break-even point is part of the financial decision-making process.

Cash-Flow Analysis

Capital is required to set up any business, and even more so in the event business, since the planning phase is often long and the period for capturing revenue very short. For example, an event team may spend a year planning an event during which period costs will be incurred, all of which have to be paid long before there is an opportunity to recoup any money. After having spent a year planning, it is possible that tickets will be sold at the venue and that all revenue will be collected on the one day. This outcome is in contrast to an everyday business in which there is a more even cash flow.

In instances in which the client is paying for the event, a deposit is generally negotiated. However, payment of the balance may not be paid to the event management company until at least a month after the event. Ideally, complete up-front payment, or a significant establishment fee, should be negotiated to alleviate cash-flow problems.

In summary, monthly expenses and projected revenue need to be entered into a spreadsheet to establish how cash flow can best be managed. A funding crisis, just days before an event, is not uncommon in this industry.

The illustration in Figure 7–6 provides an example of an event held in March, generating very little income until the month and days before the event. Only small amounts in the form of grants and sponsorships are shown as income during the planning phase in October, November, and December. Meanwhile, expenses were incurred from the beginning of the planning process, peaking in January and February when suppliers were becoming demanding. Expenses include salaries for staff, office expenses, deposits, and up-front payments to

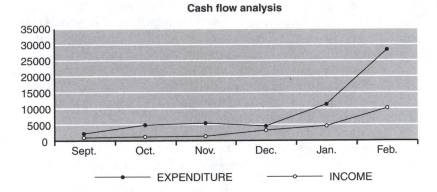

Figure 7–6   Cash-Flow Analysis

subcontractors for catering and equipment rental. The gap between expenditure and income is the cash shortfall, which in this example was particularly problematic in January and February.

Profit and Loss Statement

The profit and loss statement is a list of an organization's revenue, expenditure, and net profit (or net loss) for a specific period. In many cases, the profit and loss statement (or income statement) is prepared after the event.

In a perfect world, the profit and loss statement would match the budget. The budget is the plan, and if everything went according to plan, this outcome would be reflected in the profit and loss statement. In the event industry, the budget is generally prepared before the event and the profit and loss statement afterward, whereas in most ongoing business operations, budgets and profit and loss statements are done regularly and routinely. In an event management company, a profit and loss statement would be done for each event, as well as for the ongoing concern, the company itself. Alternatively, each event could be shown as a different cost center.

On the profit and loss statement, the most important source of revenue, such as sales of tickets, appears as the first item. If the event is paid for by a single client, this payment will be the first item, since it is the predominant source of revenue. **Gross revenue** is the total revenue before any costs have been deducted. This is a similar concept to gross wages, the amount you would receive if there weren't all sorts of deductions such as tax, worker's compensation, and the like before it reached your pocket.

If you deduct the **cost of goods sold** (also known as direct costs) from the gross revenue, you get the **gross profit.** If the gross revenue from an event were $750,000 and if the direct costs of $520,000 were deducted, the result would be a gross profit of $230,000. The cost of goods sold are those that relate directly to the revenue earned. They could include cost of venue rental, labor, and equipment rental. After calculating the gross profit, you would then deduct your **overhead costs,** such as administration costs and rent, of $165,000, and you would be left with an **operating profit** of $65,000. Finally, your **net profit** is your profit after all other costs and taxes have been deducted, in this case $41,000. This procedure is illustrated in Figure 7–7.

Balance Sheet

Whereas the profit and loss statement captures results for a given period, such as a financial year, the balance sheet gives you an idea of what a business is worth at a certain point in time. When the owners of the business have acquired assets, such as sound and lighting equipment, the acquisition becomes very relevant, and likewise, if there were outstanding bills to be paid. The balance sheet shows what the result would be if all bills were paid and everything were sold (the assets minus the liabilities). This result is the owner's equity in the business. The problem for many event management companies is that their assets, such as their reputation, are intangible!

Financial Control Systems

All purchases must be approved, and usually a requisition form is used for this purpose, meaning that the manager has the opportunity to approve costs incurred by employees. Once goods are ordered or

Profit and Loss Statement as at June 30 2004

Figure 7–7   Profit and Loss Statement

Gross revenue	$750,000.00	
Less cost of goods sold	$520,000.00	
Gross profit		**$230,000.00**
Less administrative and other overhead costs	$165,000.00	
Operating profit		**$65,000.00**
Less other income expenses (such as interest)	$6,000.00	
Profit before tax		**$59,000.00**
Less tax	$18,000.00	
Net profit for the year/event		**$41,000.00**

services provided, checks must be made that they meet specifications before the bills are paid. Fraud could occur if an employee had authority to make purchases, to record and physically handle the goods, and to pay the bills. For that reason, these roles are usually carried out by different people. In any case, the system should have checks and balances to make sure that

- purchases or other expenses are approved;
- goods and services meet specifications;
- payment is approved;
- accounts are paid;
- incoming revenue is checked and banked;
- revenue totals are recorded correctly;
- debts are met;
- all transactions are recorded and balanced;
- taxation requirements are met; and
- financial matters are correctly reported to stakeholders.

In an article appearing on July 20, 2003, in the *Milwaukee Journal Sentinel*, the four-day Jewel-Osco RiverFest was described as follows:

Entering its ninth year, the free four-day festival offers a lineup of musical entertainment and food that organizers hope will bring back the more than 55,000 who attended last year.

Dave Burch of the Rotary Club of Waukesha, which produces the festival, said the key elements for a financially successful event are in place.

More than 700 volunteers are available to help and corporate sponsors pledged about $160,000 to finance this year's festival.

This is a good example of a major community-wide event with several objectives which was being successfully staged and financially well managed.

Panic Payments

This unusual accounting term is not exclusive to the event industry, but this industry is one in which inflated panic prices are often paid. In an ideal world, the event manager has all quotes sewn up and the budget locked in long before the event. There should be few unforeseen contingencies—but don't forget this line in your budgets!

In reality, Murphy's Law dictates that something will always go wrong. And the closer it is to the event, the more difficult it is to ne-

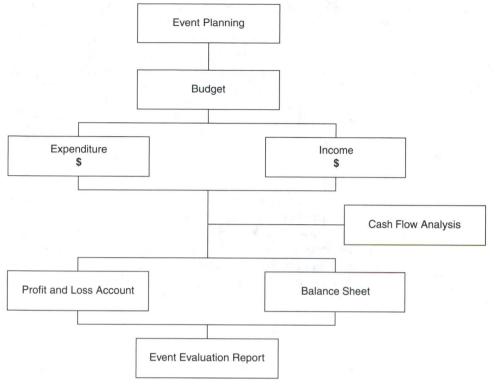

Figure 7–8   Planning, Budgeting, and Reporting Process

gotiate a reasonable price for what you require to put it right. In fact, if it is a last-minute crisis, it could easily lead to a price with a high premium—a panic payment. Essentially, the supplier has the event manager over a barrel. Careful planning and detailed contracts negotiated well in advance can prevent this situation from occurring.

Case Study

Your event business, Rave Reviews, has the opportunity to quote for two major parties. Having experienced some financial difficulties in your first year of operation, you want to ensure that you choose the most feasible of these for which to prepare a proposal and produce the winning quote.

The first party is for a top celebrity and will be held at her beachfront mansion. The party will be outdoors, and the goal is to transform the garden area through the use of a spectacular theme. The party will be attended by 350 guests, and a lavish dinner is expected.

Summary

This chapter has covered the important subject of financial management. We have learned that the budget developed prior to an event must anticipate all revenues and expenditures and that steps should be taken to finalize contracts as early as possible to ensure that expenses do not exceed budget forecasts. The event manager also needs to take into account the cash-flow situation in the lead-up to an event, since most expenses occur early in the planning process whereas the bulk of the revenue is generally collected close to, or during, the event. We have touched on profit and loss statements and balance sheets, and have emphasized the importance of financial control systems for managing expenditure and revenue from sales. Reporting systems need to be in place so that complete and accurate records are available for the final postevent report.

The second party is much larger, since 500 to 600 people will be invited. The company is giving the party to celebrate its fiftieth year of tractor and farming equipment operations. The party will be held in a large airport hangar out in the country. Food will be pretty basic, and alcohol will be very plentiful. Decor is not important, but the entertainment will be the focal point of the event.

Discuss which of these two events you would choose in terms of its ease of financial management and its potential profitability.

Activity

Prepare a budget for the promotion of a local fund-raising event. You can use any number of promotional strategies, including various forms of advertising. Make sure that you include the time taken to prepare the communication messages and designs for these materials. In the case of brochures, there may be design and print costs as well as distribution costs. Your budget should comprehensively cover all activities and expenses associated with promotion, including any salaries or wages involved.

Links

www.eventsx.com (Events Xtraordinaire)

Chapter Eight ➤
RISK MANAGEMENT

It began back in the late 1970s when someone wondered who was the best all-around motorcycle racer and from which discipline would he come. Would it be a road racer, an off-road racer or perhaps a flat track pilot? From that was born the notion of a new type of motorcycle race. It was first called Superbikers and it blended on- and off-road racing by featuring a track comprised of both pavement and dirt. Motocross bikes proved to be the best choice for this new form of racing and with minimal modifications a racer could easily build a competitive mount. The discipline prospered in the United States for awhile and then disappeared, perhaps because of the trend towards specialization. It found a home in Europe and grew modestly. Stateside, local clubs began to emerge as interest returned. Now, in a big way, Supermoto returns to where it all started in the form of and all new national series called the AMA Red Bull Supermoto Championship.

Reproduced with permission of AMA ProRacing
(www.amaproracing.com)

On completion of this chapter, you will be able to

- identify the risks associated with an event;
- assess the risks and prioritize the risks;
- manage the risks by prevention or contingency planning; and
- develop a risk management plan.

*A*lthough not everyone's choice of event, the Supermoto is extremely popular, attracting crowds of enthusiastic fans. Crowds at events such as the Supermoto have been described as highly spirited, so that the event's organizer often insists on rules in an effort to minimize risk. Typical rules state that the following cannot be brought in: alcohol, glass bottles; pets, fireworks, weapons, and drugs. See Figure 8–1.

All event organizers face a range of risks, and in this chapter we will look at ways in which these risks can be identified, analyzed, prioritized, minimized, and monitored. First, however, it is essential to define risk management.

Risk is the chance that something will go wrong. Event organizers often think of risk in terms of safety and security, but risk is much broader than that concept. It may include a cash-flow crisis, a staff strike, poor publicity or, of course, bad weather. The last of these

Rules of Road America

1.0 All persons entering the Road America Race Track will have one of the following:
  1.1 A current—Valid spectator ticket.
    1.1.1. A ticket with stub(s) upon entering.
    1.1.2 A ticket and a valid "Pass-Out" upon re-entering.
  1.2 A Valid credential (accompanied by a signed insurance-waiver witness by Road America/Club Staff personnel (Participants only).
    1.2.1 Road America credential.
    1.2.2 Event sponsoring club credential, properly validated.
    1.2.3 Appropriate weekend wrist band.
2.0 Unlicensed vehicles are not allowed to be operated on Road America property, with the following exceptions:
  2.1 Race Vehicles being used in the race event.
  2.2 Authorized Road America Vehicles with a current year sticker.
  2.3 Participants may use light vehicles.
    2.3.1 Furnish proof of vehicle insurance, if requested.
    2.3.2 Wisconsin State Law requires that all ATVs must be licensed.
  2.4 Rollerblades, skate boards, non-motorized scooters and roller skates are not permitted on Road America property.
  2.5 Riding bicycles in the competition paddock area is prohibited with the exception of race crew and race officials.
3.0 All operators of any motor vehicles (including golf carts) on Road America property must posses a valid state-issued driver's license.
  3.1 At no time in anyone allowed to park in fire lanes. Violators will be towed.
4.0 Consumption of alcoholic beverages is prohibited within the competition paddock until after all race events have concluded for the day.

4.1 Spectators may only consume alcoholic beverages in the North Paddock, and other spectator areas.
5.0 Race engines may not be run without Road America permission:
  5.1 Before 8:00 am weekends/8:30 am weekdays.
  5.2 After 6:00 pm weekends/5:00 weekdays.
  5.3 Car Clubs must vacate property by 7:00 pm each day.
  5.4 On-Track Operations 8:00 am to 6:00 pm weekends/ 8:30 am to 5:00 pm weekdays.
6.0 All vehicles or tents remaining overnight on Road America property must have:
  6.1 A valid Road America overnight camping permit properly displayed.
  6.2 Overnight stays are not permitted without formal tent or motorhome equipment.
7.0 No pets are allowed on the Road America property without Road America permission. Pets allowed on the property must either be:
  7.1 Kept within the vehicle with adequate ventilation and fresh drinking water.
  7.2 Kept under control of a leash.
8.0 Fires, when conditions permit, must:
  8.1 Be used for cooking only.
  8.2 Be contained within a device designed for containing a fire.
  8.3 Be completely extinguished before the coals, ashes and remains are discarded.
  8.4 Not be within 10 feet of spectator containment fence.
  8.5 Not be within 100 feet of an occupied Road America concession stand.
  8.6 Not be near competitor's gasoline storage areas.
9.0 At no time shall a vehicle be permitted to travel counter clockwise on the track.

Figure 8–1 Elkhart Lake's Road America
Source: Reproduced with permission from Road America.

is the event manager's greatest risk. Even if it does not have a direct impact on the event, poor weather will reduce the number of people attending an event unless adequate weather protection is provided. Rainy or stormy weather also has an impact on people's mood and motivation, making it a serious concern for which careful planning is required. **Risk management is the process of identifying such risks, assessing these risks, and managing these risks.**

In the case of the Supermoto, the potential for bad crowd behavior, the negative publicity that could result, as well as the liability involved, is no doubt the reason for the organizers to have established strict rules of entry to this event. At a broader level, any negative behavior and publicity could have a negative impact on AMA Pro Racing (American Motorcycle Association) as well as on the host cities where the Supermoto is being held. (The Supermoto's rounds are held in various cities across the country.)

The following risks need to be considered if relevant to the event you are planning.

Natural Disasters

Heavy rain is a disaster for an outdoor event, as too are hail, snow, and extreme heat. Freak acts of nature such as hurricanes and tornadoes can land smack in the middle of an event such as the one that hit Salt Lake City on August 11, 1999. According to a report in *USA Today,* "A rare tornado touched down without warning Wednesday in downtown Salt Lake City, killing one person and injuring more than 100. The black, swirling cloud struck about 1 p.m., uprooting trees and temporary buildings set up for a retailer's convention." Flooding can affect event venues, particularly temporary ones, and it can also cause damage to electrical wiring—potentially a very serious risk. Of course, fire is one of the risks that most venue managers fear and must plan for, since evacuation of large crowds is extremely difficult.

Financial Risk

Financial risk may involve unforeseen costs, lower than expected revenue, high exchange rates, general decline in economic circumstances and disposable income, fraud, fines, and cash-flow problems.

Legal Risk

Legal risks include disputes over contracts between the event organizer and the client and/or between the event organizer and a subcontractor. These can occur if expectations are unrealistic or if a gap develops between what the client had in mind and the product that the event organizer can produce for the price negotiated. Disputes can also occur if the venue does not meet the required standards in terms of such things as reliable electricity supply and suitable access for delivery vehicles. Breach of legal requirements is another form of legal risk, an example being a venue losing its liquor license for a violation of the liquor laws, such as selling alcohol to underage drinkers.

Technology-Related Risks

Technological failure is an increasing risk for high-profile events that are extremely reliant on computer programming and computer networks operating successfully. For example, a problem with guest registration at a trade exhibition would prevent the successful capture of attendee data, which are essential information for all exhibitors. For the exhibition organizer, the attendance list (generated during registration) is his or her most valuable asset. It would be made available to current exhibitors wanting to follow up on contacts, as well as being used by the event organizer in the advertising drive for the next event of a similar nature.

New Year's Eve and Fourth of July fireworks displays are two events nationwide that are most reliant on highly sophisticated technology. No doubt the pyrotechnics planners for the New Year's Eve fireworks displays scheduled throughout the world on December 31, 1999, had a number of backup systems in place for the Y2K situation that could have left the millennial celebrations in darkness.

Technology-related risks of this magnitude are of increasing concern for the event management team. *Source:* EyeWire Collection/Photodisc.

Mismanagement

A successful event requires good management, detailed planning, and sound interpersonal relationships at all levels. Mismanagement can prevent an event from reaching its objectives; so, too, can people-related problems, such as disputes at the top management levels, leading to the dismissal of key personnel. Both are potentially serious risks.

Safety and Security Risk

Accidents, riots, terrorism, and sabotage are all safety and security risks. Safety and security measures will be described in Chapter 15 in more detail.

Risk at Sporting Events

The risks associated with most community, commercial, and entertainment events are largely financial; however, with sporting events, there is the additional risk of danger to the participants and, in some cases, to the audience. For example, most bike and car races carry the risk of injury to both drivers and spectators, whether on the track or off-road. Bike races and even fun runs, such as the Nationwide Insurance Hood to Coast Relay, the largest relay race in North America, stretching 195 miles from the top of Oregon's Mt. Hood down to the Pacific Ocean, generally experience a number of medical emergencies and the occasional fatal heart attack. The challenge for

Bike races carry risk for both the competitors and the audience.
Source: Gary Conner/ PhotoEdit.

organizers of such events is to reduce the risk to an acceptable level by careful planning and by introducing new procedures and technologies when available, since safety standards change over time. Working out the safety standards for a particular sporting event at a particular time involves looking at a number of factors:

- perceived level of acceptable risk of participants and audience
- current legislation and legal precedents
- availability of risk management solutions
- development and implementation of plans, procedures, and control mechanisms

The last of these is extremely important for event organizers, for if they can show that their procedures for managing risk were well considered and well implemented, this preplanning would stand them in good stead if a charge of negligence were laid.

From the www.roadatlanta.com Web site we find evidence that the issue of risk is always on the agenda for the organizers of this race and that change is something that they have to deal with.

Road Atlanta has taken proactive steps to increase rider safety during its professional and amateur motorcycle races by re-designing the Turn 3-4 complex of its 2.54-mile Grand Prix course.

"Responding to concerns of riders and AMA Pro Racing, Road Atlanta has taken these proactive steps to increase safety and provide the riders a more exciting venue," says Mike Swaine, president and general manager of Road Atlanta.

Another important risk issue for event organizers concerns temporary fencing, staging, and seating. There have been numerous accidents where temporary seating stands have collapsed at special events, resulting in injury to participants and the audience. When temporary fencing, staging, or seating is used, a structural engineer should be consulted, and steps must be in place to ensure that correct safety standards are met.

Process of Risk Management

Risk management involves a three-step process:

1. Identify risks and hazards.
2. Assess the risks and hazards.
3. Manage the risks and hazards.

This sporting venue is well designed, not only for the comfort and convenience of the audience and the sportspeople, but also for the excellent facilities provided for the organizers and contractors. First-class facilities help to improve safety.
Source: AP/Wide World Photos.

This process allows the event organizer to establish and prioritize the risks, to take steps to prevent problems from occurring, and to make contingency plans if problems do occur.

Identifying Risks and Hazards

The first step is identifying the risk or hazard and ascertaining when and how a problem might occur. It is important to view risks broadly, in terms of the risk factors listed at the beginning of this chapter. The next step is to analyze the likelihood of problems arising, as well as the resulting consequences. As an example, mismanagement by a senior staff member, such as the person responsible for sponsorship, could have dire financial repercussions; on the other hand, poor performance by a junior member of the event team could probably be managed and resolved without serious consequence.

In terms of hazards that represent potential risk, these include the following:

- fire
- plant and equipment
- hazardous substances
- electrical equipment
- spills
- stacking of unbalanced heavy items
- temporary fencing, staging, seating, and other venue features
- moving vehicles

Brainstorming by the event management team will help enormously in identifying potential risks. Research of written material and Web site information, such as current legislative requirements, as well as conversations with organizers and managers of similar events, will also contribute to a detailed list of possible problems. For major events, a risk management consultant is recommended.

Assessing the Risks and Hazards

Once potential risks and hazards have been identified, their likelihood of occurring needs to be evaluated. This process allows the team to prioritize the issues for attention. It is a good idea to set up a committee to manage risk, safety, and security issues, and to establish operational guidelines for operating equipment, testing schedules, and the like. The following questions need to be asked (you might wish to consider heavy rain as an example of a risk factor when looking at each of these questions):

- What is the likelihood of this risk happening?
- Who will be exposed to the risk?
- What impact has this risk had in similar circumstances?
- How will people react to this risk/hazard?

With hazards that might pose a risk to health and safety, the following three classifications are recommended:

Class A hazard. Exists when a risk of death or grievous injury or illness is likely or very likely, or serious injury or illness is very likely.

Class B hazard. Exists when a risk of death or grievous injury or illness is not likely to occur but is possible, or when serious injury or illness is likely, or moderate injury or illness is very likely.

Class C hazard. Exists when a risk of serious injury or illness is not likely, but is possible, or when moderate injury or illness is or is not likely, but is possible.

(From the *Corrective Action Handbook,* 2002, U.S. Consumer Product Safety Commission)

Although this classification refers mainly to injury, the principle of looking at potential consequences is well illustrated. The potential consequences of fire, flooding, bombs, and computer failure can be evaluated in the same way.

Managing the Risks and Hazards

Once the risks and hazards have been prioritized, the final step is to look at the most effective ways of managing them. Control measures include the following:

1. Elimination plans to eliminate the risk altogether (for example, erecting covered walkways to protect spectators from rain).
2. Substitution plans (such as looking for a better-designed grandstand).
3. Isolation plans (for example, isolating dangerous or noisy equipment).
4. Engineering controls (for example, using safety barriers and fences to limit access and to control crowds).
5. Administrative controls (for example, erecting warning signs and training staff well in procedures).
6. Contingency plans (for example, developing evacuation plans for situations in which risk cannot be completely avoided).

Here, fencing has been erected to limit access to machinery and equipment.

Incident Reporting

Incident reporting is an important risk control process, and it is essential that every member of the event team is familiar with this process. An incident report card similar to the one included in Figure 8–2 should be completed for every problem that occurs, from customer complaints to slips and falls. On receipt of the incident report cards, management staff can look for patterns in the incidents and for ways in which these risks can be better managed.

There are several reasons for maintaining all documentation relating to risk:

- to demonstrate that an appropriate process was in place
- to provide a record of incidents and responses
- to allow for monitoring, review, and improvement

The results of such an approach include the following:

- reduction in problems, accidents, and incidents
- improved legislative compliance
- decrease in potential liability
- improved workplace performance
- customer satisfaction
- avoidance of controversial issues and negative media exposure

Emergency Response Plans

Every event or venue should have an emergency response plan, which is usually referred to by the acronym ERP. It is usually developed in conjunction with professional consultants who also train staff on procedures, such as evacuation and the roles of everyone involved. This plan will be discussed in more detail in Chapter 16, "Crowd Management and Evacuation."

An example of a simple risk management plan is shown in Figure 8–3. This plan shows the risks anticipated by the event organizer, the potential impact of such risks, and management strategies and contingency plans put in place to control them.

Standards for Risk Management

Risk management is recognized as an integral part of good management practice. It is an iterative process consisting of steps that, when undertaken in sequence, enable continual improvement in decision

INCIDENT REPORT CARD

Time

Date

FUNCTIONAL AREA/DEPARTMENT

YOUR POSITION

YOUR NAME

NAMES OF PERSON/S INVOLVED IN THE INCIDENT

NAME AND CONTACT DETAILS OF WITNESS/ES IF ANY

INCIDENT DETAILS

TIME OF INCIDENT

LOCATION OF INCIDENT

CAUSE OF INCIDENT

CONSEQUENCES OF INCIDENT

CAN ANY ACTION BE TAKEN TO PREVENT REOCCURRENCE?

DATE AND TIME RECEIVED AND LOGGED

OUTSTANDING ACTIONS

Figure 8–2   Sample Incident Report Card

Priority	Identification: Nature of Risk	Assessment: Impact of Risk	Management: Control	Management: Contingency Planning
1	Weather: rain or extreme heat	Rain will result in poor attendance and low on-site sales; problems with long lines; potential electrical and other equipment failure.	Monitor weather reports. Provide cover (also at entrance) for spectators. Needs to be part of event promotional material. Electrical hazards must be avoided through careful planning, competent subcontractors, control systems for safety and continuous supply.	Roving staff sell ponchos if it is wet or drinks and water if it is very hot. Provide staff with free wet weather gear or water, as appropriate. Establish task force to maintain electrical supply and backup systems.
2	Fire and evacuation	Impact would be extremely serious; however risk is not high due to venue design.	Establish ERP. Continuously monitor and control, using checklists (e.g., fire equipment, access and exits). Staff training	ERP to identify clear communication with emergency services. Senior staff appropriately deployed.
3	Crowd control	Biggest potential impact is on entry to venue due to traffic delays.	Use promotional material and ticketing process to advise audience on transportation options and parking. Provide ushers, signage and crowd control barriers to avoid congestion.	The ticketed patrons will be allowed into the venue once game has started without ticket checking through turnstiles. Senior staff deployed to deal with resulting problems of gate crashers.
4	Financial management	Financial failure for event organizer, bankruptcy or breach of contract.	Financial control systems: limited authority for purchasing and expenditure. Contract and cash flow management by finance committee. Control of ticket revenue	Limited. Short-term money market. Sponsorship with VIPs.

Figure 8–3   Risk Management Plan

			and revenue from programs and catering. Security provided for transporting cash. Staff training on procedures.	
5	Staff management	Poor staff selection and training which would have impact on level of service and satisfaction. Impact on event ambience.	Development of job descriptions and specifications, recruitment drive, training and support materials provided. Leadership and control systems training for supervisors. Performance appraisal system for senior staff. Policies and procedures for staffing, performance management, dismissal, health and safety.	Agency staff. Pay for volunteers. Work experience student group. Loyalty payment on completion. Certificate of participation.
6	Occupational health and safety	Costs of litigation, poor publicity, fines.	Development of policies and procedures to reduce risk as part of workplace practice. This includes the use of licensed subcontractors, fulfilling requirements for equipment maintenance, and building temporary structures that meet required standards. Documentation and regular reviews, including inspections.	Reporting and documentation system for recording incidents relating to health and safety, including witnesses to any incidents. Emergency response plan. Legal advice.

Figure 8–3   Continued

making. Risk management is the term applied to a logical and systematic method of identifying, analyzing, evaluating, treating, monitoring, and communicating risks associated with any activity, function, or process in a way that will enable organizations to minimize losses and maximize opportunities. Risk management is as much about identifying opportunities as avoiding or mitigating losses.

Summary

This chapter has looked in detail at some of the risks associated with the staging of events. The weather is often a significant risk, since it can reduce attendance, even at indoor events. More serious risks include fire and accidents. Failure of any key system, such as event registration, ticketing, scoring, or sound, can have a major impact and can lead ultimately to financial ruin. The development of a risk management plan that anticipates and prioritizes all of the major risk factors is essential. With this as a guide, risks can be managed and contingency plans developed to deal with almost every issue that occurs.

Nonprofit Organizations

Many people who work or volunteer for a nonprofit agency believe that nonprofits operate under some form of charitable immunity. This misconception and others about nonprofit liability may jeopardize the success of nonprofits that fail to take appropriate steps to protect themselves and their stakeholders from harm. Dispelling the myths about liability is a first step in managing risk in a nonprofit organization. The Risk Management Resource Center provides information to help local government; nonprofit organizations and small businesses manage risks effectively. It is a collaborative effort of the Public Risk Management Association (PRIMA), the Nonprofit Risk Management Center (NRMC), and the Public Entity Risk Institute (PERI). For more information, go to www.eriskcenter.org.

Case Study

Conduct a risk management analysis using a table format and appropriate headings (see Figure 8-2 as an example) for at least two of the following events:

- Outdoor launch of a soft drink product, with entertainment, for a target audience of children aged nine to fourteen.
- Minor/local golf tournament for all age groups, with a handicapping system based on heat times.
- Wedding ceremony on the beach followed by a reception at a local Country Club.
- Citywide swimming competition for high school students.

Activity

Consider some of the social and legal issues relating to the use and abuse of alcohol and drugs at events. Identify some of the factors that increase the level of this risk for the event organizer. Identify ways in which this risk can be minimized and managed.

Links

www.amaproracing.com
www.roadatlanta.com
www.eriskcenter.org
www.crowdsafe.com

Chapter Nine

PLANNING

Special events are public events, solicitation or assembly held on property under the jurisdiction of the Department of Recreation and Parks, such as public parks and/or plazas. Private events with an expected attendance of 350 or more are also classified as special events. Special Events Permits are not issued to private companies or individuals when the event activities include, selling, vending, or the operation of a business for self-gain. Special Event Permits are issued to NONPROFIT ORGANIZATIONS for the purpose of fund raising (e.g., concerts, festivals, fairs, flea markets, etc.), and/or soliciation (e.g., free will donations of money, food, clothing, etc.). Special Event Applications must be submitted by the nonprofit organization. Special Events cannot promote a business or product in any manner (e.g., signs, banners, displays, giveaways, etc.). All events activities must be restricted to the location stated on the issued permit.

Special Event Applications must be submitted at least eight weeks prior to the requested event date, with a $35 non-refundable application fee (for a ONE (1) day event) clarify information, work out proposed changes, reimbursement costs or other fees associated with using the site requested. These fees may include per day fee ($10 per day for each additional event date), and area/pavilion fee ($75 to $300 per day), solid waste removal, traffic security deposit, and/or $1,000,000 liability insurance.

Reproduced with permission of the City of Baltimore, Department of Recreation and Parks.

On completion of this chapter, you will be able to

- identify the purpose, aims, and objectives of an event;
- develop an event proposal or outline;
- identify the team and the stakeholders involved in staging an event;
- plan the location and layout of an event using maps/illustrations;
- use charts and run sheets to develop timelines; and
- develop management control systems, such as checklists.

As this statement from a department of recreation and park's manual so clearly illustrates, planning and organization are the key elements that determine the success of an event. For most event organizers, the first stop is the local government. The local government will provide guidelines on the possible impact of your event, such as the impact of noise. This may be a factor even if your event is not being held at a public venue. Another useful contact is the local tourism office. This office, with links to corporate offices in each state, plays an important part in the strategic management of events and, in many cases, provides support in a number of other ways, such as listing events on their Web site. However, before making these contacts, you need to develop the event concept. As we discussed in Chapter 2, this involves defining the event's purpose and aims, as well as the specific objectives on which the success of the event will be measured. Funding for your event may come from grants or from sponsors, but all stakeholders have to be provided with a good understanding of the event concept before you proceed further. If your client is the one funding the event, the provision of a clearly developed concept, plan, and evaluation strategy will generally avoid problems down the line, including legal ones.

Develop a Mission/Purpose Statement

The first step is to develop a simple statement that summarizes the purpose or mission of the event. Too often, the purpose of the event becomes less and less clear as the event approaches. Different stakeholders have different interests, and this situation can sometimes lead to a change of focus of which most stakeholders are unaware. The purpose of an event could be, for example, "to commemorate the history of our town in a historically authentic parade that involves the community and is supported by the community." In contrast, a sporting event may have as its mission statement "to attract both loyal team supporters and first-time spectators (potential regulars) in an effort to improve ticket sales and thus the viability of the competition and venue."

Effective planning ensures the provision of all necessary services and amenities at an event.

The mission statement should ensure that planning and implementation do not get off track and that the initial intent is realized.

Establish the Aims of the Event

The purpose can be broken down further into general aims and specific measurable objectives. An event could have any one, or more, of the following aims:

- improving community attitudes to health and fitness through participation in sporting activities
- increasing civic pride
- injecting funds into the local economy
- raising funds for a charitable cause
- increasing tourist numbers to a specific destination
- extending the tourist season
- launching a new product
- raising revenue through ticket sales
- providing entertainment
- building team loyalty
- raising the profile of the town or city
- celebrating a historical event
- enhancing the reputation of a convention organizer/venue
- conducting an inspirational ceremony
- providing a unique experience
- increasing product sales
- acknowledging award winners (for example, tourism awards or staff awards)
- producing media coverage
- highlighting the main point of a conference
- raising awareness of a charitable or political campaign

Aims vary widely from one event to another, and this is one of the challenges for the event manager. One event might have a social impact focus, whereas another might be profit-oriented. It cannot be stressed enough that everything to do with the event must reinforce the purpose and the goals. Choice of colors, entertainment, presentations, and so on must all work together in order to fulfill the purpose and goals of the event. A client may arrive at a meeting with an event organizer and say, "I want a banquet for 200 people with a celebrity entertainer," and it may emerge only through questioning that the aim of the event is to recognize key staff, to present awards, and to re-inforce success. The recognition of the aim must be established early in the negotiation process and remembered during all the planning stages.

> *It has been said by many that the Gathering of Nations Powwow is the Mecca of Indian Country; while others have said that there is a magic about the "Gathering."*
>
> *Many people from around the world have made the Gathering of Nations Powwow their travel destination. The Gathering of Nations has grown to become more than just a "Powwow," **it's an experience!***
>
> *At the University of New Mexico Arena, the "Pit," the Gathering of Nations has had the opportunity to blossom into the most enjoyable, cultural, and entertaining Native festival in North America.*

The Gathering of Nations Powwow is an event with predominately social impact aims, starting as it did as a way to promote the traditions and culture of the American Indian people in the most positive manner possible. Today this event attracts visitors from across the nation and around the world. With the proceeds of this event, the nonprofit organization has been able to establish a scholarship foundation, camp fund, and Toys for Tots program, and has helped with tornado relief and a host of other charitable causes. However, although the organization has been able to achieve significant charitable and economic impact, this is not its primary aim.

In contrast, the Portland Rose Festival aims to enhance the perception of that city as a tourist destination and to achieve targets for attendance by tourists as part of its more specific objectives. The Portland Rose Festival is Oregon's premier civic celebration and has been a Northwest tradition for 97 years. This unique festival bursts into bloom each spring to celebrate the City of Roses with events, excitement, and entertainment for all ages. More than two million spectators come to the "City of Roses" annually to participate in the parades and other festivities involved with this annual event. The goals of an event provide the foundation for many aspects of the planning process. An event organizer who becomes distracted from the stated goals is likely to clash with the organizing committee and other stakeholders. When working with clients, it is therefore essential to identify the goals early and to use them to inform the planning process. Too often, enthusiasm for the theme or the entertainment overrides the goals, and planning goes awry. If, for example, the goal were to increase consumer recognition of the main sponsor, it would be necessary to develop specific objectives and to take steps to ensure that they were achieved. At the end of the event, there should be one or more measures in place to indicate the outcomes of the event, in this case the results of a survey indicating percentage levels of sponsor recognition by the event audience. As an event manager, you need to show, in a measurable way, how the goals have been achieved. Developing objectives helps you to do this.

*E*stablish the Objectives

The goals are used to develop detailed and specific objectives. Ideally, objectives should be realistic and measurable. Targets, percentages, and sales are generally the factors used to measure objectives. As an example, an objective could be "to increase the participation level in the local community's fun walk to 3,500, including a cross-section of age groups, ranging from 15 to 60 plus, this target to be reached by the 2005 event." The number of participants and the ages of participants would be measures of this objective, whereas a survey on training undertaken in preparation for the walk would indicate less tangible outcomes such as changes in community exercise patterns and attitudes toward fitness and health. As a second example, one objective of an event organizer might be to increase awareness of a sponsor's products, whereas the main objective might be to translate this awareness into sales totaling $3 million, which would be an even more successful outcome. Surveys of spectators and television viewers are used to demonstrate changes in awareness of a sponsor's products.

Evaluation of event outcomes will be covered in more detail in Chapter 17. However, evaluation is not possible if the aims and objectives are not clear in the first place.

Objectives are generally evaluated by measures such as the following:

- size of audience
- demographics (age, country, place of origin, etc.) of audience
- average expenditure of audience
- sponsor recognition levels
- sales of sponsor products
- economic impact of event
- profit

SMART objectives are **s**pecific, **m**easurable, **a**chievable, **r**ealistic, and **t**ime related.

Prepare an Event Proposal

A complete outline for an event proposal is included in Appendix 2. At this stage of event planning, however, the proposal should include the purpose and the aims and objectives of the event, as well as details on organization, physical layout, and the social, environmental, and economic impact, if applicable. The relevant headings are shown in the outline included in Figure 9–1. Maps and models are extremely useful in illustrating the event concept, and more detailed plans will ensure that the client's expectations are realistic.

Make Use of Planning Tools

Organization charts, maps and models, Gantt charts, run sheets, and checklists are useful tools for presenting material and information to your clients, members of your staff, and stakeholders. These are described and illustrated in the following sections.

EVENT PROPOSAL

EVENT DESCRIPTION
Event name
Event type
Location, suburb and county
Date(s)
Duration/timing
Overview and purpose/concept
Aims and objectives

EVENT MANAGEMENT
Management responsibility
Major stakeholders and agencies
Physical requirements
    Venue
    Route for street events
    Event map
    Event layout (indoor)
Audience
Impact
    Social
    Environmental
    Economic

Figure 9–1 Example of an Event Proposal in the Early Planning Stage

Maps and Models

Maps are a useful way to represent an event, particularly to contractors who may be required to set up the site. It may be necessary to develop more than one map or plan. Today there are a host of computer software programs that can be used to generate computer images, giving the different parties involved in the event a better understanding of the facilities. The various people might include the following:

- builders and designers
- telecommunications and electrical contractors
- emergency response teams
- spectator services hosts
- artists, entertainers, and exhibitors
- event audience

Models are also extremely useful, since most clients find it difficult to visualize three-dimensional concepts. A model can also assist in many aspects of event management, such as crowd control. In this instance, bottlenecks and other potential problems are likely to emerge from viewing a three-dimensional illustration. Most software can also present the information in this way, allowing the event management team to anticipate all design and implementation issues. Examples of maps and models are illustrated in Figures 9–2 and 9–3.

Figure 9–2   2-D drawing of a banquet facility. Computer generated images like this help event management teams visualize the setting even though they may be miles away from the actual site.
Source: Reproduced with permission of Meeting Matrix International, Inc.

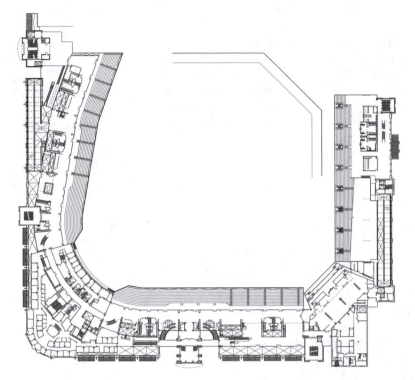

Figure 9–3   Sporting Stadiums are often used as the venue for a host of events. This shows the club level at Coor's Field in Denver.
Source: Reproduced with permission of Coor's Field.

Aerial photo of Qualcomm Stadium which is used for many events in addition to football.
Source: Reproduced with permission of Qualcomm Stadium and the city of San Diego, CA.

Gantt Charts

A Gantt chart is generally used in the **early planning days** and **in the lead-up** to an event. In this type of planning sheet, dates are listed across the top of the chart, and rules (or blocks) are used to illustrate how long each task (listed at the side of the chart) will take. The benefit of this type of chart is that the interdependence of the tasks can be clearly seen. For example, once you have plotted the process of recruiting, inducting, training, and rostering staff for an event, you may realize that the recruitment process needs to start earlier than expected to enable staff to be completely ready for the big day. Another aspect of planning is identifying the critical path: those elements of the plan that are essential to the successful outcome of the event and therefore high priority. Critical path analysis is beyond the scope of this text; however, the general principle of identifying planning elements on which all else is dependent can be done with a Gantt chart.

In the case of arrangements with sponsors, for example, these need to be finalized before any work can be done on print or promotional material because sponsors need to approve the use of their logos. If one sponsor pulls out of the arrangement, this change will have an impact on print production, which will, in turn, affect promotional activities and ticket sales. Project planning software, including specialized event planning software, is available, whereas for smaller events a spreadsheet is probably sufficient. The trick is to identify the tasks that can be clustered together and to choose the ideal level of detail required in planning the event. At the extreme, the chart can be expanded to a point where even the smallest task is shown (but at this stage, it will fill an entire wall and become unmanageable). As with maps, the Gantt chart must be a user-friendly planning tool in order to be effective.

Another point to take into account is that change is an integral part of event planning, and it may be necessary to make significant changes that immediately make all your charts redundant. An experienced event manager is able to ascertain the level of planning required to ensure that everyone is clear about his or her roles and responsibilities, while remaining reasonably open to change.

A high-level planning chart for an event is illustrated in Figure 9–4. It provides a broad overview of the main event tasks and a general timeline.

Each of these major tasks could also be used as the basis for a more detailed plan. This has been done in Figure 9–5, which shows the planning process for recruiting and training staff for the preceding event. This Gantt chart is clearly an example of a fairly detailed level of planning although, even here, the training aspect is not covered fully, because there would be many steps involved, including writing training materials and seeking approval of the content from the various functional area managers.

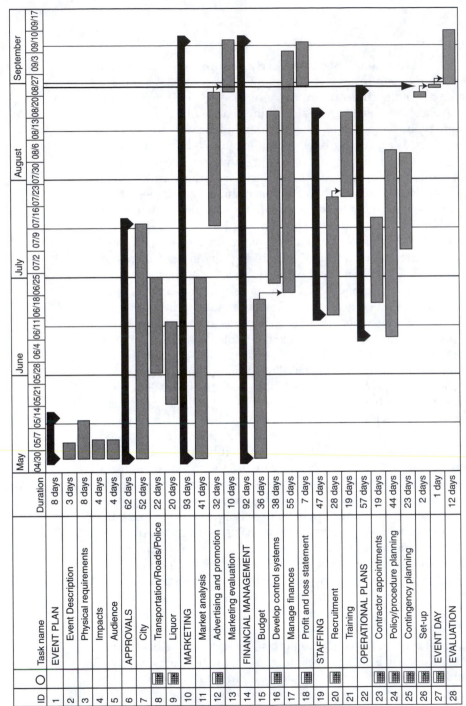

Figure 9–4 Sample Gantt Chart for Planning an Event

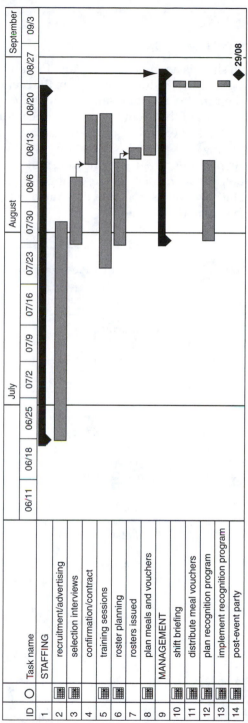

Figure 9–5 Sample Gantt Chart for Planning Staffing for an Event

Run Sheets

The run sheet is an indispensable tool for most event managers. It is the program, or schedule, of events. In the preliminary stages of planning, the run sheet is quite simple, with times allocated only to specific elements of the event (see the run sheet for a gala dinner in Figure 9–6). This overview of proceedings forms part of the event concept briefing.

As planning progresses, however, the run sheet becomes even more detailed with, for example, timings for dancers, technicians, and other staff. This development is illustrated in Figure 9–7, where setup and teardown are also shown.

7:00 pm	Guests arrive. Pre-dinner drinks in foyer.
7:30 pm	Doors open. Guests move to tables.
7:35 pm	MC welcome.
7:40 pm	Entrée served.
8:00 pm	First Championship (demonstration dance routine).
8:10 pm	Main course served. Band starts playing.
8:50 pm	Band stops. Second Championship (demo dance routine). Guests drawn onto dance floor at the end.
9:15 pm	Dessert served. Band plays.
9:40 pm	Band stops. ABTA Awards Presentation (1 award, with 2 finalists).
10:25 pm	Ms. & Mr. Sparkly awarded. Dancing for guests starts properly.
11:15 pm	MC announces final winners (all!) and last dance.
12:00 pm	Guests depart.

Figure 9–6   Preliminary Run Sheet for Gala Dinner—Concept Stage
Source: Reproduced with permission of Events Unlimited International.

8:00 am	Lay dance floor and stage, and lower vertical drapes. Scissor lift ready. Audio subcontractor commences set-up. Rear projection screen set.
9:00 am	Dance floor and stage set. Stage designer sets up stage decoration.
10:00 am	Production meeting.
11:00 am	Onstage setup commences (audio and video).
12:30 pm	Band set-up.
2:30 pm	Technical set-up complete. Table set-up can commence.
3:00 pm	Technical run-through.
5:30 pm	All decorations complete.
5:45 pm	Rehearsal with MC and SM (probably walk through with music). Band sound check.
6:30 pm	All ready.
6:45 pm	External sign turned on.
7:00–7:30 pm	Guests arrive. Pre-dinner drinks in foyer.
7:00 pm	Dancers arrive. Walk-through and music check.
7:15 pm	Pre-set lighting ON.
7:25 pm	Walk-in music ON.
7:30 pm	Doors open. Guests move to tables. All dancers ready.
7:35 pm	MC welcome.
7:40 pm	Salad served.

Figure 9–7   Complete Run Sheet for Gala Dinner
Source: Reproduced with permission of Events Unlimited International.

8:00 pm	First "Championship" (Demonstration dance routine).
8:10 pm	Main course served. Band starts playing.
8:50 pm	Band stops. Second Championship (Demo dance routine). Guests drawn onto dance floor at the end.
9:15 pm	Dessert enters and is served. Band plays.
9:40 pm	Band stops. Awards presentation (1 award, with 2 finalists).
10:25 pm	Ms. & Mr. Sparkly awarded. Dancing for guests starts.
11:55 pm	MC announces final winners (all!) and last dance.
12:00 midnight	Guests depart. Clean-up commences.
2:30 am	All clear.

Figure 9–7   Continued

Finally, an even more detailed run sheet can be developed (at this stage called the script) to identify each person's role and cues. This is illustrated in Figure 9–8 in which the timing of meal service and the cues for recommencement of the "championships" after the main course are outlined in detail.

Run sheets are an important tool for all stakeholders and participants, from the venue management team through to the subcontractors.

Organization Charts

An organization chart is another important tool used in planning. Once all tasks have been identified and grouped logically, the staffing requirements for an event become much clearer and can be represented on an organization chart. This concept will be described and illustrated more fully in Chapter 12. However, we have illustrated an event committee structure, as an example of an organization chart, in Figure 9–9.

8:10 pm
Main course served.
As main nearly cleared

MC and dancers stand by. Dance 2 music ready.
When clear
8:50 pm
Band stops and exits.
MC mic ON.
Band Off.
MC spot ON.
House down

MC: Welcome to our next championship, The Self-Booking Samba. Amazingly the finalists are our previous winners. Please welcome them back.

Vision—Self-Booking Samba

Dance floor ON.

Dancers run on.
(2nd dance routine 10 min)

Dancers pause at end.
MC spot OFF.
Music 2 On.
MC mic OFF

When music 2 finished cue music 3.

MC: And once again it's a tie, isn't that fantastic!

Now I know that there are some aspiring champions out there who are probably thinking "I could never do that!" Well our champions have graciously agreed to teach you some of their steps, so come on up and join in . . .

MC somehow coaxes people up. When enough on dance floor he cues music with:
OK. Let's dance!
(About 10 minutes dance coaching)
MC spot ON.
MC mic ON.

House UP 1/2.

Music 3 ON.
MC mic OFF.
Kitchen advised 10 min to dessert.

At end

Dance music 3 OFF.
Cue march in—SB track 14.
Kitchen 1 min to dessert

Figure 9–8   Script for Part of Gala Dinner
Source: Reproduced with permission of Events Unlimited International.

Checklists

At the most detailed level of planning, a checklist is indispensable. It is a control tool that ensures that the individual performing the tasks has not forgotten a single detail. For example, when checking firefighting equipment and emergency exits, it is imperative that a specific checklist be followed and that it be signed and dated on completion. This is part of the record-keeping process, aimed not only at preventing potential problems but also at reducing the risk of litigation if anything should go wrong. Detailed and correctly implemented plans reassure the client, allow the event team to work effectively, and build confidence in achieving the objectives of the event. A safety checklist is illustrated in Figure 9–10.

The nature of the event business is that most of the time is spent in planning and very little is spent in the execution phase. In fact, it

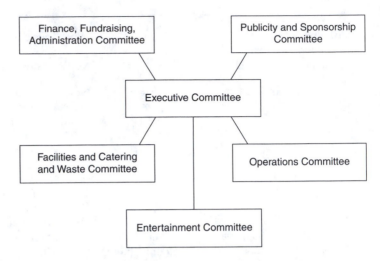

Figure 9–9   Event Committee
Structure

often comes as a shock when the event is over so quickly. Things can
go bad in an instant in the event environment, but good planning can
prevent this outcome from happening. In the best cases, the plans
have been so thoughtfully developed that the event manager's role is
simply to ensure that procedures are correctly implemented, resulting in minimal incidents and satisfied clients.

DAILY SAFETY CHECKLIST

Name   Today's date and time

Task	Check ✔ ✗	Comment	Follow up required ✔
First Aid kit fully equipped			
Flammable goods signage correct, storage away from combustible materials			
Extinguisher visible, free of obstruction			
Cleaning products labelled and stored correctly			
All electrical appliances tested and tagged within last six months			
Extension cords tested and tagged within last three months			
Extension cords not presenting a hazard over walkways			
Boxes, trash, etc. not obstructing exits or fire-fighting equipment			
Gas cut-off valve visible and not obstructed			

Figure 9–10   Daily Safety Checklist

Case Study

As the organizer of a product launch for a prestige motor car company, you need to reassure your client of your capacity to plan a successful event. Develop an **overview** of the event (event concept), a brief **run sheet,** and a series of illustrations showing the event and staging layout. Finally, prepare a timeline or **Gantt chart** to show the planning process in the lead-up to the event.

Activity

The concept "chain of events" is very relevant to event planning. Review three different types of event (such as a product launch, country arts fair, and sporting competition), and identify potential weak links in the planning process that could jeopardize each of the events if they were not thoroughly considered. For example, the lack of a backup system for electrical supplies at an outdoor venue could jeopardize the event.

Links

www.ganttcharts.com
www.eventsunlimited.com.au

Summary

In this chapter we have explained the differences among the purpose, the aims, and the objectives of an event, and have stressed the importance of these being clearly stated and adhered to. Using maps, diagrams, charts, and checklists, the event manager can show how the event can be achieved within the allocated time period. Unlike most other projects, deadlines in event management cannot be postponed, since the date must be advertised and the event venue booked. The planning tools described and illustrated in this chapter will help to meet these deadlines, particularly since each aspect of an event is generally contingent upon another. Nevertheless, planning needs to remain flexible, since this is a very dynamic industry in which change is inevitable.

Chapter Ten

PROTOCOL

We had the entire evening planned, including the seating chart for the banquet dinner. About four hours before the event was to begin, we got word that the governor was going to be able to make it. Suddenly we were faced with a number of special considerations. How should we address him? Where should we seat him? Will he have security people with him? Where should we seat his wife? Do we need to ask permission before our photographer takes photos? Will he want to address the crowd? Our list of questions went on and on.

Event Organizer

On completion of this chapter, you will be able to

- explain the concept of protocol;
- identify protocol associated with a range of events;
- identify sources of information regarding event protocol;
- avoid a breach of protocol; and
- use national symbols correctly.

The term "protocol" comes from the Greek and means "first glue." It may be said that protocol is the "glue" that holds official life in our society together.

Protocol is the set of traditional practices that have long been accepted and used when dealing with and meeting with others. Protocol reflects mutual respect and consideration and is especially important when bringing together dignitaries between nations. It also encompasses religious and cultural traditions. Protocol includes the proper way of addressing dignitaries, to the way to dress for an event. It also includes where to seat your guests at a dinner and how to fly the flag.

Titles

Style guides, available in most public libraries, provide guidelines on the correct titles for people.

Rolling out the red carpet is usually associated with formal or ceremonial events.

If high-ranking overseas visitors were attending an event, an event organizer would contact the relevant embassy to obtain information on the table of precedence and the titles to be used. See Figure 10–1.

This section provides the correct forms of address for U.S. public officials, diplomats, religious leaders, royalty, and military personnel. For each personage the chart gives the appropriate form or forms to be used in addressing letters, in letter salutations, in direct conversation, and in more formal introductions.

In diplomatic and other public circles, "Sir" is generally considered an acceptable alternative to the formal address in both written and spoken greetings; this rule does not apply to religious or titled persons. The use of "Madam" or "Ma'am" for a female addressee is less customary but still acceptable, especially for high officeholders ("Madam Governor"). This rule also holds for high officials of foreign countries.

For greetings in which "Mr." is used, the feminine equivalent may be "Madam" or, less formally, "Mrs.," "Miss," or "Ms." Although there is no formal rule for the use of "Ms.," the preference of the addressee should be respected. Figure 10–1 gives a host of examples for both written and spoken greetings.

Person	Letter Address	Letter Greeting	Spoken Greeting	Formal Introduction
President of the United States	The President The White House Washington, DC 20500	Dear Mr. (or Madam) President	Mr. (or Madam) President	The President or the President of the United States
Former President	The Honorable John J. Jones Current address	Dear Mr. (Mrs., Ms.) Jones	Mr. (Mrs., Ms.) Jones	The Honorable John J. Jones
Vice President	The Vice President Executive Office Building Washington, DC 20501	Dear Mr. (or Madam) Vice President	Mr. (or Madam) Vice President	The Vice President or the Vice President of the United States
Cabinet members	The Honorable John (or Jane) Jones The Secretary of _____ or The Attorney General Washington, DC	Dear Mr. (or Madam) Secretary	Mr. (or Madam) Secretary	The Secretary of _____
Chief Justice	The Chief Justice The Supreme Court Washington, DC 20543	Dear Mr. (or Madam) Justice or Dear Mr. (or Madam) Chief Justice	Mr. (or Madam) Chief Justice	The Chief Justice
Associate Justice	Mr. Justice Jones or Madam Justice Jones The Supreme Court Washington, DC 20543	Dear Mr. (or Madam) Justice	Mr. Justice or Mr. Justice Jones; Madam Justice or Madam Justice Jones	Mr. Justice Jones; Madam Justice Jones
United States Senator	The Honorable John (or Jane) Jones United States Senate Washington, DC 20510	Dear Senator Jones	Senator Jones	Senator Jones from Nebraska
Speaker of the House	The Honorable John (or Jane) Jones Speaker of the House of Representatives United States House of Representatives Washington, DC 20515	Dear Mr. (or Madam) Speaker	Mr. Speaker; Madam Speaker	The Speaker of the House of Representatives
United States Representative	The Honorable John (or Jane) Jones United States House of Representatives Washington, DC 20515	Dear Mr. (or Mrs., Ms.) Jones	Mr. (or Mrs., Ms.) Jones	Representative Jones from New Jersey

Figure 10–1 Spoken and Written Forms of Address for U.S. Government Officials, Military Personnel, Foreign Officials, Nobility, and Religious Officials
Source: Reproduced with permission of www.cftech.com.

(continued)

Person	Letter Address	Letter Greeting	Spoken Greeting	Formal Introduction
	United Nations Ambassador	The Honorable John (or Jane) Jones U.S. Ambassador to the United Nations United Nations Plaza New York, NY 10017	Dear (or Madam) Ambassador	The United States Ambassador to the United Nations
Ambassador	The Honorable John (or Jane) Jones Ambassador of the United States American Embassy Address goes here	Dear Mr. (or Madam) Ambassador	Mr. (or Madam) Ambassador	The American Ambassador The Ambassador of The United States of America
Consul-General	The Honorable John (or Jane) Jones American Consul General Address goes here	Dear Mr. (or Mrs., Ms.) Jones	Mr. (or Mrs., Ms.) Jones	Mr. (or Mrs., Ms.) Jones
Foreign Ambassador	His (or Her) Excellency John (or Jean) Johnson The Ambassador of _____ Address goes here	Excellency or Dear Mr. (or Madam) Ambassador	Excellency; or Mr. (or Madam) Ambassador	The Ambassador of _____
Secretary-General of the United Nations	His (or Her) Excellency Milo (or Mara) Jones Secretary-General of the United Nations United Nations Plaza New York, NY 10017	Dear Mr. (or Madam) Secretary-General	Mr. (or Madam) Secretary-General	The Secretary-General of the United Nations
Governor	The Honorable John (or Jane) Jones Governor of _____ State Capitol Address goes here	Dear Governor Jones	Governor or Governor Jones	The Governor of Maine; Governor Jones of Maine
State legislators	The Honorable John (or Jane) Jones Address goes here	Dear Mr. (or Mrs., Ms.) Jones	Mr. (or Mrs., Ms.) Jones	Mr. (or Mrs., Ms.) Jones
Judges	The Honorable John J. Jones Justice, Appellate Division Supreme Court of the State of _____ Address goes here	Dear Judge Jones	Justice or Judge Jones; Madam Justice or Judge Jones	The Honorable John (or Jane) Jones; Mr. Justice Jones or Judge Jones; Madam Justice Jones or Judge Jones

Figure 10–1   Continued

Person	Letter Address	Letter Greeting	Spoken Greeting	Formal Introduction
Mayor	The Honorable John (or Jane) Jones; His (or Her) Honor the Mayor City Hall Address goes here	Dear Mayor Jones	Mayor Jones; Mr. (or Madam) Mayor; Your Honor	Mayor Jones; The Mayor
The Pope	His Holiness, the Pope or His Holiness, Pope John XII Vatican City Rome, Italy	Your Holiness or Most Holy Father	Your Holiness or Most Holy Father	His Holiness, the Holy Father; the Pope; the Pontiff
Cardinals	His Eminence, John Cardinal Jones, Archbishop of _____ Address goes here	Your Eminence or Dear Cardinal Jones	Your Eminence or Cardinal Jones	His Eminence, Cardinal Jones
Bishops	The Most Reverend John Jones, Bishop (or Archbishop) of _____ Address goes here	Your Excellency or Dear Bishop (Archbishop) Jones	Your Excellency or Bishop (Archbishop) Jones	Bishop Jones
Monsignor	The Reverend Monsignor James Harding Address goes here	Reverend Monsignor or Dear Monsignor	Monsignor Harding or Monsignor	Monsignor Harding
Priest	The Reverend John Jones Address goes here	Reverend Father or Dear Father Jones	Father or Father Jones	Father Jones
Brother	Brother John or Brother John Jones Address goes here	Dear Brother John or Dear Brother	Brother John or Brother	Brother John
Sister	Sister Mary Marshall	Dear Sister Mary Marshall or Dear Sister	Sister Mary Marshall or Sister	Sister Mary Marshall
Prostestant Clergy	The Reverend John (or Jane) Jones*	Dear Dr. (or Mr., Ms.) Jones	Dr. (or Mrs., Ms.) Jones	The Reverend (or Dr.) John Jones
Bishop (Episcopal)	The Right Reverend John Jones* Bishop of _____ Address goes here	Dear Bishop Jones	Bishop Jones	The Right Reverend John Jones, Bishop or Detroit
Rabbi	Rabbi Arthur (or Anne) Schwartz Address goes here	Dear Rabbi Schwartz	Rabbi Schwartz or Rabbi	Rabbi Arthur Schwartz

Figure 10–1   Continued

Person	Letter Address	Letter Greeting	Spoken Greeting	Formal Introduction
King or Queen	His (Her) Majesty King (Queen) ——————— Address (letters traditionally are sent to reigning monarchs not directly but via the private secretary)	Your Majesty; Sir or Madam	Varies depending on titles, holdings, etc.	Varies depending on titles, holdings, etc.
Other royalty	His (Her) Royal Highness, the Prince (Princess) of ——————— Address goes here	Your Royal Highness	Your Royal Highness; Sir or Madam	His (Her) Royal Highness, the Duke (Duchess) of Gloucester
Duke/Duchess	His/Her Grace, the D ——————— of ———————	My Lord Duke/Madam or Dear Duke of ———————/ Dear Duchess	Your Grace or Duke/Duchess	His/Her Grace, the Duke/Duchess of Bridgeport
Marquess/ Marchioness	The Most Honorable the M ——————— of Bridgeport	My Lord/Madam or Dear Lord/Lady Bridgeport	Lord/Lady Bridgeport	Lord/Lady Bridgeport
Earl	The Right Honorable the Earl of Franklin	My Lord or Dear Lord Franklin	Lord Franklin	Lord Franklin
Countess (wife of an earl)	The Right Honorable the Countess of Franklin	Madam or Dear Lady Franklin	Lady Franklin	Lady Franklin
Viscount/Viscountess	The Right honorable the V ——————— Tyburn	My Lord/Lady or Dear Lord/Lady Tyburn	Lord/Lady Tyburn	Lord/Lady Tyburn
Baron/Baroness	The Right Honorable Lord/Lady Austin	My Lord/Madam or Dear Lord/Lady Austin	Lord/Lady Austin	Lord/Lady Austin
Baronet	Sir John Jones, Bt.	Dear Sir or Dear Sir John	Sir John	Sir John Jones
Wife of Baronet	Lady Jones	Dear Madam or Dear Lady Jones	Lady Jones	Lady Jones
Knight	Sir John Jones	Dear Sir or Dear Sir Jones	Sir John	Sir John Jones
Wife of Knight	Dear Madam or Dear Lady Jones	Lady Jones	Lady Jones	Lady Jones
Military Personnel	For commissioned officers in the U.S. Armed services, the full rank is used as a title only in addressing letters and in formal introductions: one writes to Major General Sarah Miller, U.S. Army, and introduces her as Major General Miller. In greetings the full rank is shortened to General: "Dear General Miller." Similar acceptable shortened greetings follow categorized by *full rank* then *greetings*:			

Figure 10–1   Continued

Person	Letter Address	Letter Greeting	Spoken Greeting	Formal Introduction
Army, Air Force, Marines	General of the Army Lieutenant General Brigadier General Lieutenant Colonel First Lieutenant Second Lieutenant		General General General Colonel Lieutenant Lieutenant	
Navy, Coast Guard	Fleet Admiral Vice Admiral Rear Admiral Lieutenant Commander Lieutenant, Junior Grade		Admiral Admiral Admiral Commander Lieutenant	
	For enlisted personnel, a similar principle applies. Sergeants—whether staff sergeants, gunnery sergeants, or first sergeants—are greeted simply as "Sergeant"; privates first class are referred to as "Private"; and, in the Navy and Coast Guard, chief petty officers are referred to as "Chief." Other noncommissioned officers are greeted by their ranks, although, informally, lower grades may be referred to generically as "Soldier" or "Sailor." The universal terms of respect that lower ranks must use when addressing senior officers are "Sir" and "Madam." These terms are not applied to noncommissioned officers, however; the appropriate affirmative response to a sergeant, for example, is "Yes, Sergeant."			

Figure 10–1   Continued

Dress for Formal Occasions

The appropriate dress for formal occasions should be included on the invitation. This might include business attire for formal day functions or black tie (or sometimes white) for formal evening events. Name badges should be worn on the right-hand side so that when the hand is extended for a handshake, the name badge is easily readable.

Protocol for Speakers

Speakers need to be briefed in advance and provided with a list of the guests to be welcomed, in order of precedence. The timing and the length of speeches need to be discussed with the speakers before the event and must also be canvassed with the chef so that food production coincides with the event plan and speakers are not disturbed by food service or clearing of plates.

Seating Protocol

Correct seating arrangements for occasions such as awards ceremonies and formal dinners must be observed by the event organizer.

Knowing who is to sit where can often be a touchy business. Precedence at table can lead to hurt feelings and indignation among families as well as diplomats.

A handbook of precedence and protocol can be a handy tool when making the determination of who is to sit where if you happen to be hosting an official state function. Once you have determined who is of higher rank, then it is just a matter of placing people around a table. There are a few simple rules that apply to most situations:

1. *When there is but a single table, the host and hostess usually sit at opposite ends, or occasionally in the center of the table facing each other. When multiple tables are needed, the host and hostess may be at separate tables in which case you may wish to opt for a cohost and cohostess.*

2. *The highest-ranking male generally sits to the right of the hostess. The wife of the highest-ranking man, or the highest-ranking woman herself sits to the right of the host. The second ranking male will usually sit to the left of the hostess. Now the seating should be arranged such that no two women set side by side and no two men sit side by side. This will prove a difficult feat when the number of guests is evenly divisible by four, so try to avoid this possibility, but should it happen, it is common to swap the spot of the hostess and the highest-ranking male.*

3. *A rule that has all kinds of interesting psychological implications says that married people are never seated side by side, but those engaged are seated side by side whenever possible.*

4. *The ranks for various persons is determined by the President of the United States. The list is fairly long and complex and occasionally changes. It is kept on file at the State Department.*

5. *If you happen to be in the military, there is a good book to help you sort this kind of thing out,* Service Etiquette, *by Oretha D. Swartz. It also covers other military social relationships. It is a handy book to have around when you may be hobnobbing with the brass.*

Try to seat people to best stimulate pleasant conversation and to facilitate the feeding of young children. This means not hemming young parents into corners where they can't quickly handle the inevitable emergency created by the three year olds.

Though appointing the seating for your guests may seem stuffy, it generally puts guests at ease. People like to know where the host wants them to sit and will often ask before being seated if the place they have chosen is all right. Name cards are not necessary, but can be fun. If a guest objects to the seating you have chosen, simply make a quick change.

Whatever you decide to do, choose your seating arrangement
with care as at larger dinner parties it can make a difference.

Reprinted with permission of www.holidaycook.com

Religious and Cultural Protocol

Formalities attach to most religious and cultural ceremonies, although these may or may not be observed by the client. The event organizer may therefore be required to assist with the protocol for such an event or to provide advice if the client wants a more relaxed arrangement.

Following are examples of traditions associated with a number of wedding ceremonies from around the world.

Scottish Wedding

The stag night is a tradition of Scottish weddings, male friends taking the groom out to celebrate with lots of drinking and practical jokes at the expense of the groom. Another old Scottish custom requires the groom to carry a basket of stones on his back until the bride can be persuaded to kiss him. The groom and his groomsmen often wear kilts to the wedding (traditionally with no undergarments), and the groom may present the bride with an engraved silver teaspoon on their wedding day as a pledge that they will never go hungry. A traditional sword dance is sometimes performed at the wedding reception.

Greek Orthodox Wedding

There are two parts to this service: the betrothal ceremony and the marriage ceremony. During the marriage ceremony, the priest crowns both the bride and the groom three times, and all three people parade around the altar table three times. The entrance of the families of the bride and the groom to the reception area, as well as the arrival of the bride and groom at the reception, is greeted with a fanfare.

Japanese Wedding

The bride's wedding gown is often a traditional wedding kimono. The first sip of sake drunk by the bride and the groom at the wedding ceremony symbolizes the official union of marriage. The ceremony is generally quite small and is held at a Shinto shrine, Buddhist temple, or in a chapel. Guests invited to the wedding reception make gifts of money to the couple, and the guests, in turn, are given a gift to take home.

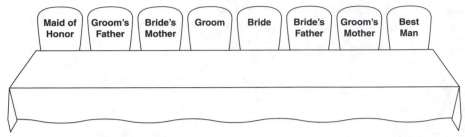

Figure 10–2   Seating Plan for Bridal Table

Macedonian Wedding

Prior to the wedding ceremony, an unmarried relative or friend of the family makes a loaf of bread and decorates it with sweets. Once the bread is cooked, the family members dance and sing, and then give the loaf to the best man, who carries it to the reception. Toward the end of the reception, the bread is taken apart by all the single males. The story goes that if they eat some and keep some under their pillow, they will see their future wife.

The formalities for weddings of different nationalities can often be found on the Internet (see one such Web site at the end of this chapter) or from the many books on wedding etiquette available in bookstores.

For the modern bride and groom, there are many variations on the old traditions, and these must be discussed with them before the ceremony. For the organizer of the wedding, the most crucial elements are the timing of the music, the speeches, and the meal at the reception. From a planning perspective, there are many details that need to be agreed upon, including the following:

- decor
- seating plans for the bridal party (see Figure 10–2) and other guests
- timing and duration of the reception
- menu and special food requirements
- beverages and payment for beverages
- timing of food service, speeches, dancing, and so on
- music, sound system, and microphones for those giving speeches
- rooms where the bride and groom can change

A run sheet (see Chapter 9) for a wedding reception would need to include the following steps and the timing of these steps:

- music on arrival
- arrival of guests
- drink service commences (generally champagne, wine, beer, and soft drinks)
- arrival of bride's and groom's families
- guests seated
- entry and introduction of the bridal party approximately half an hour later
- entrée served, starting with the bridal table
- main course served, starting with the bridal table

Approximately two hours after commencement, the following occur:

- all guests being served champagne in anticipation of the speeches and toasts
- speeches by father of the bride, the groom, and the best man (this may vary)
- cutting of the cake
- bridal waltz
- dessert and coffee being served
- dancing
- throwing of garter and bouquet
- farewell of bride and groom through an arch formed by guests
- closing of bar and music stopping
- guests leaving

Note that an open bar (which does not generally include spirits) may extend only for a number of hours, after which guests pay for their drinks.

Protocol for Sporting Ceremonies

There are a number of formalities for sporting events, including the awarding of trophies or medals at the ceremony held soon after the event has finished. Traditionally, in team sports, the press interviews the team captain of the runner-up before the winner is announced. However, different sports have different conventions. For example, at motor racing events, champagne is sprayed over spectators by the winner, and this ritual is followed by a press conference at which the drivers remain seated. Press interviews for a number of other sports take place in the locker rooms.

Preparing for Dignitaries

Since the Revolutionary War, the citizens of Alexandria, Virginia, have been celebrating the birthday of George Washington. The celebrations were organized by soldiers and citizens who were volunteers; and today (although they get terrific support from the Alexandria City Government) the Celebration is still organized by volunteers. Culminating on the third Monday in February, volunteers put together a mega-event to honor our first president. The event encompasses a 10-K race, birthday party, "birthnight" ball, and encampment, as well as a parade, among other activities.

A look at the group's parade logistics shows the provisions that have been made to accommodate any dignitaries who will be a part of the event. Study Figure 10–3 to see what steps have been taken.

Rules of Flag Flying

Event managers must know the proper protocol for flying the flag.
Source: Adrian Neal/Getty Images Inc./Stone Allstock.

Oftentimes the flag is used in association with an event. It is important to understand the proper protocol for displaying the flag.

How to Display the Flag

1. *When the flag is displayed over the middle of the street, it should be suspended vertically with the union to the north in an east and west street or to the east in a north and south street. (Union refers to the stars section of the flag)*
2. *The flag of the United States of America, when it is displayed with another flag against a wall from crossed staffs, should be on the right, the flag's own right and its staff should be in front of the staff of the other flag.*
3. *The flag, when flown at half-staff, should be first hoisted to the peak for an instant and then lowered to the half-staff position. The flag should be again raised to the peak before it is lowered for the day. By "half-staff" is meant lowering the flag to one-half the distance between the top and bottom of the staff. Crepe streamers may be affixed to spear heads or flagstaffs in a parade only by order of the President of the United States.*
4. *When flags of States, cities, or localities, or pennants of societies are flown on the same halyard with the flag of the United States, the latter should always be at the peak. When the flags are flown from adjacent staffs, the flag of the United States should be hoisted first and lowered last. No such flag or pennant may be placed above the flag of the United States or to the right of the flag of the United States.*

Officials Schedule
February 17, 2003

9–9:30 a.m. Marshals Meet at American Legion (400 Cameron Street, Lower Level).

10:00 a.m. Parking Restrictions go into effect.

☐ Police Barricades established.
☐ Begin Physical set up.
☐ Reviewing Stand & Start Point Crews start their work.

10:30 a.m. Parade Physical set up completed:

☐ Information Booth up.
☐ Reviewing Stand up.
☐ Communications Truck up.
☐ Delivery of Vehicle Signs to Dignitary Division.

11:00 a.m. All Parade Officials Brief Meeting at the Start Point.

☐ Pick up Division Signs, hat, badge, clipboard, list, and maps.
☐ Marshals Take Assigned Stations and put Division Signs in place.
☐ Dignitary Vehicles arrive for Dignitary Division.

11:30 a.m. Participant check-in begins.

☐ Place all Dignitary Vehicle signs on the appropriate vehicle.
☐ All Division Signs should be in place.

12 noon Marshals begin to put units in Parade Order.

12:30 p.m. Dignitaries arrive in Dignitary Division.

☐ All Parade Units should be at their Division sites.
☐ Marshals check every unit against Parade Order.

12:45 p.m. Marshals Parade Order Report to Communications.

12:55 p.m. March Order changes sent to Reviewing Stand.

☐ Parade Announcers in Place.

1:00 p.m. Parade Begins.

☐ Parade Units begin to pass by the Duke Street Check Point.

1:15 p.m. Jackie Sings the National Anthem.

1:20 p.m. Parade first passes the reviewing stand.

3:00 p.m. Post-Parade & Awards Reception, American Legion Ballroom.

Parade Committee

Parade Director

Parade Chief Marshals
Parade Start-point Control—*William Snyder & Marvin Heinz*
Dignitary Vehicle Coordination—*Quentin Tabscott*
Dignitary Drivers Coordination—*Sharon Lawler*
Parade Route Marshalling—*Thomas Fulham & Sharon Lawler*
Parade End-point Disbursement—*Marvin Heinz*

Parade Set-up Crew Chiefs
Reviewing Stand—*Thomas Fulham*
Start Point—*Marvin Heinz*

Parade Communications
Karen & Richard Bunn
Alexandria Radio Club & Mount Vernon Radio Club

Parade Information
Patches Distribution—*Lucian Guthrie*

Parade Reviewing Stand
Announcing—*Hugh Barton & Janet Barnett*
Postparade Reception Coordination—*Hugh Barton*

Parade Awards Judging
Marilyn Dean

Parade Dignitary Coordination
Michael Oliver

Figure 10–3 George Washington Birthday Celebration Parade
Source: Reproduced with permission of the George Washington Birthday Celebration Committee Alexandria, VA.

5. When the flag is suspended over a sidewalk from a rope extending from a house to a pole at the edge of the sidewalk, the flag should be hoisted out, union first, from the building.

6. When the flag of the United States is displayed from a staff projecting horizontally or at an angle from the window sill, balcony, or front of a building, the union of the flag should be placed at the peak of the staff unless the flag is at half-staff.

7. When the flag is used to cover a casket, it should be so placed that the union is at the head and over the left shoulder. The flag should not be lowered into the grave or allowed to touch the ground.

8. When the flag is displayed in a manner other than by being flown from a staff, it should be displayed flat, whether indoors or out. When displayed either horizontally or vertically against a wall, the union should be uppermost and to the flag's own right, that is, to the observer's left. When displayed in a window it should be displayed in the same way, that is with the union or blue field to the left of the observer in the street. When festoons, rosettes or drapings are desired, bunting of blue, white and red should be used, but never the flag.

9. The flag, when carried in a procession with another flag, or flags, should be either on the marching right; that is, the flag's own right, or, if there is a line of other flags, in front of the center of that line.

10. The flag of the United States of America should be at the center and at the highest point of the group when a number of flags of States or localities or pennants of societies are grouped and displayed from staffs.

11. When flags of two or more nations are displayed, they are to be flown from separate staffs of the same height. The flags should be of approximately equal size. International usage forbids the display of the flag of one nation above that of another nation in time of peace.

12. When displayed from a staff in a church or public auditorium on or off a podium, the flag of the United States of America should hold the position of superior prominence, in advance of the audience, and in the position of honor at the clergyman's or speaker's right as he faces the audience. Any other flag so displayed should be placed on the left of the clergyman or speaker (to the right of the audience).

13. When the flag is displayed on a car, the staff shall be fixed firmly to the chassis or clamped to the right fender.

14. When hung in a window, place the blue union in the upper left, as viewed by the street.

Activity

You have been asked to run an event with a patriotic theme for a senior Japanese executive who is about to return to Japan after working in San Francisco, California, for three years. This event will be held outdoors, and up to 400 staff members will attend. The American patriotic theme should be evident in all aspects of the event, including the decor, music, food, and beverage. Since this is a large multinational company and the media will no doubt attend the event, you must observe the correct protocol for use of American symbols. You also need to ensure that you do not breach copyright in your use of images, music, and so on, and seek permission for usage or pay licensing fees as necessary.

- Expand on the approach to the theme of this event.
- Explain how you will use patriotic images and music.
- Illustrate your use of the flag of the United States of America.

Links

www.cftech.com
www.holidaycook.com
www.chicagomarriage.com/wedding_traditions.htm
   (wedding tradition)
www.ushistory.org
www.washingtonbirthday.com

Summary

This chapter has dealt with the topic of event protocol. Protocol encompasses the traditions associated with government functions, official ceremonies, sporting events, weddings, and the like. Such rules and guidelines assist event planners in working out seating arrangements, making introductions, and protecting the privacy and security of VIPs, such as overseas dignitaries. Our national symbols often form part of event decor, and an event manager needs to be aware of the rules pertaining to their use. Awareness of the importance of protocol and the ability to locate the relevant information prior to the event will ensure that the event runs smoothly.

Chapter Eleven

STAGING

The Annual Community Theatre Drama Festival is held each spring. The popular 4–5 day event, with an average of 20 participating groups, entertains as well as educates. View a wide range of theatre and learn from professionals who adjudicate the productions presented.

The Festival is highlighted by the Sunday evening Finals session, featuring the top 3–4 (depending on # of participants) productions chosen by the Festival adjudicators, as well as the closing awards ceremony, citing groups and individuals in the festival for outstanding performance and theatre excellence. Everyone waits anxiously as the special Finals Guest Adjudicator ultimately announces the Best Production Award.

Our community theatre festival dates back to 1954 and is the oldest and one of the largest state community theatre festivals in the United States. Starting with three theatre groups who performed one-act plays, it has broadened to many more participants who perform not only one-act plays, but scenes, condensations and excerpts from full-length plays and musicals.

This festival also ties into a biennial New England Regional Festival (NERF), which features the winning productions of community theatre festivals which are held in several of the New England states. The winner of the Regional Festival represents New England in a National Festival of Community Theatres, also held biennially, sponsored by AACT.

Reprinted with permission of Eastern Massachusetts Association of Community Theaters (www.emact.org)

On completion of this chapter, you will be able to

- evaluate an event site to assess its suitability;
- select a theme and plan the decor;
- plan all staging elements, including lighting and sound;
- plan all event services, such as catering; and
- understand the roles of staging subcontractors.

The previous example of a drama festival provides an introduction to the issues associated with staging. The staging of an event incorporates all aspects of the event that enable the performance to go ahead. Broadly speaking, by performance we mean entertainment: the sport, the parade, the ceremony. The topics covered in this chapter, such as theme, venue, sound and lighting, as well as all the essential services, are relevant to many free and ticketed events and festivals. Organizers have to look at issues such as capacity, seating arrangements, emergency access, and stage requirements and staffing. Staging is an ancient concept: the Roman gladiatorial events were staged in spectacular, albeit gruesome, fashion, but these events certainly had the enthusiastic atmosphere that every modern event organizer aspires to, although the modern audience would be unlikely to enjoy the same level of bloodshed.

Choosing the Event Site

Selection of an event venue must take the needs of all stakeholders into account. Stakeholders include emergency services, catering staff, entertainers, participants, and clients.

Frequently, the client has an unusual idea for a venue, but however imaginative this may be, selection of the site must be tempered with rational decision making. Although a parking lot could be transformed into an interesting place to have a party, it would have no essential services, such as electricity, and would present enormously expensive logistical problems. An existing event venue, such as a conference center, could more easily lend itself to transformation using decoration and props. Figure 11–1 and Figure 11–2 illustrate useful information about the Moscone Center in San Francisco, California, such as hall size and capacity and the layout of facilities. Most venues and convention centers offer similar information on their Web sites.

Choosing a venue that is consistent with the event purpose and theme is essential. It can also lead to cost savings, since there is far less expense in transforming it into what the client wants.

The major considerations for selecting an event venue include the following:

- size of the event (including the size of the audience)
- layout of the site and its suitability for the event
- stage, field of play, or performance area
- transport and parking
- proximity to accommodation and attractions
- supply issues for goods and services providers, such as caterers
- technical support
- venue management

An inspection of the site should reveal any limitations, the aspects to consider including these:

Room	Square Feet	Size	Ceiling Height	Theater/ Reception	Schoolroom	Banquet	10' X 10' Booths
Hall A	94,980	275' X 298'	37'	6,758	4,232	3,900	463
Hall B	50,500	275' X 180'	37'	4,070	2,576	2,600	256
Hall C	110,965	275' X 358'	37'	8,580	5,152	4,880	561
Halls A–B	140,890	275' X 478'	37'	9,400	4,000	5,500	719
Halls B–C	152,760	275' X 538'	37'	10,400	4,800	6,200	817
Halls A–C	260,560	275' X 836'	37'	16,200	7,000	9,100	1,305
Hall D	138,684	270' X 514'	28'				711
Hall E	37,360	188' X 226' 8"	24'	4,924	2,900	2,530	198
Halls D–E	181,440	N/A	24'	N/A	N/A	N/A	976
Halls A–E	442,000	N/A	N/A	N/A	N/A	N/A	2281
West Level 1	96,660	290' X 315'	27'	N/A	N/A	N/A	510
West Level 2	99,716	290' X 305'	27'	7,000	6,780	4,480	532
West Level 3	99,716	290' X 305'	27'	N/A	N/A	N/A	532

Figure 11–1 Example of Information, Such as Hall Size and Capacity, Provided by Venue Providers on the Internet
Source: Reproduced with permission of the Moscone Center.

- compatibility with the event theme
- audience comfort
- visibility for the audience (line of sight)
- storage areas
- entrances and exits
- stage area (where relevant)
- equipment
- cover in case of poor weather
- safety and security
- access for emergency vehicles
- evacuation routes

In viewing a potential event site, there are three major stakeholders who need to be considered and whose perspectives could be quite different: **the performers, the audience,** and **the organizers.** By performers, we mean those in the limelight, whether this involves providing an educational talk, dancing in a parade, presenting an award. Performers have specific needs that are fundamental to their success, such as the level of intimacy with the audience (often the

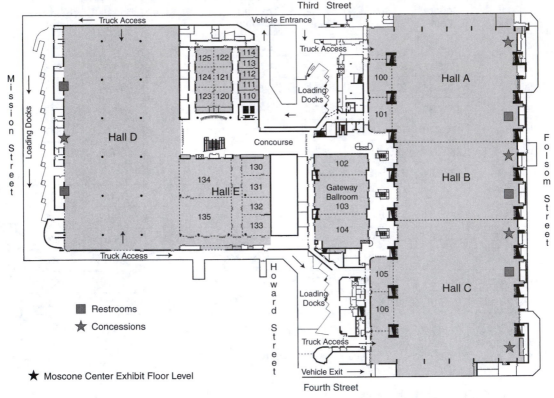

Figure 11–2   Layout of Halls and Facilities of a Convention Center Available on the Internet
Source: Reproduced with permission of the Moscone Center.

result of the distance from the audience) or the volume of the sound. Secondly, the audience has needs, the primary one being to see what is going on! An illustration of line of sight is shown in Figure 11–3. The level of lighting and sound, as well as access to and comfort of the seats, also contributes to audience satisfaction. Catering and facilities are generally secondary. Finally, from a management perspective, the venue must help to minimize risks, such as adverse weather, power failure, accidents, and emergencies.

Developing the Theme

As we have mentioned several times, the theme of an event must be supported in every aspect, including the decor, lighting, sound, and special effects. The theme may be quite subtle: for example, in the case of a high-tech theme for a conference, the audience would be only subliminally aware of aspects of the theme, such as the color

Many events involve theatrical presentations.
Source: Andy Crawford/Dorling Kindersley Media Library.

scheme. In more dramatic cases, guests might be asked to support the theme by dressing appropriately or participating in entertainment that is consistent with the theme. Themes may be tried and tested, or unique.

A theme can be reinforced through such creative elements as the following:

- color
- landscape and/or location
- film/theater/art/dance
- humor
- fantasy

Following are important aspects of the theme that need to be carefully considered by the event organizer. As you will see, there are many decisions to make!

Entertainment

There is a wide range of acts that can be used to enhance the theme of an event; and corporate events, in particular, often employ interesting performers such as snake charmers, hypnotists, and belly

The Moscone Center can accommodate large meetings.

dancers. Entertainment companies have a wealth of ideas and these can be investigated on the Web sites listed at the end of this chapter. Such companies need to be briefed in the early planning stages so that they become familiar with the event purpose and the event audience. They can then look at the event theme and come up with a range of concepts to suit the theme. If a band is recommended, the specific technical requirements should be discussed at this stage. (One event organizer illustrated the importance of briefing the entertainment provider by describing her own experience in organizing an event for a young audience. When the teenager's parents heard that one of the band members had stripped, they were furious with the event organizer!)

Figure 11–3   Line of sight.

Visible area of screen

Area outside line of sight range (obscured by person in front)

A large trade show at the Moscone Center.

Decor

Lena Malouf, the former president of the International Special Events Society (ISES) and a leading event designer, has recently earned two awards, the first for Best Event Produced for a Corporation or Association (overall budget $200,000 to $500,000) and the second for Best Theme Decor (decor budget over $50,000). Her guests were submerged in a magical "underwater" world reminiscent of the fantastical journey in the children's classic *Bedknobs and Broomsticks*. Malouf's events are characterized by extravagant displays, including imaginative moving art pieces that tie in perfectly with the chosen theme, her main aim being to surprise and transport the audience. Her book *Behind the Scenes at Special Events* (1998) is recommended for those interested in specializing in event design.

Decor encompasses many things, from the color scheme to the drapes, props, and floral arrangements. The challenge is to bring them all together into a cohesive theme. Staging rental companies can be extremely helpful with this task.

Layout

The layout of the event venue is clearly integral to the success of the event. Anyone who has worked on conferences and formal dinners knows that table layout is something that needs to be negotiated with the client well in advance. With large dinner events in large venues,

The limited space offered by this portable tent emphasizes the need for effective planning of seating.

all too often the audience at the back of the room has very limited vision of the stage. If this limitation is compounded by poor sound and too much alcohol, it does not take long before the presenter is drowned out by the clink of glasses and the hum of conversation. This situation can be very embarrassing.

When planning an event at which guests are seated around a table, it is essential to plan the layout according to scale. If the dimensions of the tables and chairs are not considered, as well as the space taken by seated guests, there may prove to be no room for waiters or guests to move around. A number of common table and seating layouts are illustrated in Figure 11–4. For each of these, a scale drawing would be used to calculate the capacity of the room and the appropriate use of furnishings.

Lighting and Special Effects

Lighting can be used to spectacular effect, and for this reason, events held at night provide the opportunity for more dramatic results than those held during the day. Lighting can be used both to create the general ambience and to highlight particular features. It is often synchronized with sound for special effect at dances and fireworks displays, and can also be used to highlight sponsor advertising. As with sound, lighting is used to create a particular mood, although it is important to remember that this must be consistent with the event theme. Subtlety is required, for there has been a tendency recently to use some of the latest patterning techniques too often. Professional advice from a lighting designer is recommended because lighting is more often than not one of the main contributors to staging a successful event.

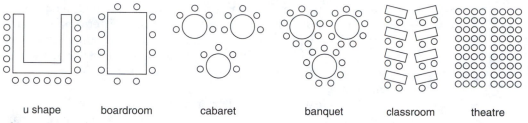

| u shape | boardroom | cabaret | banquet | classroom | theatre |

Figure 11–4   Table and Seating Layouts

Sound

Music is a powerful creator of mood. It can excite or calm an audience; moreover, particular pieces can be highly emotive. The volume needs to be pitched at just the right level, and all members of the audience need to be able to hear clearly, particularly if the event is being staged in a large stadium. Professional sound engineers can be relied upon to give advice on equipment and the acoustic qualities of a venue. For example, a concrete venue with little or no carpeting or curtaining has a negative effect on sound, but this disadvantage can be remedied by the incorporation of drapes in the design.

Vision

Vision incorporates all projected images, such as replays of sporting highlights on large screens or scoreboards. Video projectors, slide projectors, and data projectors can project images onto screens for dramatic effect, and this can be extended to live broadcasts with satellite links. A wall of monitors can be used to project one large image across the whole monitor wall, achieving the effect of a large screen. The splitting of the image between monitors is done by computer programming.

Backup projectors and duplicate copies of videos, slides, DVDs, and so on are essential. When using computer-aided programs such as Microsoft PowerPoint, a test run should be made to make sure all is in working order before it is needed. Most business and academic presentations use computer software packages to improve the visual quality of the images.

Although computer-generated slide shows such as Microsoft PowerPoint look highly professional, there is a tendency for some users to become too excited by the features provided, changing colors and effects all too often. Bullet points coming in from all directions can distract the audience, while the use of multiple fade-in and fade-out effects only add to the problem.

Another pitfall in this type of presentation is the lack of spontaneity. Presenters are bound by their scripts. Keep in mind that most presenters bring their own laptop computers and need to have adequate time allotted for setup and testing of their equipment. It is always a good idea to suggest to the presenter that his or her computer-generated slide show be put onto overhead transparencies or printed in a booklet form for the audience, just in case of an equipment failure.

There are a number of alternatives to computer-generated slide shows, such as flip charts and slide shows. In some arenas, these are returning to favor as the novelty value increases and the "wow" factor of computer-generated presentations wear off.

Stage

The stage is used for many reasons, including performances, prize-giving, and presentations. Equipment rental companies can provide advice on the size and shape of the stage, as well as on screens and other devices on which to project images from the rear of the stage.

However, the needs of the audience are the most important consideration, particularly the line of sight, which must be considered when deciding on the size and shape of the stage and the placing of lecterns or screens.

Set

The set includes all objects on the stage: props, flats, lecterns, stairs, curtains, and so on. Sometimes these can be rented; at other times they must be built.

The **cyclorama** is the drape at the back of the stage used to create a sense of distance, special lighting of the cyclorama providing different colored backgrounds. **Legs** (vertical) and **teasers** (horizontal) are used to mask parts of the rigging system and to trim the sight-lines so that only the set may be seen by the audience. A **traveler** is a type of curtain that moves along a track. Often it is used as the main stage curtain, being configured so that one operating line moves curtains from both sides of the stage simultaneously.

Field of Play

Each sporting event has specific requirements. These may include gymnastics equipment, which must be properly set up to very clear specifications. Another example is a baseball or softball field, which must be chalked properly with the batting box outlined in the proper dimensions. The infield often needs "wetting" down to eliminate the dust, but not too much to create a muddy situation. The quality of the grass field is important for many sports. For this reason, sporting fields are often covered to protect them when there is inclement weather or when they are used for other events. However, while the cover protects the surface, it also blocks out the light so that damage can still be caused to the field. These days, professional grass specialists can replace an entire field within hours, but that is a very costly exercise.

Line of sight is clearly important for sporting enthusiasts, and one cannot afford to sell seats from which visibility is impaired. The placement of media equipment is often the cause of this type of problem, and discussions must be held before tickets go on sale to establish the proposed position of cameras and sound equipment. The same holds true for processions and parades where an elevated position is preferable for camera crews. The positioning may require authorization by the local authority, and accreditation may be necessary for those eligible to enter the media area.

Finally, the use of giant screens with rear screen projectors need to be considered for large venues where there is a risk that members of the audience will not be able to readily see the stage or field of play. Figure 11–5 shows the technical team that is often needed to stage a large event.

*C*onducting *R*ehearsals

The importance of rehearsal cannot be underestimated. This is the opportunity for all involved to integrate their efforts—everyone from the stage manager (who calls the shots for the presentation) to the technical support staff (who follow the appropriate cues for lighting and sound). A technical run-through allows the staff involved to test the setup and to make sure that all elements work satisfactorily.

The production, or staging, of an event involves many specialists. As an example, members of the technical team supporting a performance would include the following:

- Artistic Director
- Production Manager
- Technical Director
- Stage Manager
- Choreographer
- Scriptwriter
- Lighting Designer
- Lighting Operator
- Sound Designer
- Sound Operator
- Vision Designer
- Vision Operator
- Front-of-House Manager
- Floor Manager

The following staff would support the performance indirectly:

- Venue Manager
- Operations Manager
- Logistics Manager
- Catering Manager
- Cleaning and Waste Manager

Figure 11–5   The Technical Team

Technical glitches at an event are unprofessional, to say the least, so a backup plan for all aspects of the presentation is absolutely essential. This includes two copies of each video or sound clip, slide presentations in more than one format, and multiple microphones. Every potential problem should have a ready solution. The final aspect, over which the event manager has little control, is the quality of the presentation given by the speaker, particularly at business and academic conferences. Giving some basic advice and encouragement beforehand can assist a presenter enormously. If rehearsals have been conducted and everything is under control, speakers are far less nervous and far less likely to feel uncomfortable under the spotlight. A "ready room" where the speaker can set up and test the presentation before going on stage is recommended. See Figure 11–6 for staging terms.

Performance

Management and agent	Take care of performers' interests
Talent	Person who is not the main performer (demeaning term)
Green room	Area where performers wait and watch monitors
Dressing room	Area where performers dress and are made up
Wings	Area used for assembling performers and props
Stage-in-the-round	Circular stage allowing 360 degree views for the audience
Proscenium arch	Traditional theater style, curtains at side and above
Thrust	Stage projecting into the audience, such as at fashion parades
Tracks	Fixed tracks used to move props
Lectern	Stand for speaker

Lighting

Light board	Where the lighting engineer controls lighting effects, adjusting colors, brightness and special effects; also where the sound engineer controls sound, including volume and switchover between music and microphone
Rigging	Overhead truss
Light poles	Upright stand for lights
Floodlight	Wide light
Spotlight	Narrow light
Fresnel	Circular soft-edged beam (can go from spot to medium flood)
Cyclorama	Curved white screen at the back of the stage for light projections
Parcan	Fixed beam with soft edge, cheaper than floodlight, usually above the front of the stage and usually used in groups of four
Lighting gels	Slip-over colors used to change the color of spotlights and parcans
Wash light	General area cover
Key light	Used for highlighting an object
Back light	Rear lighting effect (should use for speakers)

Figure 11–6 Staging Terms

House light	Lighting provided by venue
Sound	
Sound cue sheet	Specifies the sound requirements for a particular group or performance
Sound amplifier	Used to project the sound (microphones are plugged into amplifiers which power up the sound and send it to the speakers)
Out-front speakers	Speakers which face the audience
Sound monitors	Positioned on stage, facing the performers, to help performers hear themselves
Microphones	Include battery, stage (dynamic voice), headset and lectern
Exhibitions	
Floor plan	Two-dimensional layout of the venue
CAD drawing	Computer-generated, three-dimensional drawing of the design for a stand
Booth	Usually 10 ft by 10 ft stand at an exhibition
Corinthian	Walling covered with fabric to which Velcro will adhere
Pit	Service duct located in the floor, providing power and telephone cables (for some indoor and outdoor events, water and compressed air and gas can also be provided in this way)
Tracker/reader	Device for scanning visitor cards to capture their data
General	
Pyrotechnics	Fireworks

Figure 11–6   Continued

Providing Services

The supply of water, power, and gas; a communications network; and transport and traffic management is essential to the staging of most events.

Essential Services

Essential services include power, water, and gas. Although the provision of these may sound simple, various different electrical sources are often required, including three-phase power for some equipment and power backup in case of emergency. Providing the venue kitchen with gas can also be a challenge. The choice of a complex site can add to the difficulties of providing these essential services to the event venue.

Communications

Many events have particular requirements for communications, which may even include the installation of a complete telephone and communications network. Where there is a high level of demand on the

Rehearsals lead to perfection.

communications network, the issue of bandwidth must be resolved, particularly if there is a significant amount of data being transmitted. A stadium often requires its own mobile phone base station owing to the number of people using mobile telephones, particularly at the end of an event.

Transportation and Traffic Management

Transportation to the event, including air, rail, bus, train, and taxi, all need to be considered. So, too, does the issue of parking and its impact on local traffic. In some cases, streets have to be closed, traffic diverted, and special permission sought for this purpose, the event plan being an important part of the submission to the relevant authorities. Thought must also be given to access for people with disabilities, marshaling of crowds, and notifying of businesses affected by any disruptions.

Arranging Catering

A catering contractor usually does the catering for an event, taking care of food orders, food production, and service staff. These contractors (or the venue catering staff) should provide menus and costs relevant to the style of service required. Photographs of previous catering and food presentation styles can be helpful in making a decision.

There are many approaches to event catering, the most common being the following:

- set menu, with table service
- buffet

- finger food
- fast food

The style of cooking and the type of service have the main impact on cost. Food that is prepared off-site and heated or deep-fried on-site can be very cost effective as long as safe food handling practices are followed. If fully qualified chefs are to provide quality fresh food with superb presentation and if the guests are to be served by silver-service-trained waiting staff, then clearly the costs will escalate enormously.

When discussing catering contracts, the event organizer needs to be very explicit about food quantities, speed of service, and type of food required. Despite expression of interest in healthier food at sporting events, findings show that the old favorites, such as burgers and French fries, are still popular and that fruit salad and sandwiches do not sell as well. A food safety plan is another essential item when planning an event. Food safety involves protecting the customer from food poisoning by implementing a plan to prevent cross-contamination and other factors that cause bacterial growth. For example, food needs to be kept at the correct temperature all the way from the factory/market to the store, into the kitchen, and onto the buffet. Food safety plans look at every aspect of food handling and, if well implemented, ensure the measurement of temperatures at key points in the process in accordance with the guidelines of the plan. The best kitchens have refrigerated delivery areas and separate storage for vegetables, meat, seafood, and other products at the correct temperatures. Planned food production processes, including plating food in a refrigerated area, can further reduce the risk of bacterial growth. Finally, it is essential for the food safety specialist to consider the length of time taken for the food to reach the customer (perhaps at the other side of the stadium) and the length of time before it is consumed. Health authorities in the various states and counties monitor food safety.

Catering for an event is extremely demanding for those in the kitchen. Producing several hundred hot meals is not for the fainthearted. The chef should be aware of the planned time for service of all courses, and this should be confirmed at an early stage of the planning. Most floor managers will ask the chef how much notice is needed for service of the main course, and they will monitor proceedings and advise the chef accordingly. Beverage supplied at functions and banquets usually come with a number of options. One option is a "no-host bar" where both alcoholic and nonalcoholic beverage service is available for guests to purchase. Some organizers prefer to provide complimentary soft drinks, wine, or beer (spirits aren't generally included). At more formal functions, a hosted full-service bar is the norm.

Organizing Accommodations

For many conferences, exhibitions, shows, and sporting events, accommodations are an essential part of the package. The packaging of air travel and accommodations demand that planning for such events occur well in advance in order to acquire discounted air fares and attractive room rates. If such rate reductions are essential to favorable pricing of the event, it is preferable to hold the event in an off-peak season. However, as soon as an event such as the Superbowl reaches a city, discounted rates are often out of the question, since accommodations in the destination city will be fully booked.

The following extract illustrates the response of many accommodation providers as soon as they get wind of an event, although this approach to pricing is generally counterproductive. The negative image created by overpricing can have an impact on tourism in the long term.

The normally sleepy town of Mongu (in Zambia) is about to come alive this weekend for the Kuomboka ceremony. The ceremony stretches back several centuries and is about moving Lozi people from the flooded Zambezi Plains to the plateau. Hotel owners in Mongu say they immediately hiked room rates as soon as the announcement of the event was made, by between 600 and even 1000 percent in some cases. They are also quoting their room rates in United States dollars as they expect more than 5000 tourists to witness Zambia's foremost traditional event.

The holding of the ceremony is dictated by the amount of rain that falls in a particular season. So much rain has fallen this year that staging the ceremony was never in doubt.

Sunday Independent, South Africa, March 25, 2001

This is a most unusual event—most event organizers dread the prospect of rain, whereas those organizing this event require rain to ensure its success!

Managing the Environment

Waste management is an important consideration for all event organizers.

Pollution

Methods for reducing the environmental impact of noise, air, and water pollution should be part of the planning process, and advice on these can be obtained from the Environmental Protection Agency, which has offices in each state. Professional contractors can advise you on the correct disposal of cooking oils and other toxic waste that could affect our water supply. As we all know, clearly marked bins should be provided to facilitate recycling of waste products. With regard to air pollution, releasing helium balloons into the atmosphere has been shown to be environmentally unfriendly and therefore this practice is slowly dying out around the world.

Restroom Facilities

Restroom facilities include those at the venue and any temporary facilities required. The number and type of toilets to be provided at an event, including the number allocated to men, women, and people with disabilities, is another part of the decision-making process. The composition of the event audience—the number of men and women attending—and the average time taken by each person also need to be considered! Theater management has been working on this requirement for years. Every woman has faced the problem of long lines during intermission and, believe it or not, there is a formula for working out how many toilets are required! (Men have experienced this problem too, but in most cases the line to the women's restroom far exceeds the line to the men's room.) Too many events provide substandard restroom facilities that cannot meet the demand.

It is essential to discuss the requirements for any event that you are planning with a restroom facilities rental company, since they are the experts.

Cleaning

There are a number of cleaning contractors that specialize in events. In most cases, cleaning is done before and after the event. Maintaining cleanliness during peak times is challenging, particularly if there is only a short changeover time between event sessions. In that case, you have to get one audience out, the cleaning and replenishment of stocks done, and the next audience in on time. The timing of this is part of logistics planning, which we will cover in detail in Chapter 14. Cleaning staff should be treated as part of the event staff and receive appropriate training so that they can answer questions from the people attending the event.

Summary

In this chapter we have looked in detail at the staging of an event, including layout, decor, sound, lighting, and vision. The staff and subcontractors have also been identified, and the services required at an event, including catering, cleaning, waste management, and communications, have been discussed. Staging an event is probably the most creative aspect of event management, and there is enormous scope for making an event memorable by using the best combination of staging elements. The selection of the right site for an event is essential, since this can have an enormous impact on the cost of staging the event and the level of creativity that can be employed in developing the theme.

As you can see from the above, staging an event involves a myriad of tasks for the event organizer. With some events, the staging process may even include managing the fans that wait in line for days before the event for places at the event. At the Academy Awards, for example, the area designated for fans is occupied for up to two weeks before the big night, since one of the fans receives a free grandstand seat overlooking the red carpet. According to the *London Daily Telegraph*, April 20, 2001, "The commitment of Oscar followers makes Wimbledon campers look like amateurs. A thriving industry has developed around their needs, from food stands to camping equipment."

Case Study

As an introduction to an academic awards ceremony in the Town Hall, you have been asked to organize a performance by contemporary or indigenous dancers. Unfortunately, the Town Hall is a large space, with limitations in terms of lighting effects. There will also be a significant difference between the requirements of the performance and the requirements of the awards presentation, which is a formal, traditional daytime event. Investigate the options for props and drapes, and/or create a model of the stage setup for the dance production. Remember that the set will have to be easily removed or somehow integrated with the awards presentation.

Activities

Develop a checklist for a venue inspection, and then visit two or three venues and compare their various merits and limitations. In order to do this, you will need to have a specific event in mind, for example, a sporting event, a party, a conference, or a wedding.

Watch a video of *Gladiator,* and review the staging and the audience response to the events portrayed.

Links

www.emact.org (Eastern Massachesetts Association of Community Theaters)

www.aact.org (American Association of Community Theaters)

www.moscone.org (Moscone Convention Center, San Francisco, California)

www.specialevents.com (online special events magazine)

www.onsiterentals.com (portable restrooms and other rental equipment)

www.ises.com (International Special Events Society)

Chapter Twelve

STAFFING

There were two training sessions for volunteers. The first was very general and did not answer any of my questions. In fact, I was so confused I almost didn't return for the second session. All I really wanted was a realistic idea of where I would be and what I would do. Instead we were told about reporting relationships, incident reporting and emergency evacuation. When they started to talk about the ERP (Emergency Response Plan) and the chain of command I was totally lost. The final straw came when the manager talked about the contractors "attempting to pull back service in response to price gouging." I had absolutely no idea what he was saying. All I really wanted was a map and my job description.

Volunteer Event Usher

On completion of this chapter, you will be able to

- develop an event organization chart;
- write job descriptions and specifications;
- conduct recruitment and selection;
- plan induction and training;
- manage volunteers;
- plan recognition strategies;
- prepare staffing policies; and
- manage industrial relations and occupational health and safety.

*T*his comment, made by a new volunteer usher, illustrates the importance of effective communication and of understanding the listener's needs and expectations. In this chapter we will look at two important staff planning processes: developing organization charts so that people understand their reporting relationships and developing job descriptions so that people understand their specific roles, thus avoiding situations such as the one outlined in the quotation. The human resource functions of recruitment, selection, training, and performance management will then all fit into place.

Developing Organization Charts

Organization planning for events can be complex, since generally several organization charts are required, one for each different stage or task.

Pre-event Charts

Prior to the event, the focus is on planning, and, as we know, this lead time can be quite long. The charts required during this period show the following:

- All those responsible for the primary functions during the planning stage, such as finance, marketing, entertainment, catering, and human resource management. For example, the core event team for a local comedy festival includes the Festival Director, General Manager, Marketing Manager, Development Manager, Marketing Executive, Marketing Coordinator, Ticketing Manager, Office Manager, Production and Technical Manager, Artist Coordinator, Senior Producer, and Producer's Assistant.
- Small cross-functional teams that manage specific issues such as safety and customer service.
- The stakeholders committee (including external contractors, suppliers, and public bodies).

Charts during the Event

When staffing levels for an event expand to the requirements of a full-scale operation, the size of the organization generally increases enormously. In some cases, there may be more than one venue involved, so that each of the functional areas, such as the catering manager for each event venue, needs to be indicated on the chart. Charts should show the following:

- Full staff complement, together with reporting relationships for the overall event operations.
- Emergency reporting relationships (simplified and streamlined for immediate response).

Post-event Charts

After the event, the team frequently disperses, leaving only a few individuals and a chart showing key personnel involved with evaluation, financial reporting, and outstanding issues.

An organization chart can also include a brief list of tasks performed by individuals or the people performing each role. This list clarifies roles and improves communication. An organization chart for a team involved in a product launch is illustrated in Figure 12–1. Figure 12–2 is the organization chart for Keep America Beautiful. More

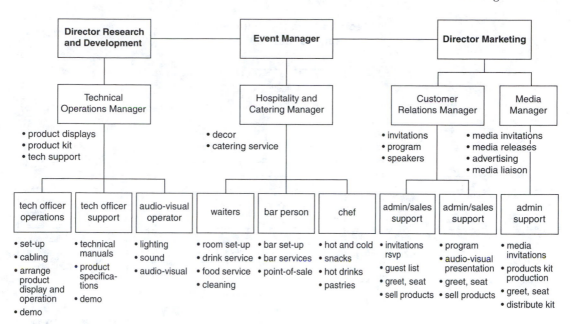

Figure 12–1   Organization Chart for a Product Launch

than 2.3 million volunteers turned up for the 2002 Great American Clean-up™ sponsored by this organization.

Preparing Job Descriptions

A job description, outlining the tasks that need to be performed, is required for each role. This document should show the position title, the reporting relationships, and the duties. A position summary is optional. In addition to the sections shown in the job description for a Catering Services Manager in Figure 12–3, there should be a section showing the terms and conditions of employment. This job description would indicate the salary applicable, whereas those for many other positions would show the award and the pay rate under the award. Since this position is likely to be a temporary one, the job description should also show the start and finish dates.

As you can see from the job description, this person will not have a direct role in catering. Instead, he or she will be managing catering subcontractors; therefore, experience in selecting organizations for the catering contracts and managing the supply of products promised in the contracts would be essential.

Once the job description is complete, it is necessary to develop a person specification, as shown in Figure 12–4. This identifies the

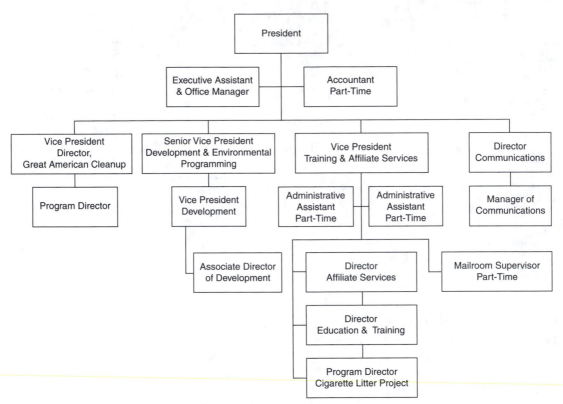

**Keep America Beautiful, Inc.
National Staff 2003**

Figure 12–2   Organization Chart for Keep America Beautiful, Inc., National Staff 2003
Source: Reproduced with the permission of Keep America Beautiful, Inc.

skills, knowledge, and experience required for the role, and it is used to inform the selection process. In this case, experience in a similar role, particularly in relation to contract management, would be required. In addition, knowledge of menu planning and costing would be essential, as would knowledge of food hygiene planning.

Figure 12–5 outlines the volunteers' opportunities associated with "I Remember Mama," an annual Boston, Massachusetts, charitable event that honors low-income elderly people. As you can see from the requirements for the position, experience in an event environment is desirable. However, experience in managing multiple contracts, such as in a resort, hotel, or catering organization, may be relevant in the absence of event experience. Figure 12–6 gives a brief description of the various volunteer responsibilities for the event.

Job Description

Position title: Catering Services Manager

Reports to: Venue Services Manager

Responsible for: Sub-contracts with caterers/concessionaires

Position summary:
To meet the food and beverage needs of all customer groups through the selection and management of appropriate subcontractors and concessionaires. To ensure compliance with the negotiated agreements regarding menus, pricing, quality and service.

Duties:
- Develop contracts for provision of food and beverage, including bars, fast food, coffee kiosks, snack bars, VIP and staff catering.
- Select subcontractors and confirm agreements regarding menus, pricing, staffing and service levels.
- Develop operational procedures with special attention to integration of services, food hygiene plans, supply and storage of food and beverage, staffing and waste management.
- Work with venue operations on the installation of the required facilities and essential services (including power, water and gas) for food and beverage outlets.
- Monitor performance of contractors.
- Deal with daily operational and customer complaint issues.

Figure 12–3   Sample Job Description

Recruitment and Selection

Once the job description and person specification have been completed, they can be used to develop advertisements and interview questions.

The most common approach to recruitment is to advertise the position in local newspapers or major newspapers, on the Internet home page for the event or event-related sites, or on notice boards. Examples of advertisements for positions in the event industry are included in Chapter 18. Employment agencies can also provide event staff—for a placement fee. This is an attractive method of recruitment because it cuts down your work by providing you with a short list of suitable applicants, as well as managing the administrative side of employment, such as taxes and insurance.

The best places to look for volunteers are volunteer organizations, schools, colleges, and universities. When selecting paid or volunteer staff, questions should be asked to check the candidates' suitability for the position. In the case of the position outlined in Figures 12-3 and 12-4, the recruitment officer could focus on, for

Job Description

Position title: Catering Services Manager

Reports to: Venue Services Manager

Responsible for: Sub-contracts with caterers/concessionaires

Position summary:
To meet the food and beverage needs of all customer groups through the selection and management of appropriate subcontractors and concessionaires. To ensure compliance with the negotiated agreements regarding menus, pricing, quality and service.

Knowledge:
- Legal contracts (with professional advice where necessary)
- HACCP (food hygiene plans)
- Responsible alcohol service
- Catering for large numbers
- Installation and management of bar and kitchen facilities

Skills:
- High level negotiation skills
- Verbal and non-verbal communication skills
- Preparing budgets and planning
- Development of operational procedures
- Problem solving

Experience:
- Managing large-scale catering subcontracts, multiple subcontractors, concessionaires
- Menu planning and catering control systems for large-scale catering
- Operational planning for new installations

Desirable:
- Experience in an event environment

Figure 12–4   Sample Person Specification

example, food safety procedures and liquor licensing, since both are relevant to the position of catering services manager.

$\mathcal{D}$rawing $\mathcal{U}p$ $\mathcal{R}$osters

Staff planning includes the development of work rosters. This can be quite difficult, particularly if multiple sessions and multiple days are involved and interrelated tasks have to be considered, because sufficient time needs to be factored in for each task. For example, if the site crew has not completed the installation of essential equipment for a particular session, work cannot begin on related tasks. Staff scheduled to be

Volunteers of America looks forward to the participation of Fidelity Investments' employees with the execution of our annual *I Remember Mama* luncheon event. Our phones are ringing off the hook with calls from our Metro Boston moms who cannot wait for the event to take place.

Newcomer Information:

Taking place each year on the day before Mother's Day, *I Remember Mama* is a charitable luncheon event, which honors low-income isolated elderly women in the greater Boston area who may otherwise be alone on Mother's Day weekend.

I Remember Mama is made possible through our lead sponsor Fidelity Investments, additional corporate sponsorships, and individuals who sponsor a mom at the luncheon in tribute to or in memory of their own mom or loved one. The proceeds of *I Remember Mama* help cover the costs of hosting these low-income seniors on this special day and support Volunteers of America's nine human service programs throughout the year.

Two Ways You Can Help:

1. Sponsor a Mom

You may sponsor a mom with a donation of a $100 or more, with the option to make the gift in tribute to or in memory of a loved one. All sponsorship gifts are highlighted in the *I Remember Mama* program book. To support the Eighth Annual *I Remember Mama* luncheon please send a check to Volunteers of America, 441 Centre Street, Jamaica Plain, MA, 02130. If your gift is a tribute gift or memorial, please provide the name of your loved one. Credit card users may donate online at voamass.org/irm. Thank you for your sponsorship!

2. Donate your time as an *I Remember Mama* Volunteer

WHEN: Saturday, May 10, 2003, 10 AM to 2:30 PM

WHERE: Seaport Hotel (Plaza Ballroom) at the World Trade Center, Boston

Volunteer Activities:

As a volunteer, you can help make this day an extra special experience for each of the mothers who will be participating in the event. Your primary role will be to help the moms enjoy themselves at the event—talk to them, dance with them, and have fun with them. Additionally, volunteers will assist with greeting, checking in, and escorting moms to their tables.

You will be assigned to a team based on your interests. Please take a moment to let us know your interests by answering the questions below with a check mark.

Volunteer Name: _____

☐ Transportation (Bus Captain)   ☐ Escort
☐ Greeter   ☐ Coat Check
☐ Information Table   ☐ Room Set-up
☐ Gift Bag Assembly (Friday, May 9th at the Seaport Hotel)

Figure 12–5 Volunteers of America Requests Your Support of the Eighth Annual "*I Remember Mama*" Luncheon Event!

Source: Reprinted with the permission of Volunteers of America.

(continued)

Figure 12–5   Continued

on duty will stand idle and become frustrated, knowing that deadlines are slipping. Having got out of bed at 3:00 A.M. to arrive as scheduled at 4.30 A.M. to set up for the day will contribute further to their frustration. In the event environment there is often limited time for transition from one session or show to the next, and there are usually many interrelated jobs to be done, requiring extremely detailed planning and scheduling. A staffing crisis in the hours preceding an event can also contribute to the risk of accidents and poor service, again emphasizing the importance of effective planning.

Training

Event staff must be trained in three basic areas: the objectives of the event, the venue, and their specific duties.

General Outline

Staff members need to be presented with a general outline of the event, as well as its objectives and organizational structure. They need to be motivated to provide outstanding service and reliable information to every member of the event audience.

Venue Information

A tour of the venue enables staff to become familiar with the location of all facilities, functional areas and departments, and the spectator services provided. This is the ideal time to cover all emergency procedures.

Specific Job Information

Event staff members need to know what their duties are and how to perform them. Maps and checklists can be extremely useful for this purpose, whereas rehearsals and role-playing help to familiarize staff with their roles before the onslaught of the event audience.

- **TRANSPORTATION GREETERS:**
When the moms arrive they are going to be greeted by our transportation greeters. 2 People per trolley will physically help the moms get off the trolley. You will stand on each side of the trolley door. 1–2 people can lead the group inside the main doors.
  - If it appears that the moms do not have nametags, direct them to the INFORMATION booth. There are extra nametags there.
  - Entertainment and VIPs also need to be directed to the Information Table.
  - If the moms are wearing nametags, you can direct them inside and hand them off to an ESCORT. Or, if they have a coat to the COAT CHECK.
  - There will also be some individual moms who transported themselves. Greeters can assist them.

- **DOOR HOLDERS:**
The volunteers assigned to DOORS will actually hold the main doors open for the moms. There can be two people on each door.

- **ESCORTS:**
Escorts will be inside the main doors. You can line up on each side of the doors. On each mom's nametag will be: the mom's name, the housing complex, the table #, and the door #. The Escort's job will be to make sure that the moms get to the appropriate door (A, B right, B left, and C).

- **CROWNERS:**
Going along with our "crown her queen for a day" theme, at each of the four doorways to the ballroom, there will be volunteers who will crown each mom with a tiara and serve as the link between the moms and the usher.

- **USHERS:**
There will be approximately 4 ushers at each doorway who will be responsible for ushering each housing complex to their appropriate table. (Table # is on the mom's nametag—they should already be at the appropriate door).

- **INFORMATION:**
Information will be sitting at a table just inside of the main entrance. You will be equipped with extra nametags, a listing of housing complexes and which table each housing complex is located and a listing of the individuals. You will be responsible for guiding the VIPs to the VIP room. Additionally, information volunteers will direct all questions to the appropriate person.

- **COAT CHECK:**
Coat Check volunteers will assist The Seaport Hotel's coat check staff. You will stand outside of the Coat Check and help the moms remove their coats and give them to the Seaport Staff.

- **TABLE HOST:**
Every table has a TABLE HOST. If you look at your note card, you will see a star next to the table number that you were assigned. During the luncheon, Table Hosts will be responsible for giving out the gift bags to the moms. When Maria Capone Goodwin completes her speech, table hosts can go to the specific alcoves where the gift bags are stored and bring them to the moms at their tables. There will be also disposable cameras on each table. Please be sure to take pictures of the moms on your table and give the camera to the housing coordinator at the end of the luncheon.

Figure 12–6   Volunteer Responsibilities—Volunteers of America Annual "I Remember Mama" Event
Source: Used by permission of Volunteers of America.

Volunteer training session during the 2002 Winter Olympics.
Source: Used with permission IOC/Olympic Museum Collections.

Most trainees would rather move from the specific, which is more personally relevant, to the general. However, in some cases, access to the venue is permitted only at the very last minute, and training has to focus on the more general aspects first. Training days provide an ideal opportunity for team building. Team-building activities, such as quizzes, games, and competitions, should be included in all training so that comfortable relationships will develop. Such activities should be relevant to particular tasks. Event leaders need to accelerate all processes as much as possible in order to hold the attention of the trainee group and to develop team spirit.

Reinforcement is essential, and at the end of training, the event manager should be confident that all staff members have achieved the training objectives for knowledge, attitudes, and skills. Too often these sessions are a one-way process, trainees becoming bogged down with an overload of information. Training materials need to be prepared in a user-friendly, jargon-free format for participants to take home. An illustration of how to use a stopwatch is provided in Figure 12–7 to show how effectively simple training aids can support learning. A hotline staffed by volunteers who answer staff questions about rosters, roles, and transportation information, as well as site directions, is also a good idea. The following checklist covers the type of information that might be included in training manuals and training sessions.

Shift Routine and Specific Tasks

- location of check-in area and check-in procedure
- reporting for shift and briefing

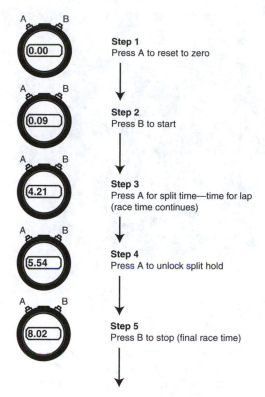

Step 1
Press A to reset to zero

Step 2
Press B to start

Step 3
Press A for split time—time for lap
(race time continues)

Step 4
Press A to unlock split hold

Step 5
Press B to stop (final race time)

Figure 12–7   A Simple Training Aid to Assist Learning

- uniforms and equipment
- incident reporting system
- supervision
- specific roles
- breaks and meals
- debriefing and check-out

Venue Operations

- venue organization and support operations
- staffing policies/rules
- emergency procedures
- radio procedures
- other relevant procedures

General Event Information

- event outline and objectives
- event audience expectations

Moving stock quickly and safely from one area to another is an important task for event staff.

- transportation
- related local services information
- contingency planning

    Customer-service training is a key component of all event training. As the general principles of quality service are well-known, the focus should be on specific information required by staff in order to

Volunteers at the 2002 Winter Olympic Games were clearly identifiable by the event audience through their distinctive uniform.
Source: Used with permission IOC/Olympic Museum Collections.

A volunteer with the Salt Lake Olympic Games helps out fellow volunteer at the Olympic Village in Salt Lake City. The volunteers came from around the world to help in making the Olympic Games go off smoothly.
Source: AP/Wide World Photos.

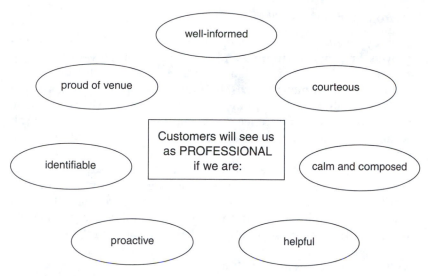

Figure 12–8   Key Aspects of Professional Customer Service

properly assist customers rather than on general skills (such as the five steps of complaint handling). Most event staff rate training on specific event information for the event audience as being the most relevant to their training needs. Staff, however well intentioned, find themselves helpless and frustrated when asked questions that they cannot answer. Figure 12–8 shows the attributes of staff that event customers value.

Briefing Staff

Briefing staff prior to every shift is essential. It is an extension of the training sessions and allows the venue or event manager to impart important, relevant information to staff before they commence work. Some information may be new, such as changes to spectator transportation arrangements, whereas other elements may be a reinforcement of key information, such as incident reporting or emergency procedures.

Managing Legal Requirements

Managers in charge of staffing need to be aware of the legal requirements of employing staff. The two main areas of concern are payroll deductions and occupational health and safety.

Payroll Deductions

Employers must complete a range of payroll deductions for each employee. Employers withhold and pay for their employees FICA (social security and Medicare), as well as a federal, state, and where applicable, local income taxes. In addition, employers must match the amount that employees pay for FICA and pay all federal and state unemployment insurance fees. The employer is responsible for collecting and remitting the respective fees and taxes and for filing them on a quarterly basis.

In addition, employers must keep a record of these payments and must supply the employee with an accounting for any payments filed during each year. Employers must supply an appropriate IRS form (W2) to each employee. For that reason, many employers enlist the help of a payroll service or accounting firm to handle all payroll deductions.

Occupational Safety and Health

The topic of occupational safety and health is covered in detail in Chapter 15. The most important element of this legislation is the responsibility it places on the event organizer for training and supervision of staff.

Employers have a duty of care for the health and safety of employees. Any issue that places employees in the workplace at risk should be considered a duty of care issue, including matters not typically seen as OSHA (Occupational Safety and Health Administration) issues, such as aggression from customers, working alone at night, or working long hours with limited rest periods. An employer's responsibilities include the provision of a safe place of work and training in safe systems of work.

A five-step approach is recommended in implementing an OSHA system. The five steps are as follows:

1. Develop OSHA policies.
2. Set up consultation meetings with employees.
3. Establish training programs and communication plans (including posters).
4. Establish a hazard identification process.
5. Develop, implement, and continuously improve risk control strategies.

Preparing Staffing Policies

Staffing policies should be developed as part of any human resource planning strategy and should cover such aspects as health and safety, misconduct, poor performance, sexual harassment, and violation of safety procedures. These policies are then simplified and summarized as rules for all paid and volunteer staff:

1. Work in a safe manner.
2. Do not endanger the health and safety of others.
3. Report all accidents and incidents.
4. Protect the confidentiality of the event organization and sponsors.
5. Do not say anything derogatory about any aspect of, or person involved in, the event.
6. Refer media questions to the correct person.
7. Look after equipment, uniforms, and other assets.
8. Act in a polite and courteous way to spectators and team members.
9. Use and abuse of alcohol or drugs while on duty is prohibited.
10. Act in a financially responsible manner.
11. Follow reasonable instructions of supervisors and senior event staff.

Developing Recognition Strategies

Recognition of the work of both paid and volunteer staff can have a huge impact on motivation. One of the most effective strategies is the development of realistic goals for staff because this allows individuals to see that their work has contributed to the success of the event.

Intangible rewards include the following:

- goal achievement through individual and team targets and competitions
- job rotation
- job enrichment
- meeting athletes, stars, musicians, and artists
- working with people from overseas
- providing service and information and performing other meaningful tasks
- praise and verbal recognition
- training and skill development
- opportunities for building relationships and friendships
- media recognition

Tangible rewards include these:

- merchandise
- tickets

- postevent parties
- recognition certificates
- statement of duties performed
- meals and uniforms of a high standard
- badges, memorabilia

Linking performance to individual or team goals should be considered carefully by those in charge of motivating staff. When recognition is given to individuals, it needs to be done with caution; otherwise, it can lead to accusations of inequity. Team targets are more likely to improve team performance and to develop camaraderie.

Managing Volunteers

Volunteer management is particularly relevant to the event business, since many events are staffed by volunteers. The following list offers suggestions for training and treating volunteers:

- Volunteers have the right to be treated as coworkers.
- They should be allocated a suitable assignment, task, or job.
- They should know the purpose and ground rules of the organization.
- Volunteers should receive continuing education on the job, as well as sound guidance and direction.
- They should be allocated a place to work and suitable tools and materials.
- They should be offered promotion and a variety of experience.
- Volunteers should be heard and allowed to make suggestions.
- They must be adequately insured.
- They should be given a reference at the end of the event.

In return, the event organization can expect the following:

- as much effort and service from a volunteer as a paid worker, even on a short-term basis
- conscientious work performance, punctuality, and reliability
- enthusiasm and belief in the work of the organization
- loyalty to the organization and constructive criticism only
- clear and open communication from the volunteer

The organization has the right to decide on the best placement of a volunteer, to express opinions about poor volunteer performance in a diplomatic way, and to release an inappropriate volunteer.

The roles most commonly performed by volunteers include these:

- usher
- timekeeper
- results co-coordinator
- referee
- administrator
- media co-coordinator
- protocol/public relations assistant
- logistics co-coordinator
- traffic and parking control
- information officer
- customer relations officer
- first aid officer
- medical assistance (professional health-care providers)
- access monitor/security officer
- shift co-coordinator
- uniform/accreditation officer
- safety officer

The personal benefits, as perceived by volunteers, were the following:

- personal satisfaction
- social contact
- helping others in the community
- doing something worthwhile
- personal or family involvement
- learning new skills
- using skills and experience
- being active.

A number of the benefits listed are often given as the reasons volunteers give freely of their time and efforts. In some cases, volunteering offers the opportunity for social contact and being active. In other cases, volunteers also receive rewards in the form of merchandise and meeting musicians or other interesting people associated with the event. Still others believe in the cause and want to be a part of it. Intangible rewards, such as achievement of specific service targets, should therefore form part of the motivation strategy for both

The 2003 Great American Cleanup™ was the most successful program in its eighteen-year history. We're proud that President George W. Bush served as our Honorary Chair, and that he endorsed our mission of individual responsibility. The President's call for involvement in the Great American Cleanup helped to motivate millions of volunteers nationwide to become stewards of the environment in communities across America.

The program was recently executed in all 50 states, plus Puerto Rico, District of Columbia, Winnipeg, Canada and St. John, U.S.V.I. We had continued, enthusiastic participation by a large number of National/State Parks, Monuments and Historic Sites, including: Katmai (AK), Crater Lake (OR), Craters of the Moon (ID), Acadia (ME), St. Gaudins (NH), Yellowstone (WY), Lake Mead (NV), Mt. Rushmore (SD) and Yosemite (CA).

The 2003 Great American Cleanup mobilized over 2.3 million volunteers from all walks of life to do litter cleanups, beautification and a large variety of community improvement projects in over 14,000 communities. An estimated 30,000 events were produced during the program period. The State and local activities focused on areas of greatest need in each participating community, including: Litter Cleanups; Reduce, Reuse, Recycle (e.g., clothes collection programs); Community Improvement and Beautification (e.g., Adopt-A-Spot, tree & flower planting, etc.); Playground, Park & Recreational Area Cleanup and Renewal; Roadway Cleanup and Beautification; Tire and Battery Recycling; River, Lake and Seashore Cleanups; Youth Education/Community Educational Workshops; Litter-Free Events; Special Promotions, Tours, Concerts and Parades, etc. Coordinated through our National Office, over 30,000 Great American Cleanup events were professionally produced by a network of State and local organizations across the country that knew what the communities needed and how to get it done.

Figure 12–9   The Great American Cleanup
Source: Used with permission of the The 2003 Great American Cleanup™.

paid and volunteer staff. (Figure 12–9 shows an example of the invaluable service given through volunteers).

The 2002 Winter Olympics was a monumental attempt to bring together volunteers to assist in running a mega-event. Salt Lake Olympic Committee's volunteer program had three phases with approximately 8,000 volunteers for pregame activities, 18,000 core volunteers for the Olympic Winter Games, and 6,000 volunteers for the Paralympic Winter Games. Almost every reporter commented on the amazing strength of the volunteer effort associated with the games.

Case study

You have been asked to run a tourism destination promotional forum. The aims are to do the following:

1. raise the profile of your region as a tourist destination;
2. provide a platform for the public and private sectors of the local tourism industry to gather, discuss, and address regional tourism issues; and

3. assist in the expansion of marketing networks and opportunities to promote local tourism destinations and events.

The Buyers and Sellers Business Session will enable delegates to network and conduct business with high-level government officials and representatives of the national, state, and local tourism organizations, as well as entrepreneurs, hoteliers, travel agents, tour operators, and the media. Breakout sessions, at which all delegates will be invited to voice their opinions, will aim to generate ideas and solutions. Also on the discussion table will be issues such as standards, product ranges, joint promotional efforts, and marketing opportunities and strategies.

You are to invite the following:

- tourism representatives and tourism information officers
- investors and financiers seeking new opportunities and business partners
- hoteliers, tour operators, ground transport providers, and tourism facility operators
- transport operators serving the area
- buyers and tourism suppliers
- media representatives

You have two major tasks:

- Develop an organizational chart similar to the one illustrated in Figure 12-1 in this chapter.
- Develop your own job description as "Tourism Forum Event Manager."

*A*ctivity

Become familiar with the Occupational Safety and Health Administration's Web site. In the process of this investigation, identify some potential problems related to workplace health and safety that are facing employees and their employers in the event industry.

*L*inks

www.osha.gov
www.kab.org (Keep America Beautiful/Great American Cleanup)
www.voamass.org (Volunteers of America, MA)

*S*ummary

Staffing is a very important part of event management and crucial to the smooth running of an event. In order to cover this adequately, we have discussed many topics ranging from the preparation of organization charts, which allow employees to understand their reporting relationships, to the importance of writing clear job descriptions. Recruitment and selection help to bring staff online, whereas induction and training prepare them for their event roles. These topics, too, have been covered, and we have also looked at the management of volunteers and the development of recognition strategies for paid, volunteer, and contract staff. Finally, the event manager needs to be able to manage industrial relations and occupational health and safety issues, as well as to prepare human resource policies.

Chapter Thirteen

LEADERSHIP

The volunteer took one look at the uniform, refused to wear it and walked off the job. Of the twenty people I had in my team on the first day, only six remained by day five. Three of my best people were re-assigned to another team on the second day. Some of those who remained beyond the second day found the work too hard; others found it too boring. People assume that when they work at a major event they will be directly involved in the action. We were long gone by the time the bike race began each morning, rushing ahead to set up the next night's camp. In reality most event employees work behind the scenes, handling difficult situations such as spectators trying to gain access to secure areas. In our case drunkenness, aggression and general horseplay by both riders and spectators were hard to handle. The work was physically hard too. Holding a team together is a real challenge, especially when there are many other opportunities for them, or nothing to hold them.

Cycling Event Manager

On completion of this chapter, you will be able to

- understand the time pressures that have an impact on event leaders and their leadership style;
- manage staff by planning, organizing, and controlling work processes;
- manage staff by informing, leading, and reinforcing outstanding performance;
- accelerate group development processes;
- manage diverse and temporary teams;
- manage communication effectively; and
- plan and manage meetings.

This story is indicative of the problems that face many event managers. Staff are often hard to come by owing to the short-term or unpaid nature of the work. In the preceding scenario, the event manager was struggling to keep the event team together for the duration of a six-day, long-distance bike race. Even though her team may have been enthusiastic to support the charity involved in the race, as well as excited to be on the road with the cyclists, the harsh realities are often quite different from the team's expectations.

Although the event planning team may work together for months or even years, the bulk of the event team works together for an extremely short period, ranging from one day to about one month. Staff expectations are hard to manage under these conditions, and there is little time for building relationships and skills. Therefore, the focus of the event leader should be on giving clear guidelines, facilitating efficient work, energizing people, and celebrating successes.

The event must be extremely well planned, and the event leader must concentrate on developing tools for organizing and controlling activities, as well as on innovative ways to inform, lead, and motivate employees and volunteers who may need to reach job maturity within minutes or hours.

Developing Leadership Skills

The leadership model on which this chapter is based is shown in Figure 13–1. The two main dimensions of this model are task management and people management, the basis for many other models used in organizational behavior.

Task Management

Task management involves the skills of planning, organizing, coordinating, and controlling work processes, using tools such as run charts, organization charts, and checklists.

Plan

Planning is probably the most important aspect of event management. It encompasses the development of policies and procedures to cover all situations, from disputes over ticketing/seating to summary

Figure 13–1   Leadership Model for Temporary Teams

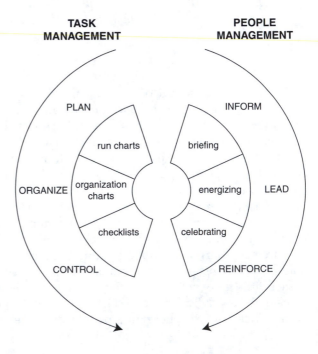

dismissal of alcohol-affected employees. Planning is necessary for the development of staff rosters and the provision of meals for paid and volunteer staff, as well as for restocking, the careful scheduling of stock being most important for multisession events. When a venue is still under construction, architectural drawings are used in logistics planning to ensure, for example, that materials and equipment can be unloaded and set up easily.

There are a number of useful tools that can facilitate the planning process. A simplified version of a run chart (see Chapter 9) is helpful for all team members, and charts and maps should be displayed and discussed during training. Sometimes it is necessary to modify them so that they can be easily understood by all event staff. Although the event management team needs to focus on the macro level of the event (the big picture), the micro level must not be ignored. It is essential that all members of the team be clear about the specific jobs that they are expected to do; otherwise, they will become frustrated, and their performance will deteriorate.

Organize

Organization charts have been covered in Chapter 9 on planning and in Chapter 12 on staffing. You will notice that including the main tasks of those involved has enhanced the chart illustrated in Figure 12–1. An organization chart enhanced with task lists is a useful tool for providing everyone with a more accurate idea of roles and responsibilities at a glance. There should be no ambiguity as to who is responsible for what. In addition to the organization chart, every person should have a job description listing his or her duties. Job rotation is an important organizational task, particularly where paid or volunteer staff are required to man remote locations. Change from one role to another during a shift can alleviate boredom and reduce feelings of inequity.

Control

Checklists are useful control mechanisms. They can be used to check cleanliness, monitor the temperature of food, check for safety or security risks, and to ensure that procedures are followed for setting up and shutting down. A completed checklist is also intrinsically satisfying for the person carrying out tasks, especially if that person's job has no visible output. Most events are high-risk, making control measures absolutely essential for risk and hazard minimization. Tours of the venue (both front- and back-of-the-house) to check that everything is safe are invaluable. Frayed carpets, loose wiring, and chairs stacked in fire exits can all be dealt with using simple control tools, such as checklists.

People Management

In terms of people management, the three skills shown in the model in Figure 13–1 include informing, leading, and reinforcing. Briefings, energizing strategies, and celebratory activities can achieve closure on short-term targets and are necessary for keeping staff interested and motivated.

People management is one of the most significant challenges for the event manager. Because of the short-term nature of events, the frontline staff does not have the commitment of employees embarking on careers with traditional organizations. A volunteer or casual employee who finds the work boring, the location unappealing, the weather unpleasant, or the food unsatisfactory may simply not return the following day. Indeed, he or she may not return from a meal break!

One college senior majoring in Japanese, volunteered to help translate at the 2002 Winter Olympics. When he found out that he would be stationed inside a small cubicle translating written documents during the entire Olympic Games, he opted out of the opportunity. He later admitted that he would have continued had he been given even one chance to catch a glimpse of the Olympic activities.

The ability to keep people informed, to inspire and motivate them through positive leadership, and to reinforce the attainment of specific results, is the key to successful people management in this fast-paced environment.

Inform

Briefings before and after shifts provide the opportunity to advise staff on the order of proceedings as well as to clarify issues of concern. If a single important piece of information is left out and if several hundred spectators ask the same question about it, it is frustrating for everyone involved and a mistake that most event managers make

One-on-one computer demonstrations are very useful for reinforcing core messages.

only once in their career. If staff understand why they are performing what appear to be unnecessary tasks, such as checking accreditation or photocopying results, they are far more likely to understand how they fit into the big picture. Well-informed staff members (including all uniformed staff who are always the target for questions from customers, regardless of their role at the event) also respond well to positive feedback from guests and spectators.

Lead

Most event staff expect to have some fun at an event, and most look forward to joining in the atmosphere. Positive actions on the part of management (including good verbal and nonverbal communication and the initiation of a range of activities to energize the team) can help to create positive staff morale. Event managers who are burned out before an event begins are unlikely to provide inspired leadership or to solve problems with tact and diplomacy. Time and stress management are vital for everyone involved. As role models, event leaders demonstrate to their staff how to provide quality service to customers. Depending on the level of formality of the event, the service provided will vary in subtle ways. Staff members look to management for these cues.

Finally, it is important that each staff member have accurate expectations of his or her role, especially the more mundane tasks. (Sometimes, jobs will be oversold and underdelivered, or undersold and overdelivered.) This circumstance provides the opportunity for the event manager to encourage the staff member to go beyond initial expectations by introducing motivational strategies such as job rotation, viewing the performance, meeting the stars and athletes, or assisting the public. Accurate expectations of the less exciting parts of the job, combined with a positive team spirit, are the outcomes of good leadership.

Reinforce

Positive reinforcement of key messages can enhance safety and service, two essential responsibilities of the whole event team. The range of ways in which core messages can be reinforced are outlined in Figure 13–2. Because event staff are well-known for their capacity to celebrate success at every stage of a project, recognition strategies for individuals and groups, including parties and prizes, are essential in this industry in which people work under tremendous pressure to pull off an event.

In summary, event leadership is about the following:

- planning for short-term assignments
- organizing and simplifying work processes
- developing checklists and other control processes

Verbal	Visual	Written	Behavioral
Briefings	Photographs	Training Material	Videos
Meetings	Displays	Memos	Working practices
Radio conversations	Models	Letters	Role modeling
One-to-one discussion	Demonstrations	E-mail	Nonverbal
Instruction	Printed slogans	Handbooks	communication
Telephone	Posters	Staff newsletters	
conversations	Videos	Reports	
Training	Internet	Information bulletins	
Word-of-mouth		Checklists	
messages			

Figure 13–2   Communication Strategies
Adapted from S. Cook, *Customer Care,* 1997.

It is also about these:

- briefing and communicating with the team
- motivating and energizing on an hourly or a daily basis
- reinforcing key messages and targets
- celebrating success

The work of the event leader may extend to some or all of the following challenging contexts that are quite unlike those of the traditional business environment:

- one shift for one day
- single or multiple venues
- single or multiple session times
- a team separated by physical distance
- routine and dull jobs away from the action
- busy, pressured, and high-stress roles in the midst of the action

And the team itself may include all or any of the following:

- contractors
- volunteers
- temporary workers
- students
- committee members
- police and other stakeholders

Long-term teams	Temporary teams
Commitment to organization's mission	Commitment to task
Decisions by consensus	Leader solves problems and makes decisions
Group cohesion over time	Limited relationship building
Career development within organization	No career/organization orientation
Intrinsic satisfaction	Tangible rewards
Empowerment	Limited responsibility
Lifelong learning	Limited learning
Positive performance management	Positive reference

Figure 13–3   Differences between Long-Term and Short-Term Teams

Managing Temporary and Diverse Teams

The characteristics of temporary groups differ dramatically from those of long-term groups. Long-term groups are able to focus on quality improvement initiatives, with quality teams contributing to ongoing improvements over a period of time. This is seldom the case for temporary teams. The differences are summarized in Figure 13–3. Not only is the event team temporary, but it is also, as a rule, extremely diverse. The general approach to managing a diverse workforce is to assimilate everyone into a strong organizational culture. When individuals share common codes of behavior and communication, and when they solve problems in routine ways, the positive benefit is consistency, and this can be achieved in the normal organizational life cycle. However, this is hard to achieve in the dynamic event environment where there tends to be more on-the-spot decision making and a wider acceptance of diverse standards of behavior. With limited time, an event leader simply does not have the opportunity to assimilate the team into a strong organizational, or group, culture. Working with a diverse range of people with wide-ranging needs and interests is inevitable.

Group Development

Studies by B. W. Tuckman as far back as 1965, and still applicable today, have shown that groups tend to go through five defined stages in their development:

1. **Forming.** This is the period during which members grow used to one another and tentatively formulate goals and behaviors that are acceptable.

2. **Storming.** In this stage there is generally some conflict over control and leadership, including informal leadership, known as sorting out "the pecking order."

3. **Norming.** Once the hierarchy and the roles of all group members have been defined, the group tends to adopt a common set of behavioral expectations.

4. **Performing.** During this productive stage, members focus on performance within the framework of the team.

5. **Adjourning.** Faced with disbandment, successful teams share a sense of loss. In this stage, feelings of achievement are tempered by sadness that the group will be disbanding.

This analysis of group development is useful to those of us who are in the event management business, because the process of group formation does require special attention in this environment. Sometimes, the early stages of group development can be accelerated so that the performing, or productive, stage is reached quite quickly. This step can be done effectively by using icebreakers in team training sessions.

When group members exhibit a wide range of individual differences, particularly in language or culture, the following strategies can help to develop effective communication between them:

1. Identify specific information needs of group members.
2. Use plain English.

Teen volunteers hear final instructions before the event begins.
Source: Mark Richards/PhotoEdit.

3. Allocate buddies or develop subteams.
4. Use graphics to impart information.
5. Rotate roles.
6. Provide all members with opportunities to participate in the group.
7. Develop group rituals and a group identity.

Geert Hofstede (1980), well-known for his work in cross-cultural communication, has identified the following value dimensions in communication.

The first value dimension he termed **power distance,** which indicates the extent to which a society accepts differences in power and authority. In some cultures, employees show a great deal of respect for authority, so Hofstede suggests that these employees have a high power distance. They would find it difficult to bring problems out into the open and to discuss them with senior staff. The low power distance prevalent in other cultures encourages closer relationships at all levels, and questions and criticism from employees are more readily accepted. As you can imagine, if employees in an event team were to come from both high power and low power distance backgrounds, the first group would be aghast at the audacity of the second group when they brazenly pointed out problems, and the low power distance employees would find it difficult to understand why the others did not speak up.

The second value dimension identified by Hofstede was **individualism/collectivism.** Some societies have a strong sense of family, and behavioral practices are based on loyalty to others. Such societies display higher conformity to group norms, and it follows that employees of these cultural backgrounds would feel comfortable in a group. In contrast, employees from highly individualistic societies would defend their own interests and show individual (as opposed to group) initiative.

These are just two cultural dimensions. There are many other variations in people's responses to situations, for example, their different attitudes towards punctuality. Hofstede suggests that the main cross-cultural skills involve the capacity to do the following:

1. communicate respect
2. be nonjudgmental
3. accept the relativity of one's own knowledge and perceptions
4. display empathy
5. be flexible
6. take turns (allow everyone to take turns in a discussion)

> *In most event situations you are running on adrenalin from the start. There is never enough time. You have to deliberately stop yourself, focus on the person, look them in the eye and use their name. It is so easy to forget to do this when you have a hundred unsolved problems and the urge is to be short with them. Something as simple as using the person's name makes the difference between a good event leader and a mediocre one. The worst event leaders are so stressed they can't remember their own names!*
>
> *Event Staffing Manager*

Figure 13–4   Statement by Event Staffing Manager

7. tolerate ambiguity (accept different interpretations of what has been said)

Improving Communication

Although the topic of event briefings has already been covered briefly, here are some additional guidelines for improved communication in the event team.

Establish the Level of Priority

It is important to establish the level of priority immediately. Emergency situations are of course the highest risk for any event, and communication about an incident or potential incident should be given top priority.

Identify the Receiver

By identifying the receiver, you will be able to match your message to the receiver's needs, thus demonstrating empathy. Your message will also reach the correct target.

Know Your Objective

Clarity in communication is often linked to the development of an action objective. If you know what you want to achieve, you will be able to express yourself more easily and clearly. Stating a problem and its ramifications is often only the first stage. By indicating what needs to be done, you can more easily achieve your objective and reach an agreed outcome.

Review the Message in Your Head

In preparing to send a message, you should structure your communication effectively. It is also useful to review the receiver's likely response.

Communicate in the Language of the Other Person

If you use examples and illustrations that the receiver will understand, your message will be more easily comprehended.

Clarify the Message

If the receiver appears from his or her nonverbal behavior not to understand your message, clarification is essential.

Do Not React Defensively to a Critical Response

Asking questions can help you to understand why your receiver has responded defensively and probably can diffuse the situation. By seeking feedback, you can ensure that you have reached a common understanding.

Time Management

To work effectively with event teams, which may be together for a very short period of time, an event manager needs to do the following:

- plan effectively
- identify critical issues and tasks
- analyze and allocate tasks
- manage work priorities
- make quick but informed decisions
- build relationships quickly
- provide timely information
- remove barriers
- simplify processes
- solve problems immediately
- manage stress for self and others
- develop creative and flexible solutions
- constantly monitor performance
- reward the achievement of outcomes

From this list, it is clear that outstanding time management skills (on a personal and a group level) are required in order to gain maximum benefit from the planning phases. An ability to develop instant rapport with new people is also essential when time is limited.

Planning and Managing Meetings

Meetings are an important feature of the management of events, starting in the early planning phases and building to pre-event briefings and post-event evaluations. Meetings can be highly productive, or they can waste an incredible amount of time. In fact, a poorly focused, poorly managed meeting will simply confuse and frustrate everyone. One event management company introduced the idea of a standing meeting to curtail the length of their meetings.

Timelines should be set and an agenda for discussion distributed beforehand with all relevant material so that everyone is prepared. During meetings a chairperson should manage the pace and outcomes of the meeting, and someone should be designated to keep notes for the record. The most important aspect of note taking is the recording of actions and deadlines for those attending. Documentation from the meeting should be distributed and actions identified, prioritized, and included in the planning process.

In addition to focusing on tasks at event meetings, focusing on people should be a priority. Meetings can be an excellent venue for relieving stress, building team spirit, and motivating all involved.

Case Study

I knew what I had to do. I had to stand at an access gate all day on my own and check staff passes. I was prepared for the boredom but I didn't bring a water bottle. Can you believe it? I wasn't given a break for six hours! By then I was really looking forward to some relief. You would think that these managers would learn something about people's basic needs. In this situation I needed to keep warm and dry. A folding chair would have made all the difference.

A drink and an opportunity to go to the bathroom would have been welcome! In terms of the hierarchy of needs, I wasn't expecting self-actualization but I was hoping to have my physical needs met by being given scheduled breaks and possibly having my job rotated. In fact by the time my shift was over for the day, my supervisor had long left the scene.

Event Volunteer

- How could this person's needs be better catered for?
- Are there any strategies for helping to motivate this volunteer?

- What leadership approach would you take to managing your event team?
- Is a different approach needed for managing paid staff and volunteer staff? Explain.
- Explain one way in which you would energize your staff or celebrate success.

$\mathscr{A}$*ctivity*

Select an event, and develop a list of pros and cons of working in three different roles at the event. Describe the leadership challenges and your solutions for the management team of this event.

$\mathscr{S}$*ummary*

In this chapter we have discussed the time constraints in staging an event and the temporary nature of the event workforce, both of which have a major impact on event leadership. The event staff manager must be able to plan, organize, and control tasks in such a way that all concerned are able to see their contribution to the aims and objectives of the event. In managing these temporary, and often diverse, teams, the event manager needs to accelerate group development processes, communicate effectively, lead constructively, and develop recognition and reward programs.

Chapter Fourteen
OPERATIONS AND LOGISTICS

The Western Open, sponsored by the Western Golf Association, is one of the best known golf tournaments in the US and is the third oldest golf championship in the world behind only the British Open and the US Open. Since its inception in 1899, the event has attracted many of the world's top golfers including, Walter Hagen, Byron Nelson, Ben Hogan, Arnold Palmer, Jack Nicklaus, Tom Watson, Nick Price and Tiger Woods. Television coverage of the Western Open which has been held in the Chicago vicinity since 1962 is broadcast to millions of viewers around the world. This glimpse of Chicago's lush green hillsides and booming metropolis has promoted the city of Chicago as a popular tourist destination.

www.westerngolfassociation.com

On completion of this chapter, you will be able to

- plan the logistics of an event, bringing all equipment and other resources on board at the right time;
- plan setup and teardown procedures;
- develop policies and procedures for the smooth operation of an event;
- develop performance standards to measure success against objectives;
- clarify the roles of the various functional areas during the operation of an event; and
- motivate staff to effectively implement plans and to follow through to event operation and teardown.

*A*n event such as the Western Open has many operational demands. First, a logistical plan would need to be developed to ensure that all competing golfers (and their entourage of managers, caddies, etc.) arrive as scheduled, that they are settled into the correct accommodations, and that all their golfing equipment is accounted for and secure. Second, there would be the whole process of preparing the course, which the greenskeepers would start many months before the competition. This would also involve setting up spectator stands, scoreboards, and crowd barriers closer to the actual time of the event (this could be done overnight, and adequate time would need to be allowed for this process). Finally, at the end of the competition, everything would need to be dismantled and stored, since most items would be valuable assets, and the course would be restored to its original state for normal operation. In between the setup and teardown, there is an event to run. (Naturally, with all events, the cost for the facility needs to include the time required for setup and teardown.)

Setting up crowd barriers is just one of the operational procedures for a major golf tournament such as the Western Open.
Source: Used with permission of Western Golf Association.

The focus of this chapter is the operation of an event, which is the culmination of many months, at least, of careful planning.

*L*ogistics

Simply put, logistics is about getting things organized, getting things (and people) in the right place, and tearing everything down. Rock concerts and entertainment events featuring international artists present many logistical problems, particularly if the group is on a tour of several cities. Sometimes a complex array of musical equipment, some of which might have been transported to the country only days, or even hours, before the event, has to be set up. However, in most cases, the team supporting the artists would have identified specific requirements, sometimes down to the last detail, to be met locally. (These might even include requests for exotic foods and special dietary items.) Arranging accommodation has been known to be complicated by the inclusion of a weird range of pets, not commonly cared for in five-star hotels, in the entourage.

The most amusing example of a logistical dilemma was reported by the organizers of an equestrian cross-country event. A decision had to be made as to how to manage "restroom breaks" for volunteers deployed over an enormous open venue. Should a small utility vehicle such as a "gator" be used to pick up the staff member and take him or her to the restroom facilities? No, it was decided that a roving porta-potty on the back of a small truck was the answer. Take

Operations staff is busy at the Seattle Marathon. *Source:* Used with permission of the Seattle Marathon.

the toilet to the staff member, not the staff member to the toilet! This method avoided redeployment or replacement staff.

In most cases, however, logistics planning focuses on setting up and changing sets. Athletics events are particularly challenging, since there are often several concurrent and consecutive events requiring different equipment. An event that involves catering also presents enormous demands when the product has to be served hot, often to hundreds of people in a very short time. One event co-coordinator describes an event in which there was only one set of plates for each guest so that the plates had to be washed between the entrée and the main course. "This process involved a trip up and down lots of stairs and a very tiny washing-up area with a single cold tap, placing

Adequate sanitation facilities are essential to the smooth running of an event. Water had to be transported to this event.

enormous pressure on the kitchen to plate the main course and serve it at the correct time. Cutlery (teaspoons in particular) is one of the biggest setbacks of the banquet department, because a search for matching cutlery can delay a room setup by an hour or more. Some chair covers take so long to stretch and position correctly that significant time can be lost carrying out this task (and significant labor costs incurred)." The logistics manager needs to be one of the most efficient and organized people on the event team. With event operations, work-flow planning becomes a fine art.

Setup

The process of setting up involves the installation of structures and readying the facilities for the event. For some tasks, such as installing sound and lighting equipment, the services of specialist engineers are needed. Setting up can be a time-consuming process, and a run-through must be built into planning. This step is absolutely essential, since it is imperative that all facilities and equipment work. Consider, for example, the event illustrated, which was attended by over 250 networked game players. The technical demands of this event, particularly the networking arrangements, defy description. Just for a start, each of the 250 computers required a network cable and at least two power sockets!

Teardown

The process of tearing down involves dismantling and organizing everything used in the event. If this needs to happen immediately

Networked game-playing event. A high-tech event involving numerous computers could become a logistics nightmare without proper planning.

after the audience has left, sufficient staff will be required because, at this stage, everyone is generally exhausted, thereby presenting a safety risk. If teardown does not occur immediately, security staff will be needed to monitor the site until all materials and equipment have been removed. Some items are particularly expensive, and if they are lost, stolen, or damaged, this outcome can have a dramatic effect on the bottom line of an otherwise successful event.

In most other industries, logistics involves managing the processes of manufacture, supply, and distribution (including storage and transport) of the product to the ultimate consumer. The same general principles apply in event management, requiring an organized and structured alignment of key logistics functions. Procurement, transportation, storage, inventory management, customer service, and database management are all examples of logistical aspects of event merchandise sales, such as T-shirts, caps, CDs, and programs. In the same way, the supply of food and beverage to the event audience starts right back with the producer of the food and beverage product. For most events, food supply is unproblematic. However, in the case of a very large event, provision of sufficient stock of potatoes for fries may require importation of frozen fries, while ensuring an adequate supply of lettuce may require the sourcing of this with a local produce company. For events that run over multiple days, food storage is also an issue, as is the logistics of fresh supplies needing to be delivered overnight, which has ramifications for staffing rosters and security. The disposal or distribution of leftover food is also an issue that needs carefully scrutiny.

Policies

Every event requires policies, which describe the general principles, or "what is to be done." For example, policies may be drawn up to prevent fraud, to limit misrepresentation, to manage the performance of staff, and to promote the right image for the event. Having prepared the policies, the procedures for implementing the policies are then developed. For example, there may be a policy for customer complaints and a procedure to follow in the event of a complaint. There may be a policy on the recruitment and training of time-keepers, and a procedure for reporting and recording performance times for athletes. The policy equates to "what is to be done," and the procedure equates to "how is it to be done."

A uniform policy would say that event staff are to wear specific shirt colors, that they are supplied and laundered by the event company, and that staff who lose their uniforms have to pay for replacements. The policy might also list the personal items that staff are not allowed to wear and might recommend a certain type of footwear. Uniform procedures would cover the steps involved in issuing uniforms to staff at the first training session, the steps involved in handing in and retrieving uniforms from the laundry using a ticket system, and the steps to take if a uniform were lost.

Procedures

A procedure can take the form of a list of tasks or a checklist. Once procedures have been developed and integrated across the event functions, all the pieces begin to fit together. Sometimes, the timing of a procedure needs to be modified to meet the needs of another functional area. For example, if the grass surrounding the greens of a golf course were scheduled to be mowed the day before a golfing competition, it would not be possible to erect the crowd control fencing until the mowing had been done. A procedure for entertaining sponsors for a full day is illustrated in Figure 14–1 in the form of a run sheet. A procedure for checking the safety of a kitchen could be outlined in a checklist, as shown in Figure 14–2. This procedure could also be shown as a flowchart, or it could be based on a logical tour of the kitchen, with items reordered to match the kitchen setup.

Performance Standards

By establishing performance standards and inspection schedules, the operational success of an event can be more confidently assured. For example, in the case of a contract with a cleaning company, there will be clear expectations on both sides, the result generally being excellent customer service. In the case of the cleaning contractor, specific details about the level of service required would be outlined for the following:

- preevent cleaning
- preevent day cleaning
- during session cleaning
- turnover cleaning (between sessions)
- postevent cleaning
- removal of waste materials

Start	Finish	Tasks
7.00 am		Security hand-over to Assistant Operations Manager.
7.00 am	7.30 am	Venue opened and checklists completed for safety, cleaning, layout and supplies and inventory ready.
8.00 am	8.30 am	Staff check-in and briefing.
8.30 am		Staff commence first shift. Hospitality area opened for light meals/coffee/breakfast.
10.00 am	7.00 pm	Staff break area open.
11.00 am		Entertainment staff arrive. Acts as per daily schedule held by Operations Manager.
11.00 am	3.00 pm	Lunch service.
2.00 pm		Hand-over from Assistant to Operations Manager.
		Meal numbers for following day confirmed.
3.00 pm		Second shift commences, staff briefing.
		Catering staff meeting—Operations and Kitchen production.
3.30 pm		Deadline for lunch cash reconciliation.
4.00 pm	10.00 pm	Dinner service.
11.00 pm	12.00 mid	Setup for following day service.
12.00 mid	1.00 am	Cleaning all areas, kitchen, dining area, and facilities.
2.00 am		Security lockup.

Figure 14–1   Daily Run Sheet—Sponsor Hospitality

The criteria for performance standards may include efficiency (i.e., speed of setup), accuracy (i.e., checklist 100 percent), revenue (dollar sales per outlet), or courtesy (customer feedback).

Functional Areas

Although the division of responsibilities into different functional areas has already been discussed in previous chapters, it is useful to review the roles of these areas, known in most other businesses as "departments." Each of these functional areas develops its own policies, procedures, and performance standards. Where there is more than one venue, a functional area, such as medical, may be represented at each venue.

Kitchen Safety Checklist

1 Food contact surfaces are clean and clear. ☐
2 Chopping boards for meat, chicken, vegetables are color coded. ☐
3 Nonfood surfaces clean and clear. ☐
4 Floors are clean and not slippery. ☐
5 Equipment is correctly cleaned and stored. ☐
6 Wiping cloths and cleaning equipment for different purposes correctly color coded. ☐
7 Plumbing is functional. ☐
8 Refrigerator and freezer temperatures meet standards. ☐
9 Hand-washing facilities meet standards. ☐
10 Garbage disposal containers are labeled and covered. ☐
11 Storage areas are clean and clear. ☐
12 No evidence of insects or rodents. ☐
13 Lighting and ventilation is adequate. ☐
14 Gas supply is checked. ☐
15 All cooking equipment is functional. ☐
16 First aid box is fully equipped. ☐

Figure 14–2 Checklist for Kitchen Safety Procedure

Procurement and Stores

This area is responsible for purchasing, storage, and distribution of all products required for the event. Such items may include radios, computers, sound equipment, and drapes, and are often rented or leased from specialist suppliers.

If catering, for example, were contracted out to a subcontractor, the subcontractor would be responsible for food purchasing and storage, and the same would apply to other subcontractors. They, too, would be responsible for their product or equipment procurement and storage.

One of the main roles for this functional area during an event is the supply of event merchandise to the sales outlets.

Marketing

In the time leading up to an event, this functional area is responsible for the overall strategy for product, pricing, and promotion. As the event draws near, image, sponsor liaison, and sales promotion become priorities.

Ticketing

The ticketing area looks after ticketing prior to an event and during the event. In some cases this function is managed by the local tourism information office; in other cases, tickets are sold by charitable organizations. For most profit-making events, the ticketing function is managed wholly by a major ticketing organization.

Registration

Most sporting events, particularly those with large numbers of participants, need a functional area to manage the registration of participants in the race or the event. This requirement involves completion of relevant forms by participants as well as the signatures of participants to acknowledge that participation is at their own risk.

Merchandising

The merchandising area is responsible for the sale of merchandise, ranging from caps and posters to CDs and videos. The range is frequently extensive and is sometimes advertised on the Internet.

Finance

As the event draws near, the main concern of this functional area is to maintain control processes, minimize expenditure and manage cash during the event.

Legal

In most cases, legal advice is sought before the event, and it is only with very large events that a specific functional area is established to cover this role.

Technology

Networks linking different reporting systems can be developed to include those for sales of tickets and merchandise, registration of athletes and recording of results, and managing rosters and payroll.

Media

This functional area deals directly with the media, and during an event it needs to be constantly informed of progress. If a negative incident should occur, it is the media unit that writes the press releases and briefs the press. It also manages media interviews with the stars or athletes.

Community Relations

Generally speaking, this functional area is represented only when there is a significant community role, for example, at nonprofit events.

Staffing

As the event approaches, the staffing area looks after training, uniforms, rosters and other schedules, and staff meal vouchers.

Services and Information

The provision of services and information to the event audience is obviously at its peak during the event, which requires the staff to be extremely knowledgeable and resourceful.

Cleaning and Waste Management

Very often this function rests with venue staff who undertake cleaning as a routine operation before, during, and after an event. For larger events, such as street festivals, the local government may ask current contractors to expand their role for the period of the festival. For major sporting events, contract cleaners are often called in to manage this functional area.

Catering

In most cases, venue catering is outsourced to a catering company, and there is generally a long-standing contract in place with that company. Sometimes, however, a decision needs to be made as to whether to employ one caterer to take on this role or several caterers, each offering different types of cuisine. Most event organizers leave this area to catering professionals.

All staff need to be able to provide event information to attendees.

Venue Operations

The management of the venue, in particular the operation of facilities and equipment, maintenance, and the like, is the responsibility of the venue team. Health, safety, and emergencies are the key areas of concern of this functional area.

Sport Associations

All aspects of a sporting competition, including results management and award ceremonies, are generally managed by the sport's association involved in the event. (For instance, a Little League state tournament would be under the direction of the state-chartered Little League officials.)

Medical

The medical functional area provides first aid to both spectators and athletes. In some cases, this area is responsible for drug testing.

Security

Access to the event site by accredited personnel is managed by security, which also plays an important role in crowd management.

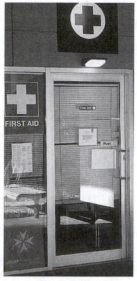

A first aid station is one of the most functional areas. If there is more than one event venue, medical facilities need to be available at all of them.

Leadership and Staff Motivation

In addition to organizing the tasks that need to be performed, an event organizer needs to focus on managing staff, volunteers, and contractors during the operational phase of the event. Since there are few

Catering for both take-out and fine dining at event venues is mostly outsourced, so that this functional area is generally managed by contractors.

long-term job prospects for most of the frontline staff working at an event, there is a higher than average chance that they might not return the next day, or that they might disappear during a break or simply walk off the job. Some of the reasons they might give include the following:

- My skills are being wasted.
- I am not suited to this job.
- I feel as if I am being used and abused.
- I feel as if my time is being wasted.
- My help is not appreciated.
- There is a lack of support.
- I don't understand how I fit in.
- The work is boring.
- I don't have all the information I need.
- I don't have the equipment I need to do the job.
- The procedures are not clear.
- I feel unwelcome and ignored.
- I don't like it.
- I got a better offer.
- I didn't expect to be doing this.
- Getting here was too difficult.

Unhappy staff say things such as the following:

"My supervisor arrived two hours late and I was kept waiting after getting up at 5 am."
"Why can't we be given more information so that we can answer questions?"
"Somebody has to keep their head and be patient."

So you can see why good leadership and an ability to motivate staff are crucial to the smooth running of an event. Some experienced event managers have made the following remarks and suggestions about staff management during the pressured moments of an event:

"Success is linked to goals, large ones and small ones. Be prepared to make the goals explicit and share achievement of these goals with your staff. This will motivate everyone."

"Give the team an identity. Establish team roles and build co-hesiveness. Games and fun are essential."

"One of the most difficult things is assigning jobs. All staff want to be able to see the show."

"A plan is a good thing, but be prepared to deviate from it."

"Nothing can prepare you for it. Being faced with huge numbers of people descending on you, filling a venue within minutes is incredible. Nothing can prepare you for the time-consuming nature of it. There are so many conflicting demands. You have to keep focused."

"There is no quicker way to destroy team morale than for the manager to complain about the situation."

"Facial messages are really important. You can ruin someone's day with the wrong expression."

"Take the time to use the person's name and give clear and concise directions."

"Once they are committed and settled, they will do anything. If you manage well, your team will walk over hot coals for you."

"Information is provided to team leaders to pass on. They need to recognize the value of getting the information to the staff at the briefing; otherwise their radio will run hot all day answering the same question."

"Sometimes it is difficult. You have a well-meaning staff member who comes to you with a suggestion. You are in the middle of doing a thousand critical things and they want your attention. You have to make time to talk to them later and explain why you can't listen right away. And you can't afford to forget to go back! If you don't, they will feel undervalued."

"Remember to be fair with recognition—you don't want to create a nasty competitive spirit in your team, especially in relation to giveaways."

"Most of the organizing committee was burnt out before the event began. Look after your physical health. It is like running a marathon. Prepare for it. Your tolerance for stress needs to be high."

"Crack a few jokes when the going gets tough; initiate a dynamic and energetic team spirit."

"Think about appreciation strategies beforehand—you have to plan celebrations for reaching milestones. This takes time and you won't have the time during the event."

"People working at events expect to enjoy themselves; if they don't, the customers won't."

Summary

This chapter has looked in more detail at logistics, including the often problematic setup and teardown phases of an event. The task of identifying resources and equipment needed, bringing them on-site, and setting up in the required time takes careful planning. The emphasis in this chapter has therefore been on organization and coordination to ensure that all functional areas work together smoothly and cooperatively through all phases of the event. The development of policies and procedures can assist in the fulfillment of this goal by outlining the interrelationship between functional areas and will also help to ensure that the event performance standards and objectives are successfully achieved.

Case Study

You are organizing a race for 20,000 runners. The biggest logistical problem you will face will be at the end of the race. At this time, runners crossing the finish line are exhausted and don't want to run or walk another step. Media members wanting to take photographs and to interview front runners compounds this problem. Enthusiastic supporters wishing to congratulate those who finish only add to it. All runners need to get across the line without hold-ups; otherwise, their times will be affected.

You need to make plans to ensure that all runners cross the line, that they are advised of their times, and that they receive free sponsor products, retrieve, their belongings, and attend the prize-giving ceremony. Some participants and spectators will not wait for the final ceremony and will wish to take the transportation provided back to the race starting point and go home.

Develop detailed operational plans for the end of the race, using estimates of finish times and crowd-flow patterns for participants and spectators.

Activities

Draw up an operational timetable for a wedding. This should include rental of all plates, silverware and glasses, table linen, candlesticks, and chair covers. It should also include organizing the ordering of the cake, car rentals, floral arrangements, and entertainment. The focus of this activity is the logistics of getting everything and everyone into place at the right time for the reception party.

Develop a midevent appreciation strategy and a plan for a postevent party in order to celebrate the success of the event with your staff.

Chapter Fifteen
SAFETY AND SECURITY

In 1979, 11 fans were crushed to death at the Who's concert in Cincinnati, OH. That event is widely regarded as one of the worst concert tragedies.

It happened again on Friday, June 31, 2000. Nine people were trampled to death at a Pearl Jam concert near Copenhagen, Denmark. Another 26 were seriously injured during a rock concert that drew 25,000 fans.

On completion of this chapter, you will be able to

- identify situations in which police or security staff are required;
- comply with laws, regulations, and standards relating to occupational health and safety;
- develop procedures to meet safety standards;
- train staff to prevent risks to health and safety;
- use systems that limit safety risks; and
- establish a system of communication for reporting incidents and emergencies.

There exists a Rock and Roll Wall of Shame that lists the names of 293 individuals who were killed since 1990 at rock concerts because of a lack of crowd management (www.crowdsafe.com/thewall.html). In the management of this type of event, careful analysis of crowd behavior and the methods proposed for controlling crowds are required. Crowd management encompasses the steps taken to organize and manage crowds, whereas crowd control is the term used for dealing with crowds that are out of control. Security staff and security organizations play a major role in crowd control, particularly in events of this nature. First aid is also a necessity.

Other events report that hundreds of thousands of people gather for celebrations throughout the U.S. with only a few minor incidents, none relating to crowd management. The behavior of event visitors thus has an important role to play in the level of potential risk at a particular event and should form part of the analysis that begins with

A well-behaved crowd at a Puerto Rican parade in New York City.
Source: © Alan Schein/ Corbis/Stock Market.

the risk management plan discussed in Chapter 8 and follows through to the contingency plans for safety and security discussed in detail in Chapter 16.

Safety of the event audience, staff, and subcontractors should be of paramount concern for every event manager, since all events carry safety risks that may result in anything from accidents to the evacuation of a venue. In this and the following chapter, we will look more closely at risks associated with the safety of the audience and staff, as well as the security procedures used to manage such risks. In addition, we will look at the potential for injury being caused by fixed or temporary structures, which may in turn be subjected to damage.

Another issue for consideration for most events is that of line management. Lines can be managed very well or very badly. The delays getting into events, such as many sporting events or concerts, are sometimes so bad that the event manager has to direct staff to stop taking tickets and simply open the gates. Clearly this situation can lead to problems inside the venue if nonticketed people manage to find their way in. On the other hand, if the sporting event has commenced, and perhaps points having been scored while the spectators remain outside, there would be little else that could be done. However, if there were a number of people without tickets outside the venue, this would not be a viable option.

The orderly management of spectators leaving the venue is just as important, with clear directions and signage necessary to guide them to public transportation and parking. Sometimes spectators enjoy themselves so much at the event that they have to be marched out by security staff.

In this chapter we will deal with general security issues, occupational safety and health, first aid, and effective communication of incidents. The topics of crowd control and emergency evacuation will be covered in more detail in the next chapter.

Security

Security is generally required for premises, equipment, cash, and other valuables, but the predominant role of most event security staff is to ensure that the correct people have access to specific areas and to act responsibly in case of accident or emergency. Identification badges (generally a tag hanging around the neck, showing the areas to which staff, media, and spectators have access) allow security staff to monitor access. Ejection of people who are behaving inappropriately—sometimes in cooperation with police personnel—is occasionally necessary.

Police officer visits with this friendly, well-behaved crowd at a Martin Luther King parade.
Source: A. Ramey/PhotoEdit.

There are several considerations in the organization of security for an event. First, it is necessary to calculate the number of trained staff required for the security role. If the venue covers a large area, vehicles and equipment may also be required. (Four-wheeled gators are usually used to deploy staff to outlying areas.) And finally, the level of threat will determine whether firearms are needed.

In all cases, security staff should be appropriately licensed, and the security company should carry the appropriate insurance.

Police Service

Local police departments often provide some of the required security services, generally at limited or no cost for community events. However, with the growth of the event industry and the increased demands on police for spectator control, charges are now being levied by some police departments for every officer attending an event. The number of police required is negotiated by the police and the event manager, the number being determined by the history of incidents associated with similar events and the availability of alcohol.

Mounted police often attend large street festivals and processions.
Source: Dorling Kindersley Media Library.

Security Services

Laws exist in relation to security service organizations and security personnel. The industry is regulated, and an event company must ensure that the appropriate licenses are secured. There are various classes of licensing requirements (commonly called Guard Cards in the industry) for the individual security officers in most but not all 50 states. All security officers are required to undergo a criminal record check.

The roles of security officers in relations to the event management industry include the following:

- acting as a bodyguard, bouncer, or crowd controller
- patrolling or protecting premises
- installing and maintaining security equipment
- providing advice on security equipment and procedures
- training staff in security procedures

Security service organizations must hold appropriate general liability insurance coverage. General liability insurance coverage is, in fact, a requirement of almost all contracts between event organizers and subcontractors. Subcontractors, including security service organizations, also need to cover their staff for work-related health and safety incidents.

Occupational Safety and Health

Employer Responsibilities

OSHA stands for the Occupational Safety and Health Administration, an agency of the U.S. Deparment of Labor. In 1970, the U.S. Congress passed the *Occupational Safety and Health Act of 1970,* known as the *OSH Act,* to assure so far as possible that every working man and woman in the nation has safe and healthful working conditions and to preserve our human resources. OSHA uses three basic strategies authorized by the *OSH Act,* to help employers and employees reduce injuries, illnesses, and deaths on the job:

- Strong, fair, and effective enforcement;
- Outreach, education, and compliance assistance; and
- Partnerships and other cooperative programs.

The *OSH Act* covers employers and employees either directly through federal OSHA or through an OSHA-approved state program.

Under the *OSH Act*, if you are an employer, you **must**

- Meet your general duty responsibility to provide a workplace free from recognized hazards;
- Keep workers informed about OSHA and safety and health matters with which they are involved;
- Comply, in a responsible manner, with standards, rules, and regulations issued under the *OSH Act*;
- Be familiar with mandatory OSHA standards;
- Make copies of standards available to employees for review upon request;
- Evaluate workplace conditions;
- Minimize or eliminate potential hazards;
- Provide employees safe, properly maintained tools and equipment, including appropriate personal protective equipment, and ensure that they use it;
- Warn employees of potential hazards;
- Establish or update operating procedures and communicate them to employees;
- Provide medical examinations when required;
- Provide training required by OSHA standards;
- Report within eight hours any accident that results in a fatality or the hospitalization of three or more employees;
- Keep OSHA-required records of work-related injuries and illnesses;
- Post a copy of OSHA 300A, Summary of Work-Related Injuries and Illnesses, for the previous year from February 1 to April 30;
- Post, at a prominent location within the workplace, the OSHA "It's the Law" poster (OSHA 3165) informing employees of their rights and responsibilities;
- Provide employees, former employees, and their representatives access to the Log of Work-Related Occupational Injuries and Illnesses (OSHA 300) at a reasonable time and in a reasonable manner;
- Provide access to employee medical records and exposure records to the employee and others as required by law;
- Cooperate with OSHA compliance officers;
- Not discriminate against employees who properly exercise their rights under the *OSH Act*;

- Post OSHA citations and abatement verification notices at or near the worksite involved; and
- Abate cited violations within the prescribed period.

Employee Rights

If you are an employee, you have the right to

- Review copies of appropriate OSHA standards, rules, regulations, and requirements that the employer should have available at the workplace;
- Request information from your employer on safety and health hazards, precautions, and emergency procedures;
- Receive adequate training and information;
- Request that OSHA investigate if you believe that hazardous conditions or violations of standards exist in your workplace;
- Have your name withheld from your employer if you file a complaint;
- Be advised of OSHA actions regarding your complaint and have an informal review of any decision not to inspect or to issue a citation;
- Have your authorized employee representative accompany the OSHA compliance office;
- Respond to questions from the OSHA compliance offer;
- Observe any monitoring or measuring of hazardous materials and see any related monitoring or medical records;
- Review the Log and Summary of Work-Related Injuries and Illnesses (OSHA 300 and 300A) at a reasonable time and in a reasonable manner;
- Request a closing discussion following an inspection;
- Submit a written request to the National Institute for Occupational Safety and Health for information on whether any substance in your workplace has potentially toxic effects in the concentrations being used and have your name withheld from your employer;
- Object to the abatement period set in a citation issued to your employer;
- Participate in hearings conducted by the Occupational Safety and Health Review Commission;
- Be notified by your employer if he or she applies for a variance and testify at a variance hearing and appeal the final decision; and

- Submit information or comments to OSHA on the issuance, modification, or revocation of OSHA standards and request a public hearing.

OSHA Acts include legislations related to clean air, safe drinking water, water pollution, toxic substances, and solid waste, to name a few topics covered.

Insurance

All employers must take out worker's compensation insurance. This covers all staff for work-related accident or injury, including their medical expenses, payment for time off work, and rehabilitation. Volunteers are not covered by this insurance because they are not, by definition, "paid workers." Volunteers are typically covered under general liability insurance for medical expenses. (Check your provider to verify.) The most important element of worker's compensation is the **responsibility placed on supervisors and managers for ensuring that employees have a safe place to work and safe systems of work. Note: Each state has its own laws regarding worker's compensation. Check with your state.**

Policies and procedures in relation to safety are essential, and these procedures need to be part of all employee training. In the following sections we will discuss the safe handling of items and the safe performance of certain activities that otherwise may be a threat to the safety of workers in the event environment.

Safe Lifting Techniques

Lifting techniques are generally part of training for anyone involved in lifting, carrying, or moving heavy objects, such as sporting equipment or display stands. Two useful training aids for this purpose are illustrated in Figure 15–1 and Figure 15–2.

The correct way to lift a heavy object is to squat close to the load, keeping your back straight. Do not stoop over the load to get a grip and pick it up. Test the weight of the object before attempting to lift it. Lift using your knees and legs (not your back) as leverage. Keep

Figure 15–1 Lifting Technique

RIGHT   WRONG

Avoid	Common Causes of Injury	Common Solutions
Lifting and moving	Lifting boxes from the floor Carrying boxes or equipment Pushing carts	Do not store items on the floor. Use proper lifting techniques. Get help or use a lifting aid. Use a cart. Avoid overreaching, twisting, or lifting overhead. Maintain casters in clean, operating condition. Match the casters to the floor type.

Figure 15–2   How to Prevent Injuries Caused by Lifting and Moving Heavy Objects

your back straight, not bent forwards or backwards. Do not twist or turn your body while carrying the object or putting it down.

From OSHA (Occupational Safety and Health Administration) come the following guidelines for the handling of heavy objects.

Lifting Heavy Loads

Some loads are too heavy for most of the population to lift, even if all lifting conditions are ideal. Extensive studies have shown that even under ideal conditions, loads heavier than about 50 to 60 pounds will increase the risk of injury. The following factors will further reduce the amount of weight that can safely be lifted:

- Bending the torso forward moves the load away from the body and forces the back to support the weight of the upper body.
- Reaching to access and lift a load also moves the load away from the body.
- Frequent repetition of lifting motions leads to poor lifting techniques and muscle fatigue.
- Twisting while lifting places the back in a less stable posture.
- Lifting for long periods of time leads to fatigue.
- Previous back injury.

Possible Solutions

- Evaluate lifting tasks to determine the maximum weight that can safely be lifted. A variety of assessment tools can be utilized to make this determination.
- Do not manually lift heavy loads. For most people loads heavier than about 50 to 60 pounds should be considered heavy.

Situations that involve awkward postures such as bending, reaching, twisting, or repetitive lifting will greatly reduce this weight.

- Use lifting assist devices to lift loads that are determined to be excessive. These devices allow loads to be lifted by mechanical means rather than forcing employees to support the weight. Some of the examples of such devices include:

  1. Powered barrel dumpers eliminate heavy lifting. Employees use a hand truck to load a heavily loaded barrel onto the device. It then automatically lifts the barrel and dumps the contents.

  2. A counterweighted device, such as a vacuum hoist, allows employees to lift significant weight. Employees must exert only a few pounds of force to guide the load around the workspace while mechanical means support most of the weight.

  3. Conveyor systems or carts allow employees to transport items around the workstation without repeated lifting and carrying.

In conclusion, OSHA suggests that a definitive, absolute safe lifting weight is not possible to determine and that a commonsense approach is required for assessing manual handling tasks. Weight should be considered, along with all other factors in the context of the task, including actions or postures, other load characteristics, the work environment, and human characteristics. (See Figures 15–1 and 15–2.)

Safety Steps for Electrical Equipment

Electrical equipment is a significant hazard in the event environment, particularly in wet weather. All safety steps must be taken to prevent accidents involving electrical equipment, including routine tagging and inspection of equipment. Many venues are extremely rigorous in their demands for documentation that demonstrates correct licensing and inspection.

The following information on workplace electrical safety was found on the National Electrical Safety Foundation's Web site at www.nesf.org and reprinted here with the organization's permission. (The organization has just been renamed the Electrical Safety Foundation International.)

Workplace Electrical Safety Tips

Adapt this list of reminders to your working environment. Be sure to consider company policies and local, state, and federal codes before establishing a written electrical safety program.

- Plan every job, and think about what could go wrong.
- Use the right tools for the job.
- Use procedures, drawings, and other documents to do the job.
- Isolate equipment from energy sources.
- Identify the electric shock and arc flash, as well as other hazards that may be present.
- Minimize hazards by guarding or establishing approach limitations.
- Test every circuit and every conductor every time before you touch it.
- Use personal protective equipment (PPE) as a last line of defense in case something goes wrong.
- Be sure you are properly trained and qualified for the job.
- Work on electrical equipment and conductors only when de-energized, unless procedures and safeguards have been established to ensure zero exposure for the worker and other people in the area.
- Lockout/tagout and ground (where appropriate) before working on equipment.
- Treat de-energized electrical equipment and conductors as energized until lockout/tagout, test, and ground procedures (where appropriate) are implemented.
- Wear protective clothing and equipment, and use insulated tools in areas where there are possible electrical hazards.
- De-energize and visibly guard (where possible) whenever contact with uninsulated overhead power lines is possible.
- Check and double-check safety regulations when a ladder or parts of any vehicle or mechanical equipment structure will be elevated near energized overhead power lines. Call your local electric utility for assistance. People standing on the ground may be particularly vulnerable to possible injury.

Cords, Equipment, and Tool Grounding

- Make sure all equipment and extension cords bear the mark of an independent testing laboratory such as UL, CSA, ETL, or MET labs.
- Protect flexible cords and cables from physical damage. Check cords for cut, broken, or cracked insulation.
- Keep slack in flexible cords to prevent tension on electrical terminals.
- Make sure the insulating qualities of a splice are equal to or greater than the original cord.

- Extension cords are for temporary use. Install permanent wiring when use is no longer temporary.
- Verify that all three-wire tools and equipment are grounded.
- Water, electrical equipment, and power cords do no mix! Use GFCI protection in wet or damp environments.
- Ground exposed parts of fixed equipment that could be energized.
- Use nonconductive tools whenever possible.
- Always double-check the operation of your voltage testers by testing a live circuit.

Other Considerations

- Verify location of all buried or embedded electrical circuits before digging or cutting.
- Determine the reason that a fuse operated or circuit breaker tripped before replacing or resetting.
- Know where your overcurrent devices are (i.e., circuit breakers and fuses) so they can be easily and quickly reached in case of an emergency.
- When replacing lamps and bulbs, verify that the replacement matches fixture requirements.

Safe Use of Machinery

Each year the use of machinery results in a number of serious injuries and fatalities. There are numerous machinery hazards such as trapping between revolving control handles and fixed part; entanglement from revolving shafts, spindles, and bars; friction or cutting from abrasive wheels; flying objects resulting from breakage of high-speed cutting tools; noise; and hot metal parts and radiation.

Many factors can cause or increase the risk, such as using the wrong machinery for the job, poor machinery maintenance, and inadequate training in the use of machinery. There are several control measures to ensure the safe use of machinery. They range from using the right equipment for the job, providing machinery guards where possible, providing maintenance and cleaning, and training and supervision of machine operators.

Safe Handling of Hazardous Substances

Because different chemicals have different safe use requirements, it is important for staff to know as much about hazardous substances used in the workplace as possible. Material Safety Data Sheets should be used to provide to staff members the following advice on these substances:

- ingredients of a product
- health effects and first-aid instructions
- precautions for use
- safe handling and storage information
- emergency procedures

Safety Signs

Safety signs are particularly important in the event workplace, since staff are generally only at the venue for a very short period. This does not allow much time for reinforcement of safety issues; however, these can be stressed during briefing sessions. Posters and safety signs can be used to reinforce key messages, helping to prevent many accidents.

First Aid

In most cases, event managers need to alert local authorities (police, fire department, ambulance services) of a planned event, although venue and event staff should also be trained in first-aid procedures. Some of these procedures will be specific to the event in question. For example, at a marathon race, common first-aid emergencies occur, including exhaustion, collapse, dehydration, road burns, and bone and muscle injuries, and therefore procedures should be in place for dealing with them. In addition, participants in races such as these sometimes do not wish to accept help, and staff would need to be trained in the correct procedure for dealing with such an occurrence.

These cylinders contain a hazardous substance, requiring clear instructions for safe handling and storage.

Incident Reporting

For any event there are standard reporting relationships on all operational issues. On the whole, these reporting relationships concur with the organization chart. However, there are many instances when communication is less formal and less structured, no less in the case of the event working environment where "mayhem" or "controlled chaos" may best describe it.

Despite some tolerance of rather haphazard communication before and during the event, **any communication relating to an incident or emergency needs to be very clear.** It must also **follow a short and specific chain of command.** The chain of command, or organization chart, for an emergency is seldom the same as the organization chart for the event as a whole. Emergency reporting tends to go through very few levels, and all staff must be trained in emergency reporting. Many stakeholders may be involved—general staff, security staff, first-aid personnel, police, emergency services—but absolute clarity is needed as to who makes key decisions and how they are to be contacted. These lines of reporting and responsibility will be reviewed in the next chapter.

Communication Methods

Most event teams use radios, since they are the most effective tool for maintaining communication. Different channels are used for different purposes, and it is essential that the correct radio procedures be followed. In Figure 15–3, radio links to the Event Operations Center are illustrated, with "Control" serving as the link to the decision makers. For example, in response to a request to remove a hazard, Control would ensure that the Site team responded to the call. If a spill were reported, Control would report to Cleaning, requesting that the spill be cleaned up. The Operations Center also has links to emergency services that can be called if required.

At some events, cell phones are used, but the drawback of this method of communication is that the information transmitted can be overheard. Networks can also become overloaded if spectators are using their cell phones too, particularly during intermission and at the end of a match or concert. This possibility is especially likely if a major emergency arises. During the "Blackout of August 2003," most

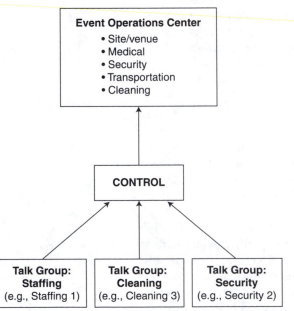

Figure 15–3 Channels of Communication for Radio Incident Reporting

A security guard in radio contact with Operations crew.
Source: Mary Kate Denny/PhotoEdit.

cell phone users in the eastern cities found that their phones quit working.

Case Study 1

The Gold Mining Company is a nightclub venue that is popular during the months of November, December, and January for its Friday night dance events. The staff working at this venue are all temporary workers, and the turnover is high. During a conversation, two of the staff, Jason and Mark, find out that they have both been mugged on

Summary

The health, safety, and security of staff and the event audience are very important concerns of the event management team. In this chapter we have discussed many measures for ensuring that these goals are achieved, including the safe handling of heavy objects and hazardous substances and the safe use of electrical equipment and machinery. Safety and security are risks that need to be dealt with by assessing the risk, managing the risk, and developing contingency plans for dealing with the risk. Not only people but also assets must be protected, and security personnel and the police are there to assist the event manager in managing these risks. Of most importance, an effective system of communication for reporting incidents will prevent the escalation of a situation and will help staff to deal promptly with any emergency.

their way home from work in the early hours of the morning, but on different Friday nights. In both cases, the perpetrators waited in a nearby alley and threatened them with knives. Jason lost his wallet and $200, and Mark broke his ankle trying to run away. Candice, another employee, has been harassed by patrons and was once burned deliberately with a cigarette by a particularly drunk and obnoxious customer. Management gave her some cash to get medical attention.

Discuss the occupational safety and health issues of the staff concerned. What are the responsibilities of the management in each of these cases? What are some solutions?

Case Study 2

The 2004 exhibition of *Designer Jewelry—Artists of the South Pacific* is being held in the foyer of a large Honolulu, Hawaii, hotel. The governor will open the exhibition, and a number of dignitaries from Tahiti, Guam, Tonga, and Samoa will be in attendance. There will be some security risks associated with the visiting guests, as well as with the items on display. Threats and protests could also disrupt the opening. Discuss the following issues:

- Who will be responsible for security (probably more than one body)?
- What are some of the potential security problems?
- What are the occupational health and safety issues?
- What steps can be taken to prevent a security incident?
- What plans should be in place should an incident occur?

Activity

Identify some of the security issues at the following events, and prepare plans to prevent or deal with these issues:

- dance party with mosh pit
- street festival
- private party for a celebrity
- product launch
- 15 K marathon race

Links

www.crowdsafe.com
www.osha.org
www.nesf.org

Chapter Sixteen
CROWD MANAGEMENT AND EVACUATION

In Rhode Island, a rock band's pyrotechnic display turned into a nightmare, killing at least 95 people and injuring 180 as a frantic mob rushed to escape. This was the deadliest US nightclub fire since 164 people were killed at the Beverly Hills Supper Club in 1977. It came less than a week after 21 people were killed in a stampede at a Chicago nightspot after Mace or pepper spray was sprayed into the crowd to quell a fight. The worst nightclub fire in the US was on November 28, 1942, when 492 people died at Boston's Coconut Grove.

The Rock band "Great White" had just started playing at the Station Concert Club in West Warwick, RI, when giant pyrotechnic sparklers began shooting up and set fire to the ceiling. The entire building was in flames within three minutes. The building was not required to have a sprinkler system because of its size. One of the band members was reported as a casualty of the terrible accident.

No license was sought for the pyrotechnic display. There were inadequate exits, in fact the only exit swung inward. The club had been cited with a safety violation for inadequate exits, but no repair had been made. According to reports most of the bodies were found near the entrance and some appeared to have been trampled.

Adapted by author from KOMO 4 News report 2-24-03; CBS News report from correspondent Lee Cowan; The Boston Phoenix 2-27-03; Fox News report 3-02-03; CBC News 2-22-03; and a report found on NFPA.org (National Fire Protection Association "Fire Safety in Assembly Occupancies")

On completion of this chapter, you will be able to

- identify the types of events and situations that might give rise to crowd management problems;
- develop crowd management and crowd control systems and procedures;
- identify the types of occurrences that may require evacuation; and
- develop procedures for evacuation.

As these reports illustrate, contingency plans need to be in place in case of emergencies at an event and, clearly, easy access for emergency services is one of the first aspects that needs to be considered. Evacuation and crowd management are others. In this chapter we will deal with all three.

The initial task of the event manager is to develop a crowd management plan.

The Crowd Management Plan

The following are the key things to consider when developing this type of plan:

- the number of people at the venue (the event audience, staff, and contractors)
- the likely behavior of spectators (especially for events with a history of crowd behavior problems)
- the timing of the event, including session times and peak periods
- the layout of the venue and/or other facilities
- the security services to be provided or contracted
- the legal requirements and general guidelines

The last of these items requires adherence to occupational health and safety legislation and the laws relating to exits, as well as to a number of guidelines provided by various agencies, if applicable to the event, such as the following:

- **NFPA Standard 126—Pyrotechnics.** The National Fire Protection Association, Standard for Use of Pyrotechnics before a Proximate Audience, is the national consensus code applicable to both indoor pyrotechnics as well as outdoor displays. Although the NFPA 1120 has not been adopted in every state, the APA deems this standard to be the prudent operator's definitive guide, and urges members of the industry to strictly comply with the standard. (For more information about safety standards for all aspects of pyrotechnics, go to www.nfpa.org or to the American Pyrotechnics Association's Web site at www.americanpyro.com.)

- **Code 5.02 (Outdoor Lighting Code Handbook)—Outdoor Sports Lighting.** From the International Dark-Sky Association's handbook come outdoor lighting codes, including the requirements for lighting levels used for training, competition, and spectator viewing for outdoor night sports. (See www.darksky.org.)

- **ANSI/IES RO-1-1993 (American National Standard Practice for Office Lighting).** This sets forth the minimum requirements for electric lighting systems within office buildings in order to provide visual conditions that facilitate for safe working conditions as well as safe movement of people in the normal use of the building. (See www.globalihs.com.)

- **OSHA Code 1910.37 (Occupational Safety and Health Administration).** This code states that each exit route must be adequately lighted so that a person with normal vision can see along the exit route. Each exit must be clearly visible and marked by a sign reading "Exit." Each exit route door must be free of decorations or signs that obscure the visibility of the exit route door. It also states that each exit sign must be illuminated to a surface value of at least five foot-candles (54 lux) by a reliable light source and be distinctive in color. (For the entire code, go to www.osha.gov.)

All of the preceding standards, as well as many more that are relevant to building permanent and temporary structures, are available on the Web sites listed at the end of this chapter. The crowd management plan covers readily available information, such as the dimensions of the venue or site, but it also goes further to encompass the probable number of spectators at particular times of the event and their flow through the site. Clearly the peaks are the most problematic from a crowd management perspective, and the plan needs to address this and other challenges by covering the following:

- Estimate the level of attendance for specific days and times.
- Estimate the number of people using public corridors, specific entrances, and specific aisles and seating at particular times.
- Estimate the number of ushers and service and security personnel needed for crowd management.
- Establish the requirements for crowd control measures, such as barriers.
- Identify the areas that need to remain restricted.
- Develop an identification process for restricted access by specific staff.
- Identify particular hazards (for example, scaffolding and temporary structures).
- Identify routes by which emergency services personnel will enter and leave the site.
- Establish the means of communication for all staff working on the site.
- Establish a chain of command for incident reporting.

- Check safety equipment (for example, the number of fire extinguishers, and check to see that inspections have been carried out according to legal requirements).
- Identify the safety needs of specific groups of people, such as people with disabilities, children, and players/performers.
- Identify first-aid requirements and provision.
- Develop an emergency response plan (ERP).
- Develop an evacuation plan, and initiate training and drills for the staff concerned.

As we know, there are many different types of event venue, each having specific features and some being safer than others. They range from outdoor environments, such as streets and parks, to aquatic centers, indoor facilities, and purpose-built venues. The last of these is generally the safest, since crowd management and evacuation would generally have been considered at the time these structures were built and would have been rehearsed again and again by the venue team. However, a crowd management and evacuation plan would still need to be developed for each event held at the venue, because factors such as crowd numbers and movement would generally be different.

Major Risks

The major incidents that need to be considered in relation to crowd management and evacuation include the following:

- fire, smoke
- bomb threat, terrorism, threats to VIPs
- flood, earthquake, or other natural disasters
- heat, failure of air-conditioning or lighting
- gas leaks or biological hazards
- crowd crush, overcrowding, congestion
- riots, protests
- vehicle accidents
- collapsing fences or other structures

For each of the above, the response of the public to the emergency should be evaluated so that the emergency team has procedures in place for preventing panic. Reassuring messages on the public address system is one way of reducing panic and ensuring orderly evacuation.

The density of this event audience illustrates the importance of appropriate crowd control measures.

Crowd Management

Once a range of risks has been identified—in particular, risks such as congestion, overcrowding, and crowd crush—the circumstances that may lead to bad or destructive behavior in these contexts needs to be analyzed. The risks then need to be prioritized and plans put in place to avoid them (known as **preventative** measures) or to deal with them should they occur (known as **contingency** measures). An example of a preventative measure for reducing congestion at turnstiles is to employ staff to assist spectators and to monitor the area. Impatient crowds, however, might simply jump over the turnstile or knock it down. There would thus need to be a contingency plan in place for dealing with this situation. Property damage by spectators would also need to be covered, and procedures would be required for ejecting the offending spectators. At worst, the police may charge them. (Streakers who disrupt play during sports matches come to mind in this instance.) The more serious risk, however, are nonticketed spectators who gain illegal entry.

The following strategies (adapted from the Web site at the end of this chapter) may help to prevent deaths and injuries suffered by fans at rock concerts and other large events:

- Review the behavior of crowds attending similar past events.
- Review crowd responses to specific bands and performers at past rock concerts.

- Conduct an evaluation of all structures available for mosh pit management.
- Obtain engineering and specialist advice.
- Isolate the mosh pit from the general audience.
- Limit mosh pit capacity and density.
- Provide easy exits from the mosh pit area.
- Ban alcohol and cigarettes from the mosh pit.
- Station special first-aid assistance near the mosh pit.
- Ban stage diving, body surfing/swimming.
- Provide specially trained private security and "peer security."
- Provide special ventilation and drinking fountains for moshers.
- Pad the floor and all hard surfaces, including barriers and railings.
- Ban certain types of clothes and accessories worn by moshers in the pit.
- Introduce mosh pit safety announcements in advance of the show and during shows.
- Seek assistance from the performers in managing or preventing moshing.

Figure 16–1 lists a number of soccer disasters that have occurred in the past, all related to crowd management.

Emergency Planning

Every business needs to have guidelines for emergencies that impact normal workplace operations. The guidelines should include communication protocols and evacuation procedures. The U.S. Department of Justice offers a sample plan. By studying this sample plan, an event management team may get ideas that will help them in formulating their own emergency plan. Following are some of the highlights of their plan.

A Crisis Management Plan (CMP) is a detailed guide outlining the policies and procedures to be followed in case there is an emergency situation. The plan suggests that a Crisis Management Team (CMT) and an Evacuation Team be assembled.

The goals of the CMP are to do the following:

- Provide guidance to managers regarding appropriate procedures and resources
- Protect the safety and well-being of all employees
- Provide for the care of employees and their families through personnel services

1971	Glasgow, Scotland. Sixty-six people were crushed to death in what became known as the Ibrox disaster when Glasgow Rangers and Celtic fans clashed after a late goal.
1976	Yaounde, Cameroon. A fight broke out between the two teams, and the president of Cameroon sent in paratroopers by helicopter. Two bystanders were killed.
1982	Moscow, Russia. Police herded a group of fans into one section of the stadium during a European Cup match between Spartak Moscow and Haarlem. They were crushed by fans returning to the ground after a late goal. Official reports say that 60 people died, but the actual number was reportedly closer to 340.
1985	Brussels, Belgium. Drunken British Liverpool fans attacked rival Italian Juventus supporters during a European Champions Cup at the Heysel Stadium. Thirty-nine people were crushed or trampled to death after a concrete wall collapsed. More than 400 were injured.
1986	Guatemala City, Guatemala. At least 82 people died and about 150 were injured by stampeding fans prior to a 1998 World Cup qualifying match between Guatemala and Costa Rica.
1989	Hillsborough Stadium, Sheffield, England. Ninety-six fans died, many by crushing and asphyxiation. Over 300 people were injured during an FA Cup semi-final.
1991	Orkney, South Africa. At least 40 people were killed when fans panicked after brawls broke out.
1996	Lusaka, Zambia. Nine fans were crushed to death, and 78 other were injured during a stampede following Zambia's victory over Sudan in a World Cup qualifying game.
1996	Guatemala. Ninety people were killed and 150 injured in a crush during a World Cup qualifier.
2000	Harare, Zimbabwe. Violence broke out during a World Cup qualifier between South Africa and Zimbabwe after a late goal. Thirteen people were trampled to death when riot police fired tear gas.
2001	Johannesburg, South Africa. Forty-three people were crushed to death, and many hundreds were injured when excited fans tried to get into a capacity stadium. Some died outside, and others died inside, crushed against barricades at the side of the field.
2001	Accra, Ghana. A stampede triggered by police antiriot tactics at a soccer match left over 120 people dead. Police responded to the disruption by firing tear gas into the stands. Thousands of fans then fled the gas attack by rushing to a pedestrian tunnel. A horrible crush resulted, according to reports from the scene.

Figure 16–1   Soccer Disasters

- Minimize posttraumatic stress reaction among employees
- Ensure that accurate and appropriate information about the incident is conveyed to appropriate audiences
- Plan the orderly return of the workplace to a normal mode of operation
- Outline preventative measures that should be taken in advance

The Crisis Management Team is the team responsible for responding to the emergency. This team could include the following personnel:

- Crises Manager
- Administrative Coordinator

- Operations Coordinator
- Employee Support Coordinator
- Technical Support Coordinator

These individuals should generally be in attendance during the hours of operation, should show leadership qualities and sound judgment under pressure, and should be able to communicate clearly. The first of these attributes is the most problematic in the event business. For leased premises, the venue team is generally limited in number, and few work for the full duration of the event. The question of availability during an event, especially one with multiple sessions, is a key consideration for the committee. There is no point in having a well-trained CMT who is not in attendance! Following are the chief roles of each person in the CMT.

Crisis Manager

During normal operations, the Crisis Manager will have the responsibility of managing the crisis on-site. The CMT will assist with the decision-making processes. The duties of the crisis manager include ascertaining the nature and location of the emergency and determining the appropriate action; ensuring that emergency services and the Evacuation Team members are advised concerning evacuation; and briefing emergency personnel on their arrival.

Administrative Coordinator

The Administrative Coordinator is responsible for all administrative support needs of the CMT and works closely with the Crisis Manager. This person will assist with notifications and mobilizing resources; tracking the situation; and collecting, organizing, and distributing documentation. The Administrative Coordinator locates, procures, and stores items listed in the emergency equipment and supplies list before any crisis.

Operations Coordinator

The Operations Coordinator acts as a liaison between the CMT and operations staff to maintain operational efficiency. In addition, this person would assess and identify the operational needs, establish alternate sites as needed, coordinate transportation, and assist in the return to normal operations.

Employee Support Coordinator

This individual would coordinate psychological services, family support, and trauma recovery. These services should be available to all victims, families, and coworkers.

Technical Support Coordinator

The Technical Support Coordinator is responsible for setting up equipment for the command center and any other areas needed. He or she would oversee the setup of computer systems; ensure that proper telecommunication lines are available; set up monitors for televised newscasts; and troubleshoot any problems with either the computers or phone lines.

In addition, a separate Evacuation Team might be implemented with the following personnel:

- Floor Monitor
- Stairwell Monitors
- Handicapped Persons Monitor

Floor Monitor

The Floor Monitor is responsible for supervising and expediting the planned and controlled movement of individuals on his or her assigned floor in an emergency. The Floor Monitor must stay in constant communication with the Stairwell Monitor through the use of 2-way radios.

Stairwell Monitor

The Stairwell Monitor is responsible for control and movement of personnel from the floor via the designated evacuation stairway. The Stairwell Monitor will be identifiable by an orange vest. This person will stay in constant communication with the Floor Monitor. This person is the last person out and will close the door upon leaving.

Handicapped Persons Monitor

Under the direction of the Floor Monitor, this person assists physically challenged, injured, or other persons needing assistance during the building evacuation process. He or she reports the status of the handicapped or injured persons to the Floor Monitor.

Implementing Emergency Procedures

In order to effectively implement emergency procedures, the following steps should be taken:

- Review implementation issues, and integrate them with all other event operational plans.

- Ensure broad awareness of the procedures through wide dissemination of information and consultation with all concerned.
- Use signage and well-designed communication materials in a simple format to provide information.
- Train all staff.
- Test the procedures by conducting evacuation exercises.
- Review procedures to check effectiveness.

Fire Procedures

There are four major steps that ideally should be initiated concurrently:

1. Ensure the safety of everyone within the vicinity of the fire.
2. Call the fire department in any circumstance in which there is suspicion of fire.
3. Conduct evacuation.
4. Fight the fire with appropriate equipment, or retreat and close all doors.

Note that there is no need for anyone to give permission for a call to the fire department. This call can be initiated by anyone.

Evacuation Procedures

All staff should be trained in their specific roles in this situation. In the event of an evacuation, it is important for staff to do the following:

- remain calm
- be observant
- listen to and follow instructions
- provide information and instructions to staff and spectators when advised to do so
- maintain radio protocol (do not block channels)
- follow all safety precautions (such as not using elevators in case of fire)

A crisis management plan is reliant on the chain of command. Early warning means fast intervention. The U.S. Department of Justice offers this sample plan (Figure 16–2).

Bomb Threat Procedures

As with fire and evacuation procedures, there is a recommended procedure for dealing with bomb threats. Details are available from the FBI Bomb Data Center, which publishes a handbook giving standard

EMERGENCY INSTRUCTIONS FOR ALL EMPLOYEES

To Report

FIRE
If you discover a fire or smoke:
1. Sound the building alarm
2. Call 911*, Building Mgt. 662-1200* and the Crisis Mgr.
3. Follow instructions for all employees

BOMB THREAT
If you receive a bomb threat:
1. Record information on FBI Data card (Appendix E)
2. Call 911*, the Crisis Mgr and Building Mgt. 662-1200
3. Follow instructions for all employees

CHEMICAL OR BIOLOGICAL THREAT
If you receive a suspicious package/item containing a powdery substance, has strange odors, stains or leaks:
1. Do not handle.
2. Isolate the package and cordon off the area closing all doors leading to the area.
3. If you handled the item, wash exposed skin areas for at least three minutes with soap and water and rinse for one minute.
4. Notify SEPS and the Crisis Manager.
5. Avoid coworkers.
6. Wait for Hazmat team for possible decontamination procedure

MEDICAL EMERGENCY
If you have, or see someone with, a medical emergency:
1. Call 911*
2. Administer first aid or request assistance.
3. Call Crisis Manager

* You must dial "9" for an outside line.
** In case of evacuation no beverages, food or bulky items are to be carried into the stairwells

Other than reporting

FIRE
All employees should:
1. Close windows and **leave doors open and unlocked**
2. Evacuate** the building in accordance with the emergency evacuation plan for the area in which you are located at the time of the alarm
3. Proceed to primary staging area at the Columbia Square corner of 12th and F Sts., NW.
4. Standby for further instructions

BOMB THREAT
All employees should:
1. If directed – search immediate area for suspicious object (voluntary basis only)
   a. If package found – do not touch
   b. Call Bomb Squad – 911*
   c. Evacuate area.
2. If evacuation** of the building is required follow the evacuation plan
3. Proceed to primary staging area at Columbia Square
4. Standby for further instructions

CHEMICAL OR BIOLOGICAL THREAT
All employees should:
1. Stay away from the suspected area and from anyone potentially exposed.
2. If an evacuation is ordered, follow normal evacuation procedures.

EARTHQUAKE
All employees should:
1. Take cover under table, desk, or in doorway.
2. **Do not** run outdoors.

SEVERE WEATHER
All employees should:
1. Prepare to move to a place of safety.
2. Stay away from large windows.
3. Standby for further instructions.

* You must dial "9" for an outside line.
** In case of evacuation no beverages, food or bulky items are to be carried into the stairwells 2

Figure 16–2   Emergency Instructions to All Employees

Available from the **Bomb Data Center** upon request.

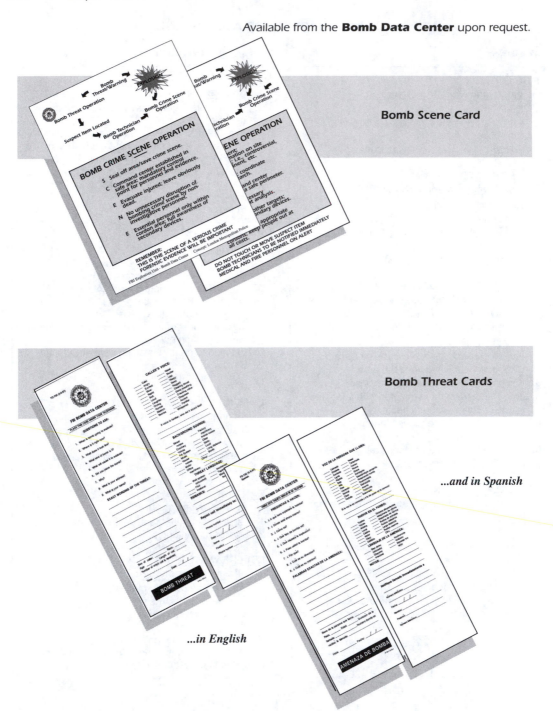

Bomb Scene Card

Bomb Threat Cards

...and in Spanish

...in English

Figure 16–3   Bomb Threat Checklist
Source: Reprinted with the permission of the FBI Bomb Threat Division.

guidelines that can be kept near all telephones. These include the following:

- evaluation (deciding whether or not to take action, and whether to search, with or without evacuation)
- notification (police should be advised)
- search (the aim is identification of the suspicious object, which should not be touched or moved)

In Figure 16–3 there is a checklist, which should also be kept near the telephone, outlining the questions to ask and information to secure about the caller.

Case Study

You are going to rent a venue for a fashion show. The venue you have in mind is an old theater that lends itself well to the event, with excellent sight lines for the audience. However, the decor and lighting planned by your artistic director for your fashion parade may compromise safety. Drapes over the ceiling area will obscure the normal lighting and will prevent the fire sensors and sprinklers from working correctly. Also, there are a number of props that may hinder access into and out of the venue. On the other hand, the audience expected is quite small. Answer the following questions:

- What are some of the safety risks associated with this event?
- Who is responsible for the safety of the venue and the audience?
- With whom should you discuss the risks associated with your event concept?
- How could the risks be reduced?
- What sorts of contingency plans could be developed?
- What should the evacuation plan include?

Activities

1. Visit www.crowdsafe.com, and list five major crowd control problems that have led to significant numbers of casualties at rock concerts.
2. Visit an event venue, and evaluate the emergency plan in terms of the following:

   - the venue's physical features and likely emergency risks

Summary

In this chapter we have dealt with one of the most problematic issues for event managers: crowd control. Unfortunately, there are many examples of events at which people have lost their lives through fire or riot, and there are many examples of near-misses. For every event, emergency response plans for crowd control and evacuation in case of fire or other major risk must be developed. These plans must comply with the relevant legislation and standards, and must be properly implemented. All possible preventative measures need to be put in place prior to the event. Staff training and contingency planning are other key aspects of the emergency response plan.

- the venue map, emergency equipment, and access for emergency services
- entrances and exits for the event audience
- the clarity of roles for staff involved
- reporting relationships
- communication technologies
- record keeping
- other legal compliance or adherence to standards

Links

www.crowdsafe.com/mosh.html (strategies for ensuring crowd safety)
www.osha.org
www.usdoj.gov

Chapter Seventeen
MONITORING, CONTROL, AND EVALUATION

The Sole Burner is an annual event for the American Cancer Society and has become the largest run/walk of its kind in Appleton, Wisconsin. It first began in 1983 with 40 participants raising $4,000.00. Throughout the years, the event has grown to be the Society's largest event of its kind in Wisconsin, with a goal of raising $255,000 for 2003. The Sole Burner is both a serious and social event. The event is designed to rally community support for the American Cancer Society and recognize Cancer survivors as well as promoting the value of a 5K run or walk.

It is also designed to raise money for American Cancer Society programs of research, education, advocacy, patient, and family services.

And lastly, it is an event that is organized and staged by volunteers. Sponsor donations help cover expenses.

Reproduced with permission of Sole Burner, www.soleburner.org

On completion of this chapter, you will be able to

- develop and implement preventative and feedback control systems;
- plan an evaluation strategy;
- use research approaches to identify the composition of an event audience;
- use research approaches to evaluate the success of an event from the customer, staff, and management viewpoints; and
- write an event evaluation report.

This is an outstanding example of event evaluation in that it demonstrates the association's achievement of its objectives, which were to raise awareness of the work of the American Cancer Society and also to raise awareness of walking and running as a viable form of exercise and to provide a motivational goal for commitment to regular exercise as an integral part of a healthy lifestyle. However, in addition to the findings that supported the health-related objectives, it was found that many of the participants were from outside the Appleton area, resulting in a positive economic impact from tourism on the region. Many of the participants saw the walk as a family outing, demonstrating a positive social impact as well.

In this chapter we will look at two aspects of event management: control and evaluation. Control systems are essential in ensuring that procedures are followed (for cash handling and recording entrants, for example) and that performance measures are achieved.

Evaluation is the process of measuring the success of an event against its objectives. The data from performance measures are used in this analysis. Using the example of the preceding run/walk, control systems would ensure that all participants were registered, whereas evaluation would involve an analysis of the questions on the registration form and feedback after the event. If a significant number of local residents joined the walk without registering, this outcome would indicate a lack of control measures and would naturally have an impact on the evaluation findings.

Monitoring and Control Systems

The challenge for the event manager is to delegate and monitor effectively and not to micromanage (become too involved with detail). While attention to detail is positive, this should be left to the event manager's team. A successful event manager needs to be aware that during the peak time of an event, nonstandard situations and incidents will require his or her time, meaning that all routine procedures and control systems need to be in place before the event. Such control systems ensure that information filtering to the top of the event organization will prompt management to make decisions to intervene only if things are not going according to plan.

Take, for example, the simple situation of T-shirts and caps being sold through an outlet at an event. How would an event manager know whether the cash passed over the counter were reaching the till or whether all the merchandise were reaching the outlet? A simple procedure for recording the number of boxes of stock issued and an hourly check of stock and cash levels would immediately show any shortfall.

Preventative Controls and Feedback Controls

There are two types of controls: preventative and feedback. A preventative control is established early in the planning process. For example, checking the quality of incoming food for a banquet is a preventative control measure, as is monitoring food temperatures to avoid food poisoning. Signed requisition forms are another preventative measure that is designed to curtail unauthorized spending and not meeting the budget. A checklist for setting up sporting equipment before an international gymnastics event is another example of a preventative control measure. This would need to be designed to ensure that setup would meet international specifications: if measurements were inaccurate, injury could be caused to an athlete or an athlete could be disqualified. In Figure 17–1 we have included an example of a site inspection checklist.

Venue Checklist	☐
Plans to scale (all venue dimensions)	☐
Disability access	☐
Capacity for seating and standing	☐
Sight lines for event audience (no pillars, obstructions)	☐
Capacity for storage	☐
Appropriate number of toilets, suitable locations	☐
Suitability of food and beverage preparation and service areas	☐
Accessibility for delivery and installation of equipment, food, etc.	☐
Correct number of tables, chairs, plates, glasses, etc.	☐
Emergency evacuation plan	☐
Safety of venue (fire equipment, entrances and exits)	☐
Preferred contractors (e.g. security, catering)	☐
Fixed and rental equipment requirements	☐
Electrical supply	
Water supply (especially for temporary kitchens)	☐
Venue limitations	☐
Outstanding issues/actions	☐

Figure 17–1   Site Inspection Checklist

Feedback controls are put in place to assist with decisions during an event. For example, feedback would be required to decide on the point at which event merchandise should be discounted to avoid having stock left over. If you discount too early, you lose revenue. If you discount too late, you find yourself with stock that has no sale value. Incident reporting is another form of feedback control: if a series of similar incidents have occurred, preventative measures need to be implemented. As an example, the reporting of a number of slips and falls in the kitchen over a period of days would require the implementation of a preventative measure, which might be thorough overnight cleaning, sandpapering the floor, and painting it with a nonstick surface or providing mats to cover the slippery areas.

In most industries, information from point-of-sale and stock control systems is the feedback used for measuring and managing sales and profit levels over a particular period. However, in the event industry, decisions about price and other product features are made before the event, with sales occurring over a very short time period, allowing little opportunity to respond to financial information during an event. For that reason, it is very important to collect and store information on aspects of an event, such as merchandise sales, for use as a precedent for the next event of a similar nature.

Operational Monitoring and Control

There are a number of issues in relation to operational procedures that need to be addressed before the event begins. These include the necessity for delegation of responsibility and flexibility in carrying out procedures, the effect of control systems on customers, and the importance of financial controls.

Implementation of Priority or High-Risk Procedures

If the procedure is one that involves high risk, it must be fixed, detailed, and well documented. There can be no deviation from this type of procedure. It must be part of training and readily available to those who need to use it. The procedure for emergency evacuation is a good example. Posters and signs must be erected to assist staff in remembering their training on evacuation, and controls must be put in place for checking on emergency systems, such as exits, firefighting equipment, announcement and crowd management equipment (for example, loudspeakers), and access for emergency vehicles.

Delegation of Decision Making

A flat organizational structure is essential for the successful operation of an event, so that some parts of the event manager's role must be delegated. At most events, the pace is so fast that it is crucial that staff be in a position to make decisions on the spot. This is particularly important for volunteers (many of whom are well qualified in other roles) who generally need to know that they have a part to play in the problem-solving process. Only decisions on such important matters as evacuation need to be referred to the more senior staff on duty. Event staff need to be trained to make decisions when minor incidents occur, and each of these incidents needs to be recorded in a log book for analysis at the end of the shift or at the end of the day. Checks and monitors will ensure that delegation is managed well, that quality service is provided, and that costs are contained.

Flexibility in Operational Procedures

Since flexibility is required in many aspects of event management, most particularly in the operational phase, it is important that the desired outcomes are fully understood by all staff. Staff, too, need to be able to think on their feet and make quick decisions about changing noncritical procedures where circumstances demand it. This ability is, in fact, one of the most desirable attributes of event operations staff.

Assuring Customer Satisfaction

In some cases, control systems can serve to frustrate customers, and at times, customers will endeavor to circumvent the system by trying, for example, to do the following:

- enter areas without accreditation
- purchase alcohol for underage drinkers
- change their seating to a better area
- break the rules for rides (about height, attire, or use of safety equipment, for example)
- cut across crowd control barriers
- stand or sit in the aisles

In each of these cases, a decision needs to be made by event staff as to what to do. If a customer is refusing to wear safety equipment for a ride, for example, customer safety considerations should come before customer satisfaction. On the other hand, if you were confronted by customers frustrated by having to walk an extra distance as a result of crowd control barriers when there are clearly no crowds, you may decide to move the barriers to allow them through.

Controlling Finances

Financial control can be assured by the following:

- using a requisition system for purchases/expenditure that limits those people authorized to spend over a certain dollar limit
- ensuring that all expenditure is accounted for and documented
- checking goods against requisition and order forms
- checking stock levels
- using financial systems that maintain up-to-date information on income and expenditure
- using financial systems to forecast cash flow
- ensuring that everyone understands the budget and current financial position

Control of point-of-sale systems, or registers, can be achieved by these measures:

- checking and securing seed money
- checking that cash received is accurately recorded and/or processed through the point-of-sale system/register

- checking that point-of-sale terminal/register printouts have been balanced against cash takings (after removing the initial seed money)
- checking that cash and documents have been securely transported and stored
- checking that banking documentation has been retained and balanced against statements issued by the bank

The following suggestions for monitoring and controlling event operations have been provided by experienced event organizers:

- **Check** everything, over and over.
- Write everything down, including promises made by your contractors and requests made by your client.
- Develop checklists for everything possible.
- Check the venue before you move in, and note any existing damage.
- Never leave the venue until the last staff member has finished.
- Check the venue before leaving—some things may have been accidentally left on (gas) or left behind (including people).
- Pay attention to detail at every stage.
- Schedule carefully, since the audience has little patience with long-winded speeches, for example.
- Maintain a contingency fund for unexpected expenses.
- Involve the sponsor at every stage.
- Get approvals for use of logos before printing.
- Don't take safety knowledge for granted; repeat often.
- Train staff to be observant.
- **Check** everything, over and over.

Evaluation

Evaluation is an area that is frequently neglected following an event. This neglect is unfortunate, because there are many benefits to be gained from a critique of the event. From a quality viewpoint, it allows those involved to learn from their experience and to improve operations. For those not involved, it provides a body of information for future planning of events. If you can't learn from your own experience, at least you can learn from someone else's.

Evaluation needs to be planned before the event, the event objectives generally guiding the evaluation process. In Chapter 9 on planning, the concept of developing event aims and objectives was introduced; and in Chapter 5 on marketing, the importance of understanding the target audience was discussed, together with the consumer's decision-making process. Now we will highlight the benefits of evaluation by sharing the objectives about The Oregon Shakespeare Festival as well as an economic impact study for the region where the festival is held (see Figures 17–2 and 17–3). Annual research into the demographics and behavior of the attendees has been a contributing factor to this outcome, allowing the event organizers to plan for the following event and to improve the figures every year.

Evaluation Methods

When planning evaluation, it is very important to work out what information you require. For example, participants entering a cycling race may be asked for their age and address, which would allow an analysis in terms of their general demographics. What a pity if they were not asked whether they had participated before, how they had heard about the event, and when they had made the decision to take part. This information would greatly assist the organizers of the next event.

Background

The Oregon Shakespeare Festival traces its roots back to the Chautauqua movement, which brought culture and entertainment to rural areas of the country in the late 19th century. Ashland's first Chautauqua building—erected in 1893, mostly by townspeople—saw its first performance on July 5. The Oregon Shakespearean Festival was officially born on July 2, 1935, with a production of *Twelfth Night*. Reserved seats cost $1, with general admission of $.50 for adults and $.25 for children. Even at those prices, the Festival covered its own expenses. It is among the oldest and largest professional regional repertory theatre companies in the United States.

Facts and Figures

- The Oregon Shakespeare Festival has the oldest existing full-scale Elizabethan stage in the Western Hemisphere, built on the site of the old Chautauqua theatre established in 1893.

- Presents an eight-month season of 11 plays—four by Shakespeare and seven by classic and contemporary playwrights—in rotating repertory in three theatres; the outdoor Elizabethan Stage (seats 1,190), the Angus Bowmer Theatre (seats 601), and the intimate New Theatre (seats 270–360).

- Offers a school visit program which annually sends actors to more than 275 schools, presenting performances and workshops in Shakespeare and modern literature to more than 150,000 students in Alaska, California, Kansas, Nevada, New Mexico, Oregon and Washington.

- Employs approximately 450 theatre professionals from all over the country.

- Has a volunteer staff of nearly 750, which received the President's Volunteer Action Award in Washington, DC in 1986.

Figure 17–2   The Oregon Shakespeare Festival
Source: Reproduced with the permission of the Oregon Shakespeare Festival.

**OREGON SHAKESPEARE FESTIVAL
ECONOMIC IMPACT – 2002**

	Festival Operations						
	Individual Parties		Groups		School Groups		
Total ticket sales for the year	307,105	77%	14,616	4%	77,889	19%	399,609
% of Visitors Who Come Specifically to Attend the Plays	257,986	84%	14,616	100%	77,889	100%	
Ticket Sales to:							
Local Groups	38,695	15%	1,900	13%	7,010	9%	
Visiting Groups	219,273	85%	12,716	87%	70.879	91%	
Average number of plays seen	3.8		2.8		2.7		
Number of Individuals Seeing the Plays is:							
Locals	10,183		679		2,596		13,458
Visitors	57,703		4,541		26,251		88,496
							101,954
Average Number of Nights Stayed							
Visitors	3.7		2.2		1.7		
Average Daily Expenditure for Visitors Excluding Theatre Tickets	$ 97.39		$ 97.39		$ 85.11		
Total Expenditures for							
Visitors	$20,792,715		$972,998		$3,798,336		$25,564,048
Fesitval's Budgeted Expenditures for the Year							$19,030,187
Total Direct Impact							$44,594,235
Oregon Multiplier						x	2.9
Total Economic Impact of Festival Operations							$129,323,300

Figure 17–3 Oregon Shakespeare Festival Economic Impact—2002
Source: Reproduced with the permission of the Oregon Shakespeare Festival.

The type of information just described can be obtained from surveys conducted before, during, and after an event by completion of forms or through personal interviews. Alternatively, a small focus group of participants can provide valuable information through group discussion.

The following are examples of questions that may be included in a customer survey for an informal postevaluation report. However, to obtain a more reliable report, the survey would need to be designed and analyzed by a market research company.

- How did you find out about this event?
- Why did you decide to come to the event?
- When did you decide to come to the event?
- Did you come to the event with other people?
- Who was the main decision maker?
- How did this event meet your expectations?
- Was the public transportation/parking adequate?
- Did you get value for money?
- Were the food and beverage adequate?
- Were the seating, sound, and vision adequate?
- Would you attend this event again?
- Why would you recommend/not recommend the event to others?
- How could the event be improved?

In the case of an exhibition, the questions would be something like the following:

- Why did you come to this exhibition?
- Do you have the authority to purchase at this exhibition?
- Did you place any orders at this exhibition?
- Do you plan to place any orders as a direct result of the exhibition?
- Did you come to this exhibition last year?
- When did you decide to come to the exhibition?
- Have you traveled from another state to visit the exhibition?
- What were the best features of the exhibition?
- How could the exhibition be improved?

Staff Debriefings

Meetings of event staff and stakeholders can generate valuable information for the evaluation report. Some of the questions addressed in this type of meeting include these:

- What went well, and why?
- What went badly, and why?

- How could operations be improved?
- Were there any significant risk factors that we did not antici-pate?
- Was there a pattern to any of the incidents reported?
- Are there any outstanding legal issues, such as injuries or accidents?
- Are there any implications for staff recruitment and training?
- How would you describe the organization and management of the event—in the planning and the operational phases?
- What can we learn from this event?

Financial Records

Audited financial records, together with a number of planning and other documents, are an essential component of postevent analysis and reporting. These include the following:

- audited financial statements
- budgets
- revenue, banking, and account details
- point-of-sale reconciliation
- payroll records
- the risk management plan
- incident reports
- minutes of meetings
- insurance policies
- contracts with other agencies and organizations, such as rental companies and cleaning companies
- asset register
- promotional materials
- operational plans
- policies and procedures
- training materials
- database of attendees/participants if possible
- record of results of competitions
- event evaluation and statistics (including attendance)
- event or sponsor report

It is one thing to know that you have managed a successful event but quite another to prove it. The event manager needs more than informal feedback from the after-event party. A summary report evaluating the event against specific aims and objectives is an absolute necessity.

The Broader Impact of Events

Events can have an economic, political, physical, and social impact on the community (Hall, 1992; McDonnell et al., 1999). The economic impact of an event can be both direct (spending by international visitors) or indirect (the flow that occurs when related businesses benefit from the expenditure of event visitors). For example, farmers, wholesale suppliers of flowers, and food production companies would benefit from increased sales, and this outcome in turn would prompt further expenditure on their past as demand for their products increased. Economists and tourism analysts have shown that events such as the Mardi Gras in New Orleans or the Superbowl have an impact on the U.S. economy. Tourism, in fact, plays a significant role in the economy. According to the Travel Industry Association of America, in 2001, the U.S. travel industry received more than $555 billion, including international passenger fares, from domestic and international travelers. These travel expenditures, in turn, generated nearly 7.9 million jobs for Americans, with nearly $174 billion in payroll income. Approximately one out of every eighteen U.S. residents in the civilian labor force was employed as a result of direct travel spending in the United States during 2001. Events such as festivals, meetings, conventions, and exhibitions that increase the level of international tourist visitation have a positive economic benefit by increasing export earnings.

Political benefits clearly accrue when events raise the profile of a town, city or country. When a region enjoys a surge in tourism, increased economic benefits and the associated reduction in unemployment lead to support for politicians at both local and state levels. Of course the reverse occurs when an event has a negative impact on the community. Events often increase community spirit, bringing social benefits as well. For example, the many multicultural events held in the United States expand our cultural perspective, whereas rave parties where drug abuse is prevalent can have a negative impact.

The physical impact of events is evident in the construction of new infrastructure, such as roads, railways, and sporting venues. However, events can have a negative environmental impact by causing damage or creating offensive noise. A good example of an event with an extremely positive environmental impact on the community is the Great American Cleanup™, our country's largest annual community involvement program. In 2002, nearly 2.3 million people

Summary

This chapter has looked at two neglected aspects of event management: control and evaluation. Control systems are necessary to ensure that plans are carried out, yet often the event deadlines draw near too soon for these systems to be developed. Preventative controls are established during the early planning phase of an event, whereas feedback controls help with decisions during the event. If control systems meet best practice standards, they will reduce risk and ensure that there will be ample evidence if a court action should occur. Evaluation is required to ensure that an event meets the aims and objectives identified in the planning strategy. The capacity to show that these objectives (for example, financial, safety, customer satisfaction) have been met is one way of guaranteeing that the event management team is selected for future events.

volunteered for the Great American Cleanup™ by renovating playgrounds, cleaning up waterways and seashores, picking up litter, planting trees, beautifying parks, removing graffiti, and restoring buildings.

Case Study

There are 28 college football bowl games held in various cities throughout the United States. From the Rose Bowl to the Fiesta Bowl, the Gator Bowl to the Liberty Bowl, the ever-increasing list of bowl games shows American's passion for football. The bowl games are generally held between December 17 and January 3, in an atmosphere of friendly competition. Many of the bowl games include numerous events leading up to the game. The Rose Bowl is part of the Tournament of Roses, which includes one of the country's most beloved parades, The Rose Parade. The Tournament is more than just a parade and football game. According to its official Web site, it has become "America's New Year Celebration," a greeting to the world on the first day of the year and a salute to the community spirit and love of pageantry that have thrived in Pasadena for more than a century.

More information can be obtained from www.tournamentofroses.com, or for information about other bowl games, visit www.football.about.com.

Take a look at one of the bowl games and some of the events held in conjunction with the game. Select one event, and develop a range of objectives for that event and a corresponding strategy for evaluating the success of the event.

Activity

Investigate a control system to be put in place at an event, and evaluate its effectiveness (or lack of it). This system may relate to the following:

- registration of participants
- cash handling
- safety
- food hygiene
- purchasing and control
- staff accreditation

inks

www.soleburner.org
www.osfashland.org (Oregon Shakespeare Festival)
www.kab.org (Keep America Beautiful and the Great American Cleanup™)
www.tournamentofroses.com
www.football.about.com

Chapter Eighteen
CAREERS IN A CHANGING ENVIRONMENT

Cultural festivals include arts festivals, popular and classical music festivals, film festivals, and dance and craft festivals. In addition to cultural events, each state hosts numerous sporting events, some with international profiles, such as the U.S. Open Grand Slam Tennis Tournament. The meetings, incentives, conference, and exhibition industry also contributes to the total number of events held in the United States, as do all product launches and large-scale private parties.

This chapter is about employment prospects and specializations for those planning a career in the event industry, which, as you can see from the preceding, is a growth area. It also covers the current issues of concern for event organizers, since up-to-date knowledge of the industry is essential for everyone involved in it.

Crowd management and crowd control are the most problematic areas. Attending or participating in an event is a risky leisure pursuit, and event organizers have ethical obligations to ensure that the latest knowledge and the latest technology are applied to ensuring the safety of staff, the audience, and the participants. Knowledge of audience psychology, as we have seen, can help to more accurately predict crowd behavior and some of the problems that might occur.

An event manager thus needs to be an expert in psychology, crowd behavior, consumer decision making, financial management, human resource management, marketing, safety, and logistics. Legal knowledge is also helpful, as is a solid understanding of risk issues. Nonetheless, the event business provides an adrenalin rush for all those involved. As happy and excited faces stream out of the venue, the memories of all those planning problems—and your tiredness— soon fade. Although the event manager's role is hardly that of party host and is more about long hours and hard work, it is still fun.

On completion of this chapter, you will be able to:

- discuss economic, social and other changes that will have an impact on the field of event management;
- discuss the attributes of a successful event manager;
- evaluate a range of career choices in the area of event management; and
- discuss the similarities and differences between event management and project management in other industries.

Job Opportunities

Apart from the position of Event Manager for which you would require education, training, and experience in other roles, there are many other jobs available in the industry. As someone wishing to enter the event industry, you could consider positions in one of the functional areas described in Chapter 14, such as venue operations, catering, technology, or registration. These positions include the following:

- Operations and Logistics Manager
- Entertainment Manager
- Sports Competition Manager
- Risk Manager
- Tourism Event Coordinator
- Security Coordinator
- Venue Manager
- Catering and Waste Manager
- Pyrotechnics Consultant
- Administration Co-coordinator
- Sponsorship Manager
- Lighting/Sound Engineer
- Technology Support Officer—Meetings
- Technology Support Officer—Exhibitions
- Event Designer
- Registration Manager
- Equipment Rental Sales Manager

The following job descriptions (lists of tasks) provide some insight into just a few of the just-mentioned positions.

Event Manager

As the overall organizer of an event, the manager performs a large number of roles. Following are some of the duties you may find in a job description for Event Manager.

Tasks

1. Develop an event concept, purpose, and objectives.
2. Establish a committee and/or event planning team if not already in place.
3. Review the feasibility of the event to maximize strengths and opportunities.
4. Conduct a risk management analysis to minimize weaknesses and risks.

There are many jobs for catering staff in the events industry.

5. Develop a marketing plan for the event.
6. Develop budget, break-even, and cash-flow analyses.
7. Prepare detailed event plans, and obtain the support of the stakeholders, as well all required approvals.
8. Organize specific theme and staging effects.
9. Recruit and select staff, train, and lead staff effectively.
10. Develop detailed plans for event safety and security, including emergencies.
11. Develop policies and procedures for event logistics and daily operation.
12. Develop monitoring and control systems, as well as evaluation procedures.
13. Write a postevent evaluation report to be presented to sponsors/ stakeholders.

Venue Manager

The Venue Manager is generally a permanent employee who is familiar with all aspects of the venue and provides a service to anyone who books the venue. It is essential that the roles of the Venue Manager and the Event Manager are clear, because these two individuals are often employed by different organizations. For example, a venue will have preferred security contractors and/or cleaning contractors, and this arrangement can sometimes lead to conflict with the event organizing committee if it, too, has preferred suppliers of these services.

Tasks

1. Develop a site diagram, site dimensions, and specifications.
2. Negotiate contracts and deposits/fees.
3. Negotiate organizational structure and staffing with the event organizer (e.g., responsibility for cleaning and/or security).
4. Discuss site needs for performers.
5. Discuss site needs for the event audience/spectators.
6. Review the feasibility of plans for logistics and operations.
7. Provide support for setup, including signs and crowd management facilities.
8. Ensure development and implementation of safety and security plans.
9. Monitor the site for health, safety, and cleanliness.
10. Work with the event team to ensure that the emergency evacuation plan is in place and that roles are clear.
11. Check entrances, exits, and equipment (i.e., public address system, security communication system).
12. Assist with teardown at the end of the event.
13. Check all assets, and monitor security during teardown.
14. Manage payment of fees.

Exhibition Registration Manager

The registration of people visiting an exhibition is a key role, and in many cases exhibition organizers do their best to register participants beforehand for two reasons: it saves time on entry to the exhibition, and it allows for the registration of participants who intend to visit but do not make it on the day. When completing the registration form, the person indicates his or her area of interest in the exhibition, and this information allows exhibitors to target this person for advertising. The database of visitors to an exhibition is a most valuable asset. Therefore, technical hitches must be avoided at all cost because they can cause delays and, at worst, loss of data. (One exhibition manager reported that the loss of his data resulted from a power surge to his computer.)

Tasks

1. Meet with the committee/organizer to establish registration requirements, in particular the system for registration and the data to be captured.

2. Develop a registration plan, including selection of software or specialist subcontractor, and a schedule for the complete process.

3. Develop an operational plan and diagram for the registration area, and review feasibility with the venue concerned, with particular emphasis on network cabling and backup electrical supply.

4. Recruit, select, and train staff for registration duties.

5. Assist with planning of advance mail-out advertising, including information on preregistration.

6. Organize name tags, magnetic cards, or other materials for registration.

7. Set up registration area.

8. Allocate duties to staff, and schedule tasks to suit level of demand.

9. Manage operational issues, questions, problems, and complaints.

10. Monitor and manage those waiting in lines.

11. Close registration, and provide required reports to exhibition managers.

The positions available in the event business are many and varied. Quite often people find themselves working on events, having come from other fields such as sport administration, entertainment, television production, and even nursing. This last example is indicative of how a medical background can be highly relevant to other roles such as first-aid training and occupational health and safety training, leading ultimately to a role in risk management. Figure 18–1 gives a sampling of actual job openings in the event management industry.

Keeping Up-to-Date

Anyone planning a career in events must stay up-to-date with trends. Fashions change rapidly, and one cannot afford to come up with stale or outdated ideas. It is thus essential to stay up-to-the-minute with trends in entertainment and the arts. The Web site for Bizbash provided at the end of this chapter is just one site that will stir your imagination. The Web site also lists a number of event fiascos from which some good lessons can be learned, such as remembering to turn off the sprinkler system before the guests assemble on the lawn! We've included a few of our favorite event bloopers in Figure 18–2. The activity

Events Managers

Expanding trade association seeks organized, creative manager to plan workshops and special events. Responsibilities include budgeting, scheduling, site selection, contract review/negotiations, catering, and all related meeting activities. Candidate must have excellent computer/communication skills; marketing background a plus.

Meeting Coordinator

A pharmaceutical industry association seeks meeting coordinator and speaker assistant. Candidate should be highly organized and able to manage multiple tasks. Support a team of meeting planners and program managers to provide administrative and logistical support for over 20 conferences and seminars ranging in size from 10–1,000 attendees; creating and distributing marketing materials; coordinating with staff, speakers, hotels, and vendors, managing accounts receivables.

Catering Manager

Candidate will coordinate catering functions at a busy convention and event center. Catering manager will work with our catering consultants who will handle all incoming catering inquiries from large conventions to wedding parties up to 3,500 guests. Responsibilities include job pricing, customer contact, follow up as well as staff training, scheduling, and overseeing jobs. Other duties include rental pricing as well as billing and receiving payments.

Exhibitor Services Manager

A business college degree and a minimum of two years of sales, convention services, or hospitality experience preferred. Customer service and telemarketing experience is paramount. This challenging position requires extraordinary interpersonal skills, oral and written communication, and the ability to exercise independent judgment

with minimal supervision. You must be a team player with the ability to perform well under pressure due to constant deadlines. Computer literacy is also a must.

Concessions Operations Manager

This manager will oversee the food and beverage operations on the three levels of general seating at a major sports arena. Duties include training of all personnel; assisting the director in all operations; maintaining and keeping accurate records; inspect all performance to ensure service standards are being achieved; work with culinary department to ensure food quantities are ready for each shift; inspect all areas for cleanliness and possible safety hazards; follow HR and Union procedures regarding hiring, discipline, and terminations; prepares weekly schedules. Employee must be available to work evenings, weekends, and holidays if necessary.

Event Supervisors

This role involves overseeing the service provided by ushers and event staff. Employee will manage a team for a minimum of three shifts over four days. Previous experience with two-way radio, large crowds, and working with volunteers would be useful. You must have excellent communication and team leadership skills.

Communication Executive

We are looking for a special person with strong communication skills to manage the content, production, and presentation of all event communication material, whether written, published, or electronically presented. You will be required to manage a comprehensive media program.

Vice President of Banquet Operations

This senior executive position is to influence restructuring of banquet and conference services for a major resort. Extensive experience required

Figure 18–1 Employment Opportunities

at premier properties in excess of 100,000 square feet of space. A very unique opportunity with major expansion planned.

Director of Sales

Convention and Visitor's Bureau is seeking a strong director of sales with convention and meeting sales experience a plus. This individual would understand citywide conventions and have a thorough understanding of vertical and geographic markets. This director will be required to direct and train a strong sales team to shift gears from current focus on corporate small business to major group and convention business.

Risk Management

Responding to a senior executive, the appointee will be responsible for the ongoing assessment of risk exposures, controls, and responses and overseeing compliance. A major focus will be the enhancement of risk management systems, policies, and strategies and the analysis and reporting of risks.

Sponsorship and Events Manager

We are a nonprofit organization. Your role would involve managing the delivery of all fund-raising activities, developing and maintaining relations with corporate sponsors, planning and budgeting, as well as management of operational committees. You must have the ability to communicate on a professional level and have experience in business development.

Promotions Coordinator

Popular bar and nightclub is seeking a creative and energetic person to develop and promote theme nights and special events. The position involves organizing promotions from concept design to execution for a facility that has a capacity to seat over 600 people. A marketing or event management background would be helpful.

Entertainment Director

Guest relations professional with flair, creativity, and initiative is required to take on a new and exciting opportunity. The position will involve creating and managing entertainment, as well as social activities for guests and assisting the sales team in liaising with journalists and photographers.

Special Events Rental Consultant

The ideal candidate will have a strong knowledge of planning and coordinating of special events. Must be able to travel within the region to conduct site surveys for tent installation, produce accurate site drawings, and be familiar with rental accessories as well as computer literate. Candidate also must be willing to put in long hours during the busy season and not be afraid to "roll up their sleeves" when needed. We offer a base salary plus end of year bonus based on performance, full health benefits, 401K, and mileage allowance.

Sponsorship Executive

In conjunction with our external consultants, you will be involved in the development of proposals and identification of prospective sponsors. You will also be responsible for developing and delivering all sponsorship benefits to a large sponsor base.

Figure 18–1   Continued

suggested at the end of this chapter involving the development of a portfolio relevant to the event industry is also designed to stimulate your creativity.

However, in addition to creative ideas, it is also essential to stay up-to-date with economic trends. Regular visits to tourism Web sites,

A successful event planner not only needs nerves of steel but also the ability to make lemonade out of lemons at a moment's notice. From bizbash .com, a Web site for event planners, come a few real-life examples of event faux pas and foibles and what the quick-thinking planners did to try to save the event or what they learned for future events.

Fishy Thank-You Gift

Karen Loftin sent this blooper from her time as director of sales for a Texas hotel: "My staff and I decided to put together an appreciation luncheon for our top clients. At each setting we spotlighted a thank-you gift of a beta fish in a beautiful glass vase. My catering director used tap water to fill the vases, and as we sat down with the clients, the fish were literally dying before our eyes. It was a lovely time as I took each vase out of the room and took out the dead fish. I handed guests their thank-you gifts (the now-empty vases) as they left, and two women really got upset about the fish dying in front of them. Needless to say, a grand time was had by all."

It's Raining Inside

The venue "Float" had a hard time living up to its name at a recent Mediabistro cocktail party. After guests were greeted by no heat in the building—on an already very chilly winter night—the club's water pipes froze and burst. That caused another problem when droplets of water from the pipes began to fall on an outdoor heat lamp, which was set up in an attempt to warm the place up, and puffs of smoke floated upward—setting off the smoke detectors and the sprinkler system. An indoor rainstorm ensued, and after ten firefighters showed up, the venue was evacuated. Party hostess and Mediabistro founder **Laurel Touby** tried to salvage the sinking event by moving it down the street to the Russian Vodka Room.

Rules of the Game

An event planner for a software company tells about a lesson learned about making rules for event games. "I planned a casino-themed party for reception during a trade show. The night was a huge hit and we had thought of *almost* everything—our own custom chips, decorations, real casino equipment, professional dealers and the right food, drink and music. Because 90 percent of the audience was government employees, the hardest part was getting the regulations and guidelines regarding acceptable gifts for them. We were able to offer significant prizes by giving everyone who attended the same number of chips at the registration table. Then they could gamble and try to increase their holdings, or just hold them until the end of the night and cash them in for raffle tickets. (Anyone who lost all their chips was given a raffle ticket anyway.) When everyone cashed in their chips, we saw that one guy had a pretty big stash, but thought nothing of it. It turns out that some of his co-workers left early and they all pooled their chips and left their co-worker to collect any winnings. When we had someone draw the winning tickets, this guy won the second time. Then he won the third time. By the fifth time, half of the crowd wanted us to confiscate his remaining tickets; the other half knew him and thought it was hilarious. There was nothing we could do—the rules we posted all around the room (per government regulations) didn't mention multiple winnings, so we had no way to take his remaining tickets. He ended up with seven prizes in all. We learned our lesson: All future contests and events have a clause saying an attendee may only win one prize at each event."

Figure 18–2   Event Bloopers
Source: Reproduced with the permission of BiZBash Media (www.bizbash.com).

particularly to the corporate planning areas, will keep you informed of the latest in strategic planning for events. Collecting this information will ensure that you are both informed and creative—an ideal combination for the rapidly changing event environment.

Case Study

Having read a number of job descriptions for event roles in this chapter, develop a letter of application and résumé for two of these jobs at any event discussed in this book. Note that each time you apply for a position, you need to modify your résumé to stress your relevant knowledge and experience. For example, one résumé might stress your knowledge of marketing principles, and the other might illuminate your understanding of operational issues. If your experience is limited, you can fabricate some relevant experience for the purpose of this exercise.

Activity

Develop a scrapbook of newspaper and magazine articles that are relevant to the event industry so that you can remain up-to-date with current trends and issues.

Links

Imaginative Ideas for Events
www.bizbash.com
Career Resources and Employment Opportunities
www.iami.org
www.acmenet.org
www.mpiweb.org

Summary

This final chapter has looked at a range of social, economic, and other changes that have had, and will continue to have, an impact on the field of event management in the future. Staying up-to-date with fashion, entertainment, tourism trends, and the like is essential. A number of employment choices are available for those considering a career in the event industry, and a number of these positions have been described in this chapter. Of most importance, the management skills developed by event managers are relevant to many other occupations in which risk is high, deadlines are tight, people management skills are a priority, and there is only one opportunity to get it right.

Appendix 1

SUPPLEMENTAL INTERNET LINKS

References were made in the text to the following Web sites.

www.aact.org (American Association of Community Theaters)

www.acmenet.org (Association for Convention Marketing Executives)

www.alaskastatefair.org (Alaska State Fair)

www.alyeskaresort.com (Winterfest; Springfest; Blueberry & Mtn. Arts Festival)

www.amaproracing.com (AMA Pro-racing)

www.anchoragederbies.com (King & Silver Salmon Derbies)

www.anchorage.net (Anchorage, Alaska, events)

www.bigtex.com (Texas State Fair)

www.bixsociety.org (Bix Beiderbecke Memorial Jazz Festival)

www.cer.org (Bear Paw Festival)

www.cfdrodeo.com (Cheyenne Frontier Day Rodeo)

www.cftech.com (Titles for dignitaries protocol)

www.chicago.il.org (Chicago, Illinois)

www.chicagomarriage.com/wedding_traditions.htm (wedding tradition)

www.conventioncenters.us (U.S. Convention Centers)

www.crowdsafe.com (Crowdsafe)

www.crowdsafe.com/mosh.html (Strategies for ensuring crowd safety)

www.emact.org (Eastern Massachusetts Association of Community Theaters)

www.epa.gov (Environmental Protection Agency)

www.eriskcenter.org (Emergency Risk Center)

www.eventsx.com (Events Xtraordinaire)

www.eventsunlimited.com.au (Events Unlimited International)

www.fanfair.com (Nashville Country Music Festival)

www.foodsafety.gov (Government food safety information)

www.football.about.com (high school, college, and pro football)

www.frederickarts.org (Frederick, Maryland, Arts Festival)

www.fstea.gov (Food Safety Training & Education Alliance)

www.ftc.gov (Federal Trade Commission)

www.furrondy.com (Winter Carnival)

www.ganttcharts.com (Gantt Charts)

www.goseawolves.com (Hockey Classic; Midnight Marthon)

www.holidaycook.com (Seating protocol)

www.iacconline.com (International Association of Conference Centers)

www.iami.org (International Association Managers, Inc.)

www.icca.nl/index.htm (larger exhibition centers)

www.iditorad.com (Iditorad Trail Sled Dog Race)

www.ises.com (International Special Event Society)

www.jrwf.org (James River Writer's Festival)

www.kab.org (Keep America Beautiful/Great American Cleanup)

www.komen.org (Susan G. Komen Association)

www.kumbhallahabad.com/ (Maha Kumbh Mela Festival)

www.lapl.org (go to databases; statistics; Databook for LA county Table II for the statistics used in Figures 3–1, 3–2, 3–3, and 3–4)

www.lasvegascomedyfestival.com (Las Vegas Comedy Festival)

www.lewisandclark200.org (National Geographic Society)

www.lewisandclarkexhibit.org (Lewis and Clark Exhibit)

www.mncn.org (Minnesota Council of Nonprofits)

www.moscone.org (Moscone Convention Center, San Francisco, California)

www.mpiweb.org (Meeting Professionals International)

www.nal.usda.gov/foodborne (Foodborne Illness Education Information Center)

www.nationalwestern.com (National Western Stockshow)

www.nesf.org (National Electric Safety Foundation—now Electric Safety Foundation International, www.esfi.org)

www.newportevents.com (Newport, Rhode Island)

www.onsiterentals.com (portable restrooms and other rental equipment)

www.osfashland.org (Oregon Shakespeare Festival)

www.osha.gov (Occupational Safety and Health Administration)

www.psfilmfest.org (Palm Springs International Film Festival)

www.raffa.com (Lists fund-raising requirements for each state)

www.ragbrai.org (The Register's Annual Great Bicycle Ride Across Iowa)

www.renolaketahoe.com (Reno/Lake Tahoe Camel Races)

www.restaurant.org (National Restaurant Association)

www.roadatlanta.com (Road Atlanta)

www.sba.gov (Small Business Administration)

www.shootout.net (Alaska College Basketball Tournament)

www.soleburner.org (Soleburner event)

www.specialevents.com (Online event magazine with buyer's guide provides links to florists, entertainers, fireworks, furniture, etc.)

www.symphonyofseafood.com (Alaska Seafood Festival)

www.tournamentofroses.com (Tournament of Roses, Pasadena, California)

www.travelsd.com (Travel South Dakota)

www.usdoj.gov/crt./ada (Americans with Disabilities Act–ADA Homepage)

www.ushistory.org (The Independence Hall Association Web site)

www.visitrhodeisland.com (Rhode Island Tourism)

www.voamass.org (Volunteers of America, Massachusetts)

www.washingtonbirthday.com (George Washington's Birthday Celebration; Alexandria, Virginia)

Appendix 2

EVENT PROPOSAL

Event Description

- Event name
- Event type
- Location
- Date(s)
- Duration/timing
- Event overview and purpose/concept
- Aims and objectives

Event Management

- Management responsibility
- Major stakeholders and agencies
- Physical requirements
  Venue
  Route for street events
  Event map
  Event layout (indoor)
- Audience
- Impact
  Social
  Environmental
  Economic

Approvals and Consultation

- State and federal government
- County, city, or town

- Roads and traffic authority
- Liquor licensing
- Police
- Building
- Insurance
- Health
- Environmental
- Entertainment
- Music licensing
- Security

Marketing

- Competitive analysis
- Market analysis and planning
  Customer segmentation
  Meeting audience needs
  Consumer decision making
  Price and ticket program
- Advertising and promotion
  Messages
  Media
  Budget
- Public relations
  Press releases
  Media briefing
- Marketing evaluation

Financial Control

- Capital and funding requirements
- Fees (police and security, local government, music, etc.)
- Costs (including insurance)
- Control systems (e.g., cash handling)
- Taxation
- Profit and loss statement
- Cash-flow analysis

Risk Management

- Identification of risks and hazards
- Assessment of risks and hazards
- Management of risks and hazards
- Incident reporting

Event Staging

- Theme
- Decor
  Layout
  Entertainment
  Special effects, lighting
  Sound
- Services
  Electricity
  Water
  Transportation (including air travel, access to and from venue)
  Traffic management
  Street closure
  Impact on local traffic
  Notification of affected businesses, etc.
  Diversions
  Security
  Support vehicles
  Parking
  Disability access
- Catering
  Providers
  Facilities
  Food safety plans
- Waste and environmental management
  Toilets
  Waste management, recycling
  Noise
  Water pollution
- Cleaning

Staffing

- Selection and recruitment
- Rosters
- Training
- Briefing
- Recognition strategies
- Industrial relations
- Recruitment of volunteers

Safety and Security

- Safety of the event audience
- Safety and security of the performers, VIPs, etc.
- Health and safety of the staff
- Security for premises, equipment, cash, etc.
- Communications
  Meetings
  Reporting relationships
  Emergency reporting relationships
  Communication methods (radio)
- Emergency access and emergency management
- First aid

Operational Plans

- Policies, e.g., complaints, crowd control
- Procedures and checklists
- Performance standards (link to objectives)
- Contingency plans
  Weather
  Electrical supply, lighting
  Fire
  Accident
  Crowd control
  Delay or cancellation
  Bomb threat or other security incident

- Logistics
  Setup/teardown
  Structures and facilities
  Lighting
  Sound
  Setup/teardown

Evaluation

- Postevent evaluation
  Objectives
  Measures
  Analysis
  Report

Appendix 3
PROFESSIONAL ASSOCIATIONS

Alliance Service Network (Service provider to meetings, convention, and tradeshow industries) www.allianceservicenetwork.com

American Association of Association Executives www.asaenet.org

American Exhibition Services, Inc. www.aesmarketing.com

American Hotel & Lodging Association www.ahla.com

American Association of Pyrotechnics www.americanpyro.com

American Society of Association Executives www.asaenet.org

Association for Convention & Marketing Executives www.acmenet.org

Association for Convention Operations Management www.acomonline.org

Association for Destination Management Executives www.adme.org

Club Managers Association of America www.cmaa.org

Council of Protocol Executives

Destinations Unlimited (offers free destination advice to event organizers) www.dudmc.com

Healthcare Convention & Exhibitors Association www.hcea.org

International Association of Convention & Visitor's Bureaus www.iacvb.org

International Festivals & Events Association www.ifea.com

International Society of Meeting Planners www.iami.org

International Special Events Society www.ises.com

Meeting Professionals International www.mpiweb.org

National Association of Catering Executives www.nace.net

National Association of Exposition Managers www.iaem.org

National Fireworks Association www.nationalfireworks.org

National Restaurant Association www.restaurant.org
National Speaker's Association www.nsaspeaker.org
Professional Convention Management Association www
.pcma.org
Society of Corporate Meeting Professionals www.scmp.org.

Appendix 4
EVENT MANAGEMENT PROGRAMS

Following are a number of schools offering programs in meeting and event management or related disciplines. This is in no way a comprehensive listing, but just a sampling. As the industry grows, so does the education program available. Students should check with any schools of interest to see whether they also have a program.

Appalachian State University, Boone, NC
(Meeting and Convention Management)
www.appstate.edu

Arizona State University, Tempe, AZ
www.asu.edu

Austin Community College, Austin, TX
(Meeting and Event Planning Certificate; Associates in Hospitality Management with specialization in Meeting and Event Planning)
www.austincc.edu/hospmgt

Baylor University, Waco, TX
(Tradeshow Marketing)
www.baylor.com

Chemeketa Community College, Salem, OR
(Meeting Planning and Convention Management)
www.hsm.org

Cloud County Community College, Concordia, KS
www.cloudccc.cc.ks.us

College of the Cariboo, Kamloops, BC
(Events and Convention Management)
www.cariboo.bc.ca

Columbia College, Columbia, MO
(Meeting and Convention Planning)
www.ccis.edu

El Paso Community College, El Paso, TX
www.epcc.edu

Florida International University, North Miami, FL
(Convention and Trade Show Management)
www.hospitality.fiu.edu

George Washington University, Washington, DC
(Event Management Certificate Program)
www.gwu.edu

Georgia State University, Atlanta, GA
(Convention and Meeting Planning)
www.robinson.gsu.edu/hospitality

Indiana University at Indianapolis, Indianapolis, IN
(Convention and Meeting Planning)
www.iupui.edu

Kansas State University, Manhattan, KS
(Convention Service and Meeting Planning)
www.ksu.edu

Keuka College, Keuka Park, NY
(Meeting and Convention Planning)
www.keuka.edu

Madison Area Technical College, Madison, WI
(Meeting and Event Management Degrees)
www.madison.tec.wi.us

Mercyhurst College, Erie, PA
(Meetings, Convention, and Trade Show Management)
www.mercyhurst.edu

Metropolitan State College, Denver, CO
(Meeting Planning)
www.mscd.edu

Mt. Hood Community College, Portland, OR
(Conventions and Meeting Management; Special Events and Attractions Management)
www.mhcc.cc.or.us

New Mexico State University, Las Cruces, NM
(Conventions and Meeting Planning; Special Events Management)
www.nmsu.edu

Niagara University, Niagara Falls, NY
(Convention Operations)
www.niagara.edu/hospitality

Northeastern State University, Tahlequah, OK
(Meetings and Destination)
www.nsuok.edu

Northern Virginia Community College, Annandale, VA
www.nv.cc.va.us

Purdue University, Lafayette, IN
(Meeting and Convention Sales and Service)
www.cfs.purdue.edu/htm

Richland College, Dallas, TX
(AAS degree in Exposition and Meeting Management)
www.rlc.dcccd.edu/travel/index.htm

Robert Morris College, Coraopolis, PA
(Convention and Group Operations)
www.robert-morris.edu

Roosevelt University, Chicago, IL
(BS degree with emphasis in Meeting Planning; Certificate
   program in Meeting Management)
www.roosevelt.edu

San Jose State University, San Jose, CA
(Conference, Convention, Meeting, and Event Planning)
www.hospitality.edu

Skyline College, San Bruno, CA
www.smcccd.cc.ca.us

Southern Illinois University at Carbondale, Carbondale, IL
(Convention and Meeting Management)
www.siu.edu

Temple University, Philadelphia, PA
(School of Tourism and Hospitality Management)
www.temple.edu/STHM/

University of Central Florida, Orlando, FL
(Event and Meeting Planning)
www.hospitality.ucf.edu

University of Houston, Houston, TX
www.hrm.uh.edu

University of Massachusetts–Amherst, Amherst, MA
(Meeting Planning)
www.umass.edu/hrta

University of Nevada, Las Vegas, Las Vegas, NV
(Undergraduate course in Event and Convention Planning;
    Distance Learning Course for Masters Program in Meetings,
    Conventions, and Events)
www.unlv.edu

University of New Hampshire, Durham, NH
(Conference and Meeting Planning)
www.fsmgt.unh.edu

University of New Orleans, New Orleans, LA
(Concentration in Conventions and Meeting Planning)
www.uno.edu

University of Phoenix, Online Program
www.uophx.edu

University of South Carolina, Columbia, SC
www.hospitality.sc.edu

University of Southern Mississippi, Long Beach, MS
www.usm.edu

Virginia Polytechnic Institute and State University,
    Blacksburg, VA
www.vp.edu

BIBLIOGRAPHY

ADA, *Americans with Disabilities Act*, www.usdoj.gov/crt/ada.

American Association of Museums, 1575 Eye St. NW, Washington, D.C., www.aam-us.org.

Axtell, R. *The Do's and Taboos of Hosting International Visitors.* John Wiley and Sons, New York, 1990.

Catherwood, D. W. and Kirk, R. L. *The Complete Guide to Special Event Management.* John Wiley and Sons, New York, 1992.

Cook, S. *Customer Care.* Kogan Page, London, 1997.

Denvy, D. *Organising Special Events and Conferences.* Pineapple Press, Sarasota, Florida, 1990.

Getz, D. *Event Management and Event Tourism.* Cognizant Communication Corporation, New York, 1997.

Goldblatt, J. J. *Special Events: Best Practices in Modern Event Management.* John Wiley and Sons, New York, 1997.

Hall, C. *Hallmark Tourist Events: Management and Planning.* Belhaven Press, London, 1992.

Handy, Charles. *Understanding Organizations.* 4th edn. Penguin Books, London, 1993.

Hofstede, G. *Culture's Consequences: International Differences in Work Related Values.* Sage, Beverly Hills, 1980.

International Special Events Society, *Code of Ethics*, www.ises.com.

McCaffree, M. and Innis, P. *Protocol: The Complete Handbook of Diplomatic, Official and Social Usage.* Prentice Hall, New York, 1977.

McDonnell, I., Allen, J. and O'Toole, W. *Festival & Special Event Management.* John Wiley and Sons, Brisbane, 1999.

McGill, M., Slocum, J. and Lei, D. "Management Practices in Learning Organizations." *Organizational Dynamics*, 42, Summer 1992.

OSHA, *Occupational Safety & Health Act of 1970*, www.osha.gov.

Malouf, L. *Behind the Scenes at Special Events.* Wiley, Brisbane, 1998.

Minnesota Council for Nonprofits 2001, *Handbook for Starting a Successful Non-profit*, www.mncn.org.

Perlman, S. and Bush, B. *Fund-Raising Regulation: A State-by-State Handook of Registration Forms, Requirements and Procedures.* John Wiley and Sons, New York, 1997.

Robbins, S. P. *Organizational Behaviour.* 8th international edn. Prentice Hall, New Jersey, 1998.

Robbins, S. and Coulter, M. *Management.* 5th edn. Prentice Hall, New Jersey, 1996.

Rocky Mountain States Hospitality News, *Utah Gears Up for the Olympics*, February 2002.

Small Business Administration, *State Requirements for Business Registration*, www.sba.gov/hotlist/license.html.

Swartz, O. D. *Service Etiquette.* 4th edn. Naval Institute Press, Annapolis, Maryland, 1988.

Tuckman, B. W. "Developmental Sequence in Small Groups." *Psychological Bulletin*, 63, 1965, pp. 384–99.

Toffler, A. *Future Shock.* Bantam Books, New York, 1990.

U.S. Census Bureau. *Demographics*, laplorg; databook for LA County Table II.

U.S. Census Bureau. *Statistical Abstract of the US*, 2002 edn.

U.S. Consumer Product Safety Commission. *Corrective Action Handbook*, 2002.

Vecchio, R., Hearn, G. and Southey, G. *Organizational Behaviour.* Harcourt Brace, Sydney, 1996.

Watt, D. *Leisure and Tourism Events Management and Organization Manual.* Longman, London, 1992.

Weaver, D. and Opperman, M. *Tourism Management.* John Wiley and Sons, Brisbane, 2000.

INDEX